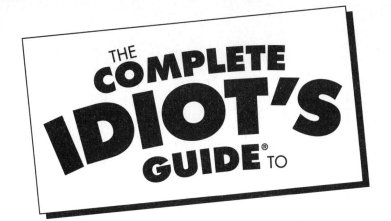

THE COMPLETE IDIOT'S GUIDE® TO

The Ultimate Reading List

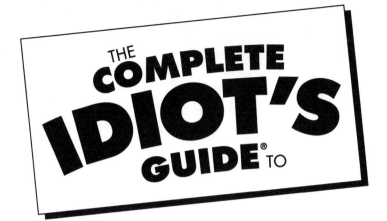

The Ultimate Reading List

by Shelley Mosley, John Charles, Joanne Hamilton-Selway, and Sandra Van Winkle

ALPHA

A member of Penguin Group (USA) Inc.

ALPHA BOOKS

Published by the Penguin Group

Penguin Group (USA) Inc., 375 Hudson Street, New York, New York 10014, USA

Penguin Group (Canada), 90 Eglinton Avenue East, Suite 700, Toronto, Ontario M4P 2Y3, Canada (a division of Pearson Penguin Canada Inc.)

Penguin Books Ltd, 80 Strand, London WC2R 0RL, England

Penguin Ireland, 25 St. Stephen's Green, Dublin 2, Ireland (a division of Penguin Books Ltd.)

Penguin Group (Australia), 250 Camberwell Road, Camberwell, Victoria 3124, Australia (a division of Pearson Australia Group Pty. Ltd.)

Penguin Books India Pvt. Ltd., 11 Community Centre, Panchsheel Park, New Delhi—110 017, India

Penguin Group (NZ), 67 Apollo Drive, Rosedale, North Shore, Auckland 1311, New Zealand (a division of Pearson New Zealand Ltd.)

Penguin Books (South Africa) (Pty.) Ltd, 24 Sturdee Avenue, Rosebank, Johannesburg 2196, South Africa

Penguin Books Ltd., Registered Offices: 80 Strand, London WC2R 0RL, England

International Standard Book Number: 978-1-59257-645-6
Library of Congress Catalog Card Number: 2006920579

09 08 07   8 7 6 5 4 3 2 1

Interpretation of the printing code: The rightmost number of the first series of numbers is the year of the book's printing; the rightmost number of the second series of numbers is the number of the book's printing. For example, a printing code of 07-1 shows that the first printing occurred in 2007.

Printed in the United States of America

Note: This publication contains the opinions and ideas of its authors. It is intended to provide helpful and informative material on the subject matter covered. It is sold with the understanding that the authors and publisher are not engaged in rendering professional services in the book. If the reader requires personal assistance or advice, a competent professional should be consulted.

The authors and publisher specifically disclaim any responsibility for any liability, loss, or risk, personal or otherwise, which is incurred as a consequence, directly or indirectly, of the use and application of any of the contents of this book.

Most Alpha books are available at special quantity discounts for bulk purchases for sales promotions, premiums, fund-raising, or educational use. Special books, or book excerpts, can also be created to fit specific needs.

For details, write: Special Markets, Alpha Books, 375 Hudson Street, New York, NY 10014.

Publisher: *Marie Butler-Knight*
Editorial Director: *Mike Sanders*
Managing Editor: *Billy Fields*
Acquisitions Editor: *Tom Stevens*
Development Editor: *Jennifer Moore*
Production Editor: *Megan Douglass*

Copy Editor: *Nancy Wagner*
Cover Designer: *Becky Harmon*
Book Designer: *Bill Thomas*
Indexer: *Brad Herriman*
Layout: *Ayanna Lacey*
Proofreader: *John Etchison*

For Louise Stephens, the bravest person we know.

Contents at a Glance

Contents

Introduction

There's nothing like a good book. It can take you to different times and different places. It can inspire you. It can make you laugh. It can make you cry. It can scare you to death.

But finding these books can be an overwhelming task. Just go into any big-box bookstore and try to pick one title out of the thousands lining the shelves. Or go to a library, where your friendly librarian will help you as soon as she unjams the copy machine, tells someone where the bathroom is, and reboots the computer.

So there you are, lost in a sea of books again. This is where our book can be your lifeline to finding that elusive literary treasure—your perfect book.

This is a collection of books both in print and out of print. Thanks to libraries, the Internet, and new and used bookstores, they're all findable. Even if a book's a little hard to locate, it's worth the extra effort if it's a great read. We enjoy these books, and we hope you will, too.

How Do You Use This Book?

We have devoted each chapter to a certain type of book. Several chapters feature popular fiction genres—mysteries, romances, chick lit and women's fiction, horror novels, fantasy novels, and westerns. Chapters dedicated to popular nonfiction titles we think you'll like range in topic from true crime to travel. Throughout you'll find a mix of classics and books fresh off the press.

Each chapter begins with a short introductory essay about the genre, and then an annotated list of books follows. Some chapters are subdivided into classics and newer titles, while others are more intermingled.

Extras

You'll find lots of sidebars—recommendations, bits of information, tips, definitions, and cautions—sprinkled throughout the book. This is what they'll look like:

An Expert Speaks

Experts in the world of books, including editors, authors, and librarians give recommendations.

You Can Book on It!

Here you'll find interesting asides, advice, and factoids.

The Rest of the Story

Additional tidbits about authors and their books will appear in these notes.

And the Award Goes to ...

Many books listed here are award winners, and we've spotlighted some of those.

Acknowledgements

Our heartfelt thanks go to the following individuals:

Tom Stevens and Mike Sanders, editors at Alpha Books, who had a vision of this book and the faith that we could make it a reality.

Kris Ramsdell, writer and librarian, who shared her unmatched knowledge of the romance genre and advised us in other subject areas, too.

Dorchester editor Leah Hultenschmidt, who graciously offered us advice, support, and possible titles when we were just getting started.

Award-winning author Jayne Ann Krentz, who inspired and advised us, and who has led the way in preserving genre fiction for generations to come.

Publishers and editors who shared their advice and favorite titles: Paula Eykelhof, Katherine Johnson, Chris Keesar, Susan McCarty, Joyce Saricks, Donna Seaman, Kim Tabor, Bill Ott, Blanche Woolls, Brianna Yamashita.

David Mosley, our favorite Trekkie, and expert for the "science fiction" chapter.

Former cowboy and rodeo rider Fred Wann and Arizona historian Sandra Mofford Lagesse, our official consultants on the western chapter.

Librarian Lynne Welsh for helping us add some magic to the fantasy chapter.

Volunteer *par excellence* Jennie Burrell, who gave much advice on good titles for the true crime chapter.

Fellow writer Marion Ekholm (also our official proofer), who did many early-morning brainstorming sessions with us.

Author Lynn Kerstan, librarian Suella Baird, and fellow writer Rose Jackson, who generously polled friends, family, and colleagues for us.

Librarian Lisa Colcord and fellow writer Jo Manning, who even annotated their lists of suggestions.

Authors who took a break from their manuscripts to recommend titles: Stephanie Bond, Connie Brockway, Laurie Schnebly Campbell, Christina Dodd, Gwynne Forster, Roz Denny Fox, Jocelyn Kelley, Leigh Greenwood, Carolyn Hart, Sandra Hill, Vicky Hinshaw, Kristine Hughes, Eloisa James, Beth Kendrick, Jill Marie Landis, Cathie Linz, Deborah Mazoyer, Judi McCoy, Teresa Medeiros, Stevi Mittman, Sophia Nash, Brenda Novak, Tara Taylor Quinn, Linda Rising, Sharon Swearengen, Vicki Lewis Thompson, Susan Vreeland, Karen Witmer.

Librarians who shared their suggestions: José Aguiñaga, Stephanie Allen, Anna Caggiano, Charlotte Cohen, Dianna Dwyer, Mark Floor, Frank Gonzalez, Julie Havir, Mary Johnson, Lee Kornblum, Frieda Ling, Nicole Lohrbeer, Bonnie Moon, Joanna Morrison, Steve Paschold, David Rodriguez, Russell Sears, Bette Sharpe, Louise Stephens, Dennis Tucker, Kris Vanderlee.

Avid readers who were more than willing to name their favorites: Dorothea Abbott, Marty Applebaum, Andy Baird, Larry Baird, Evelyn Barnett, Belva Barrick, Vicki Burrell, Judy Cassell, Richard Cassell, Janice Schallenberger Coe, Jessica Collins, Justine Cornelius, Mia Elmsäter, Mary Forester, Michelle Gregory, Belva Hall, Marilyn Hall, Karen Lusher, Brian Mazoyer, Katie Mazoyer, Tony Moke, Andy Mosley, Jennifer Mosley, Jessica Mosley, Janet Munsil, Joshua Munsil, Kerri Munsil, Wes Munsil, Martha Jo Russell, Ruth Russell, Lyn Souter, Wade Stephens, Pamela Wertz.

Trademarks

All terms mentioned in this book that are known to be or are suspected of being trademarks or service marks have been appropriately capitalized. Alpha Books and Penguin Group (USA) Inc. cannot attest to the accuracy of this information. Use of a term in this book should not be regarded as affecting the validity of any trademark or service mark.

Historical Fiction: Bringing the Past to Life

In This Chapter

- ◆ Classics: too good to miss
- ◆ Ancient world: how now, brown mammoth?
- ◆ Medieval Europe: Middle Ages crisis
- ◆ Europe: royalty rocks—peasants roll
- ◆ United States: red, white, and new
- ◆ Asia: views from the East
- ◆ Middle East/Africa: desert dramas

Do you like the drama and richness of history but can't stomach the dusty historical tomes in the nonfiction section of your library? While your friends are watching *Desperate Housewives*, are you watching recorded episodes of *Masterpiece Theater*? Do you secretly wish horses and buggies would come back into fashion? If so, do we have hours of wonderful reading for you!

Historical fiction is an easy way to learn about our fascinating past, because authors often populate their stories with a mix of real and fictional characters. For its backdrops, the genre draws from all time periods; however, a novel is only truly considered historical fiction if its setting is at least 50 years before the book itself is written.

With some fiction genres, one name often stands out as the "king" or "queen" of the genre. However, with historical fiction, coronating a single author as king or queen becomes much more difficult simply because this genre has so many talented authors. Readers often put James Michener at the top of their favorites lists, but not everyone likes the way Michener always begins his books by going back to the beginning of time when dinosaurs ruled and the earth was young. Although Jean Plaidy may have cornered the market on "royal" historical fiction, some readers may find a bit too much romance mixed with the history in her work. Margaret Mitchell is another possibility for the title of best historical fiction writer ever. Unfortunately, she only wrote the one book, *Gone with the Wind*. So we give you our favorites. Who rules this genre? You be the judge.

Classics

The Agony and the Ecstasy, Irving Stone, 1961

No one, before or after, has done a better job of bringing the complex personality of Michelangelo to life. From the intricate setting of Renaissance Italy and its politics to the relationship of Michelangelo to his art, Stone has created his finest work, an enormous and brilliant book about the art world's greatest genius. Even readers who know nothing about art will devour this novel.

The Far Pavilions, M. M. Kaye, 1978

Ashton "Ash" Pelham-Martyn once worked as a servant for the Raj, but when he returns to India years later as a British officer, he discovers one of his new duties is to escort two royal brides to their weddings. Unfortunately, one of the women is none other than Princess Anjuli, his one true love. It's easy to get lost in this tragic saga of lovers torn between desire and duty set amidst the rich lushness of India.

Forever Amber, Kathleen Winsor, 1944

Amber St. Clare must use her wits, beauty, and courage to survive tempestuous and licentious Restoration England. While she will eventually become mistress to many, including King Charles II, Amber will only love one man. When it first debuted, *Forever Amber* caused a scandal for its sexual tone and "promiscuous" heroine and, of course, was an immediate hit with readers. But there's more to this popular best-seller than sex; Winsor spent five years researching *Forever Amber*, and it shows in her convincing portrait of a long-gone era of British history.

Gone with the Wind, Margaret Mitchell, 1936

What can we say about *Gone with the Wind?* Combine a beautiful, spoiled, and scheming heroine, Scarlett O'Hara; the ultimate—not to mention handsome— hero, Rhett Butler; *and* the Civil War, and presto: you have the perfect book that will keep you up all night. And you will want to reread it every year. Face it—this book is addictive! *Atlanta Journalist* reporter Mitchell's first and only novel was not only an immediate best-seller, with more than one million copies sold in less than a year. Mitchell's version of the South might be romanticized, but she has few rivals when it comes to creating compelling characters and a vivid story.

> **The Rest of the Story**
>
> It has been reported that more hardback copies of *Gone with the Wind* were sold than any other book except the *Bible*.

Hawaii, James Michener, 1959

Michener uses his trademark, a detailed approach to history, to craft the story of Hawaii from its geological beginnings through its achieving statehood in 1959. In *Hawaii*, Michener is particularly brilliant at bringing many cultures and a huge cast of characters of this region together into one spellbinding story. Michener has also written about such varied locales as Israel (*The Source*), the American West (*Centennial*), and Africa (*The Covenant*). However, start with *Hawaii* to read him at his very best.

I, Claudius, Robert Graves, 1934

This is the story of supposedly "dimwitted" stutterer Claudius, who survived the reigns of the first three Roman emperors and later became emperor himself. With a sharp wit and clever characterizations, distinguished academic Graves writes with a commanding authority about ancient Rome, the ultimate setting for power politics where rivals often ended up dead. The equally fascinating sequel is *Claudius the God*, in which Claudius becomes emperor.

Katherine, Anya Seton, 1954

Katherine is the story of the romance between Chaucer's sister-in-law, Katherine Swynford, and John of Gaunt, Duke of Lancaster. Considered the best of Seton's many outstanding historical novels, *Katherine* has all the ingredients of a best-seller: fascinating characters, star-crossed lovers, and a vividly evoked historical setting. Seton's books have an excellent sense of time and place, but her gift of bringing her characters to life is what readers remember most.

The King Must Die, Mary Renault, 1958

With a superb sense of the past, Renault brilliantly recreates the legendary story of the Athenian Theseus, from his meeting with Medea to his journey to Crete, where with Ariadne's help he kills the mysterious Minotaur. Inspired by Greek mythology and archaeology, Renault wrote a number of historical novels, including *The Bull from the Sea*, which continues Theseus's adventures.

Lady in the Tower, Jean Plaidy, 1986

Beautiful, ambitious, cunning Anne Boleyn tells how she refused to settle for being Henry VIII's mistress, insisting instead on being his queen, with famously tragic results. Plaidy is one of the pseudonyms for popular, prolific English author Eleanor Hibbert, who also wrote as Victoria Holt and Phillipa Carr. As Plaidy, she earned a loyal following of readers for her meticulously researched, yet wonderfully readable, novels that covered the range of British history. If you like this book, you're in luck—Plaidy wrote enough novels for several years of reading.

Shogun, James Clavell, 1975

After being shipwrecked off Japan, English navigator John Blackthorne learns the complex ways of the Japanese from Lady Mariko and becomes involved in the power struggle between two rival warlords, Toranaga and Ishido, both of whom want to be the next shogun, or military leader. Clavell was a movie screenwriter before writing this best-selling epic of love, honor, and courage, and uses those skills to bring the world of the shogun to life.

Ancient World

The Assyrian, Nicholas Guild, 1987

In ancient Ashur, brothers Tiglath and Esarhaddon, sons of the aging king Sennacherib, grow up as friends but later become dangerous rivals when both become involved in a deadly struggle for the throne as well as the love of the same woman. In this captivating novel, Guild skillfully recreates the brutal and bloody—and yet in some ways quite modern—world of ancient Assyria. Tiglath's adventures in the ancient world continue in *Blood Star*.

The Beacon at Alexandria, Gillian Bradshaw, 1986

The Greek maiden Charis flees an arranged betrothal to a man she hates and finds her way to Alexandria, where she adopts a disguise and begins studying medicine. Bradshaw neatly integrates the political intrigues and deadly dangers of the Roman Empire into her compelling tale of a strong, independent woman who isn't content to settle for the roles allotted to women in classical times.

The Clan of the Cave Bear, Jean Auel, 1980

A group of Neanderthals, the Clan of the Cave Bear, take in Ayla, a young Cro-Magnon woman, after the other members of her tribe are killed in an earthquake. The tribe distrusts Ayla because of her "different looks," but she's finally accepted as the "Woman Who Hunts." This book, the first in Auel's "Earth's Children" series, is enriched by the author's extensive research on daily life in Ice Age Europe. Occasionally anachronistic but always entertaining, this book was tremendously popular when it first came out and practically created the prehistoric fiction subgenre.

Gates of Fire, Steven Pressfield, 1998

Xeones, sole survivor among the 300 Spartan warriors at the classical infantry battle of Thermopylae, tells Xerxes how the Spartans managed to hold back the invading Persian army for nearly a week, which proved to be long enough to later ensure a victory for the Greeks. Pressfield writes convincingly about the brutality and courage of the battlefield. Few writers can match his grasp of ancient warfare.

The Gilded Chamber, Rebecca Kohn, 2004

Kohn retells the tale of Jewish heroine Esther, who first became the concubine, and later the wife, of Persian King Xerxes, and the sacrifices this brave woman took on to help save her people. This beautifully evoked novel brings new depth to the story of this legendary biblical queen.

Hippopotamus Marsh, Pauline Gedge, 1999

A group of Egyptian princes, led by the Tao family, risks everything to overthrow the Hyksos, a group of foreigners who have controlled their country for the last 200 years. Gedge's richly detailed, yet leisurely paced, historical novels are filled with intriguing facts about warfare, religion, politics, and life in Ancient Egypt.

King and Goddess, Judith Tarr, 1996

In this spellbinding story, Queen Hatshepsut, with the help of her loyal scribe and later royal lover, Senemut, takes control of the throne to become Egypt's first female pharaoh. Tarr, who started writing in the fantasy genre, has conquered historical fiction as well. A fascinating tale of history with a remarkable heroine, this book will make you want to read all of Tarr's books.

Pompeii, Robert Harris, 2003

In this unforgettable novel, Harris creates a fast-paced plot and a compelling cast of characters, and then throws in one of the ancient world's most spectacular disasters. Roman engineer Marcus Attilius Primus is sent to take charge of the Aqua Augusta in Naples after the chief engineer disappears. Once he arrives there, Marcus discovers a bigger problem—a volcano ready to erupt.

The Red Tent, Anita Diamant, 1997

A popular reading group selection, *The Red Tent* is the fascinating story of the biblical Dinah, who learns both the art of midwifery and the secrets women share in the Red Tent, a place they go during their menstrual cycles. Diamant skillfully blends biblical characters with those of her own creation in this captivating story of courage, sorrow, happiness, and friendship.

> ### The Rest of the Story
>
> The biblical account of Dinah, known as the "Rape of Dinah," is found in Chapter 34 of Genesis. In the Bible, Dinah maintains her silence through the atrocities committed by Jacob's sons, but Diamant's tale gives her a voice.

Sarum, Edward Rutherfurd, 1987

Drawing on the stories of five different families, Rutherford recreates the history of the English town of Salisbury from the Ice Age to the twentieth century. Rutherfurd's sweeping, sagalike approach to historical fiction proved irresistible to readers, and he was quickly hailed as the heir to James Michener's crown.

Medieval Europe

The Innocent, Posie Graeme-Evans, 2004

In fourteenth-century England, young peasant Anne's knowledge of herbs brings her to the attention of the queen of England, but her beauty captures the interest of King Edward IV. Australian author Graeme-Evans was a television producer and director before penning this book, the first in a trilogy, which continues the story of star-crossed lovers Anne and her king.

Jerusalem, Cecelia Holland, 1996

Crusaders, Knights Templar, and the battle for control of the Holy Land are at the center of Holland's story of Rannulf Fitzwilliam and a group of warrior monks who become involved in a struggle for control of Jerusalem between the Christians and the Muslims. Not as well known as other historical fiction writers, Holland deserves a place on your reading list for her meticulous research, vivid characters, and multilevel plots. This book is for those who loved the movie *Kingdom of Heaven.*

The Name of the Rose, Umberto Ecco, 1983

When Brother William of Baskerville visits a Benedictine abbey to investigate charges of heresy, he becomes involved in a series of murders connected to a book by Aristotle. Italian philosopher Ecco's first novel became an international runaway best-seller. We call this "mensa" fiction, due to the obscure literary references. Have an encyclopedia handy.

The Sunne in Splendour, Sharon Kay Penman, 1982

In Penman's revisionist look at the Lancasters and the Yorks, Richard III is not a villain and did not murder the boys in the tower. He is the protector and supporter of his elder brother, King Edward IV, and is later forced to claim the throne when his brother dies and his heirs are declared illegitimate. Considered to be one of the best novels about Richard III, this huge book will keep you captivated until the final page.

A Vision of Light, Judith Merkle Riley, 1989

Inspired by a vision of light, Margaret of Ashbury hires a reluctant Brother Gregory to write her life story. Riley's captivating tale of a medieval woman who refuses to accept her traditional role in society will please readers who like adventurous historical fiction featuring a strong-willed, rebellious heroine. Margaret and Brother Gregory's story is continued in *In Pursuit of the Green Lion*, and concludes in *The Water Devil*.

The Winter Mantle, Elizabeth Chadwick, 2003

Waltheof Siwardsson falls in love with and eventually marries Lady Judith, one of William the Conqueror's nieces. However, Waltheof soon finds his allegiance to William difficult to honor once he, prompted by his new wife, agrees to lead a revolt against the Norman king. Award-winning British author Chadwick is known for her historical novels set in medieval England. Fans of historical romances also enjoy her books, due to their strong romantic elements.

The Year of Wonders, Geraldine Brooks, 2001

When the bubonic plague strikes a remote English village, the residents, including 18-year-old widow and servant Anna Frith, agree to sacrifice themselves and save the surrounding villages by isolating their town and its inhabitants. Based on a true story of a village in Derbyshire, Brooks movingly recounts a brutal and harsh time in history. This is a perfect choice for literary fiction readers who haven't read much historical fiction.

The Rest of the Story _____

> After writing *The Year of Wonders*, Geraldine Brooks won the National Book Award with her next novel, *March*, the story of Louisa May Alcott's father and the time he spent away from his family during the Civil War.

Royalty Rocks

The Alchemist's Daughter, Katherine McMahon, 2006

Trained in the forbidden science of alchemy by her father, brilliant but naïve Emelie Selden is lured away from her home by a charming adventurer. Thinking she's found true love, Emelie soon discovers her marriage is less than golden. Set in Elizabethan England, this book superbly captures the plight of women during that period.

The Autobiography of Henry VIII, with Notes by His Fool, Will Somers, Margaret George, 1986

Henry VIII's memoirs, as he himself might have told them, are blended with irreverent and acerbic comments from his court jester. This book created a huge stir in the publishing world when it debuted, and quickly found favor among fans of such PBS series as *The Six Wives of Henry VIII* and *Elizabeth R.*

You Can Book on It! _____

> Each of Margaret George's historical novels (she has written books about Cleopatra, Mary, Queen of Scots, and even Helen of Troy) is a rich literary feast of fascinating historical details and captivating storytelling.

The Birth of Venus, Sarah Dunant, 2003

Mystery writer Dunant shows that she's equally gifted when it comes to historical fiction with *Birth of Venus*, a bewitching novel set in fourteenth-century Florence. In the best opening chapter we've read in a while, the sisters of St. Vitella's prepare the body of Sister Lucrezia when they find the tattoo of a snake covering her entire torso. Lucrezia used to be Alessandra Cecchi, a Renaissance beauty whose love for an artist is the core of this passionate page-turner about art, love, and betrayal.

Circle of Pearls, Rosalind Laker, 1990

When Julia Pallister is born one October day in 1641, she's given a rare and beautiful pearl, which will bind together three generations of Pallisters. Think *Lifestyles of the Rich and Famous* set in seventeenth-century England, as the feisty Julia overcomes numerous obstacles, including Puritans, the Black Plague, and the Great Fire of London, to save her family's cherished estate.

The Crimson Petal and the White, Michel Faber, 2002

In Victorian England, Sugar tries to escape her life as a London prostitute by becoming the mistress of William Rackham, writer and heir to his family's perfume business. Critics compared Faber to Dickens when this dense and complex novel, filled with a wide-ranging cast of characters, was first published.

Fingersmith, Sarah Waters, 2002

Sue Trinder tries to pay back the family of thieves who raised her by assisting in their scheme to con a fortune out of heiress Maude Lilly. But when Sue, posing as a maid, meets Maude and finds herself attracted to her, the carefully constructed plan begins to unravel. Waters shares Charles Dickens's ability to craft a large cast of completely different yet equally entertaining characters. Filled with many distinctive details about Victorian England, both upstairs and downstairs, *Fingersmith* has a vivid sense of place and time.

The Game of Kings,
Dorothy Dunnett, 1961

Exiled from Scotland as a rebel, Francis Crawford of Lymond, a Scottish nobleman and soldier of fortune, finds himself involved in a number of different plots to upset the balance of power in sixteenth-century Europe. Dunnett skillfully recreates the deadly world of European politics in this swashbuckling tale of danger, deception, and desire. *The Game of Kings* is the first in a series of six books cleverly linked together by the game of chess.

An Expert Speaks

"I've read all my life, but nothing has given me greater reading pleasure than Dorothy Dunnett."

—Lynn Kerstan, author

The Girl with a Pearl Earring, Tracy Chevalier, 1999

In seventeenth-century Holland, a young girl goes to work as a maid to the famous painter Vermeer and winds up becoming the inspiration for Vermeer's masterpiece. An exquisitely crafted jewel of a book, Chevalier proves that historical fiction doesn't have to be the size of a doorstop to be engrossing.

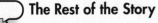

The Rest of the Story _____

The Girl with a Pearl Earring (Het meisje met de parel) is the name of a Vermeer portrait, a novel, and a movie. Despite these multiple treatments, many mysteries still remain. Who was the girl? Why is she wearing a turban? Is the pearl real, and where did it come from?

The Lady's Maid, Margaret Forester, 1991

The story of Elizabeth Barrett Browning's courtship and marriage is narrated by her private maid, Elizabeth Wilson. In this literary equivalent of *Upstairs Downstairs* meets *Gosford Park*, Forester, who has also written a biography of Barrett Browning, uses the historical facts of Elizabeth and Robert Browning's lives to lend realism to her quietly compelling story of a servant and her famous, invalid employer.

The Many Lives and Secret Sorrows of Josephine B., Sandra Gulland, 1999

This is the fictionalized diary of Josephine Bonaparte, who journeys from Martinique to worn-torn France, where she meets Napoleon, a man who dreams of one day ruling all of Europe. Gulland takes a literary approach to historical fiction in the first of a trilogy about France's ill-fated empress.

Master and Commander, Patrick O'Brian, 1990

Captain Jack Aubrey, R.N., has just received command of his first ship, the HMS *Sophie*, when he meets Stephen Maturin, his new ship's surgeon, naturalist, and intelligence agent. O'Brian is unrivaled at capturing shipboard life and warfare during the Napoleonic era in exquisite detail. His 21-book series featuring the adventures of Aubrey and Maturin is an excellent choice for readers who like plenty of action and danger.

Mr. Midshipman Hornblower, C. S. Forester, 1950

These short stories focus on the beginnings of Horatio Hornblower's career in His Majesty's Navy, as he receives his first assignment on the HMS *Justinian*, fights in the French and Spanish Wars, and eventually earns the title of Lieutenant. Forester was one of the first to popularize nautical fiction. His Hornblower books remain the standard for the subgenre.

The Other Boleyn Girl, Philippa Gregory, 2002

Sisters Mary and Anne Boleyn both become rivals and mistresses of King Henry VIII, but the king ultimately chooses Anne as his next queen. Known both for her brilliant use of someone on the "margins" of history as her protagonist and her ability to effectively blend fact and fiction, Gregory has written other historical novels, but her favorite era seems to be the tempestuous, color-ful reign of the Tudors. *The Other Boleyn Girl*, the book that first brought her fame, is an excellent introduction to her beguiling brand of historical fiction.

Penmarric, Susan Howatch, 1988

Penmarric is the gloomy, decaying estate in Cornwall that is home to the Castallack family. Howatch chronicles the secrets, petty feuds, and betrayals that almost destroy the family. This sweeping saga of Cornwall from the 1890s through the 1940s is an engrossing precursor to the multi-generational epics of Barbara Taylor Bradford and the early Elizabeth Adler.

Sails on the Horizon, Jay Worrall, 2005

Second Lieutenant Charles Edgemont assumes command of the *Argonaut* dur-ing a battle with the Spanish. His bravery earns him wealth and the title of Commander, but what Edgemont really wants is to win the love of Penelope Brown. If you love the action and adventure of other Napoleonic- era nautical novels, such as those by Patrick O'Brian, you'll go for this one.

The Secret Diary of Anne Boleyn, Robin Maxwell, 1997

Just as the newly crowned Queen Elizabeth I has decided to succumb to the temptation of an illicit affair, she is given the diary of her mother, Anne Boleyn, who gave her heart to Henry VIII and died for it. Maxwell's first novel is a deliciously juicy chronicle of the lives and loves of two of England's most famous—and misunderstood—women.

Sharpe's Tiger, Bernard Cornwell, 1999

Cornwell is best known for his series featuring Private Richard Sharpe, a rifle-man in the future Duke of Wellington's army. Cornwell bases each of the Sharpe books on a real military campaign or battle. In *Sharpe's Tiger*, Sharpe's efforts to contact a spy are complicated by the 1799 siege of Seringapatam. Cornwell's research is so thorough and his writing is so skillful that you feel you are fighting alongside Sharpe.

Through a Glass Darkly, Karleen Koen, 1986

When *Through a Glass Darkly* was released in 1986, it was the summer's big blockbuster hit. In the novel, 16-year-old Barbara Alderley is betrothed by her autocratic grandmother to the much older Roger Montgeoffrey, Earl Devane. Barbara's marriage proves to be no love match once she learns her husband married her only for her family's estate. Few writers have captured the glittering and decadent world of the Restoration Era and beyond as well as Koen, both in this book and its sequel, *Now Face to Face*.

United States

Ahab's Wife, Sena Jeter Naslund, 1999

Inspired by a single sentence in Melville's *Moby Dick,* Naslund fashions the fascinating tale of Captain Ahab's much younger second wife, Una, who journeys from rural Kentucky, disguises herself as a boy on a whaler, and eventually marries Ahab, her soul mate. Naslund deftly incorporates many of the crucial issues of the nineteenth century (slavery, women's rights) into the plot. We think Una is one of the most intriguing heroines to grace the pages of historical fiction in quite a few years.

An Expert Speaks

"Beginning with the startling line, 'Captain Ahab was neither my first husband nor my last', this is the saga of a strong and rare woman in search of a spiritually satisfying life. An adventure tale, a trio of romances, a woman's self-discovery, a compelling narrative with read-twice sentences of absolute brilliance, a tour de force of originality—*Ahab's Wife* is all of these."

—Susan Vreeland, author

The Alienist, Caleb Carr, 1994

Asked by New York police commissioner Teddy Roosevelt to investigate a series of brutal serial killings, psychologist (known as an "alienist" in that time) Dr. Lazlo Kriezler teams up with a reporter to find the killer. Part mystery, part historical novel, *The Alienist* is the best of both worlds.

Beloved, Toni Morrison, 1987

In a horrific act of sacrifice, runaway slave Sethe murders her infant daughter rather than allow her to be captured and returned to slavery. The act haunts her—literally—for the rest of her life and prevents her from any chance of a happy future. Morrison is an exceptional writer. This is probably her masterpiece, but it's not an easy read—the story shifts back and forth in time. This book will stay with you long after you've closed the cover.

Brookland, Emily Barton, 2006

This grand novel features Prue Winship, the oldest of three sisters, who takes over the family gin distillery business in late eighteenth-century New York. But Prue's dreams go beyond running a successful business. She wants to build a bridge from her home in Brooklyn (then known as Brookland) to Manhattan. Using her letters to her daughter to tell her story, this extraordinary woman's vision makes for a dynamic epic novel, filled with vivid historical details and heartbreaking characters.

An Expert Speaks

"Even though it has appeared at the top of several 'best' book lists lately, I have to say that *Beloved* by Toni Morrison really is the best novel I've read. At times difficult to read because the events recounted are so grim, it still drew me in and made me care deeply for the characters—Sethe, Denver, Paul D., Beloved, and the others—and the universal human beings they represent. This novel encapsulates the American experience as no other novel, partly because it's about those who are more often omitted or marginalized—African Americans and women."

—Katherine Johnson, editor

City of Light, Lauren Belfer, 1999

As Buffalo, New York, plans for the Grand Pan-American Exposition of 1901, Louisa Barrett, a headmistress of a local girls' school, is forced to examine the choices she has made in life after a mysterious death occurs at the city's power plant. With a richly detailed cast of characters and a unique setting, this massive novel sweeps the reader into the turbulent world of turn-of-the-century America.

The Rest of the Story

The Grand Pan-American Exposition of 1901 took place on 350 acres in Buffalo, New York. No ordinary affair, John Philip Sousa wrote "The Invincible Eagle" especially for it. The Exposition zoomed to the top of the news when President McKinley was shot there by an anarchist on September 6, 1901. He died eight days later.

Cold Mountain, Charles Frazier, 1997

With the help of no-nonsense, hardworking Ruby, former pampered socialite Ada tries to save her family's farm on Cold Mountain even as wounded Confederate soldier W.P. Inman struggles to return home to Ada, the woman he loves. In chapters that alternate between Inman's journey home and Ada's efforts to restore their family farm, Frazier writes in a quietly powerful and brilliantly poignant way about the personal costs of the American Civil War. In *Cold Mountain,* the literary novel meets historical fiction.

The Color Purple, Alice Walker, 1992

This will be *the* novel Walker will be remembered for (and how they made a musical out of it is still a mystery!). Set in the first half of the twentieth century, two sisters, Celie and Nettie, share their sorrows and joys (more sorrows than joys) through letters to each other and to God. If you are feeling the tiniest bit depressed, you might want to wait until you can stand the pain—but it's worth it!

Creek Mary's Blood, Dee Brown, 1980

In 1905, a Washington, D.C., journalist travels to Montana and interviews 91-year-old Dane, who recounts the story of his grandmother, the legendary Creek Mary Kingsley. The fictionalized reminiscences reflect the real experiences of Native Americans during the western expansion. Brown, best known for his nonfiction work, *Bury My Heart at Wounded Knee*, meticulously researched this riveting saga. Sounds heavy, but it's a darned good read.

Daughter of Fortune, Isabel Allende, 1999

Written in Allende's trademark lyrical style, *Daughter of Fortune* tells the story of Eliza Sommers, who follows her wayward husband from their home in Chile to California, meeting her soul mate, a Chinese shipboard cook, on the way. Oprah included this novel in her book club, so you know you're going to need a box of tissues while reading it.

Enemy Women, Paulette Jiles, 2002

When Adair Colley is arrested and imprisoned as a Confederate spy, she not only manages to survive imprisonment but also finds love with her Union captor, Major William Neumann. Poet and memoirist Jiles takes an unusual aspect of the Civil War—the imprisonment of women—and creates an unsentimental historical novel that beautifully explores such topics as courage and love.

Into the Wilderness, Sara Donati, 1998

Elizabeth Middleton leaves England with her brother to live with their father in America, where she plans to open a school. But her plans take an unexpected turn when she falls in love with Nathaniel Bonner, a Scotsman raised by the Mohawks. If you loved the Daniel Day-Lewis version of *Last of the Mohicans*, this book is for you. A little romance, a lot of history, and three more in the series!

The Killer Angels, Michael Shaara, 1974

Characters from both the Union and Confederate armies tell the tragic story of the bloody battle of Gettysburg. Few writers have so expertly captured both the brutality and the nobility of war like Shaara, who won the Pulitzer Prize for this book. The movie *Glory* was based on *The Killer Angels*.

The Known World, Edward P. Jones, 2003

Henry Townsend, a former slave who eventually purchases his own freedom, becomes a slave owner himself in Virginia, but the slave riots threaten to destroy everything for which he has worked. This powerful book won the Pulitzer Prize in 2004 and truly deserved it.

Lincoln, Gore Vidal, 1984

Powerful and surprisingly subtle (for Vidal, anyway), this fictionalized biography centers around Lincoln's political skills, which allowed him not only to win the presidency, but also to keep the Union together during the difficult days of the Civil War. Even though you know how the story will end (or at least you should if you paid attention during American History 101!), Vidal's enthralling story still shocks and saddens.

North and South, John Jakes, 1982

In this character-rich page-turner, Jakes traces the fates of two families—the rich, plantation-owning Mains and the Pennsylvania iron industrialists Hazards—through the Civil War. Jakes has written in other genres, but he's best known for his historical fiction, including this one, the first in a trilogy about the Main and Hazard families.

People of the Wolf, W. Michael Gear and Kathleen O'Neal Gear, 1990

Born into an Ice Age clan, two brothers, Runs-in-Light and Raven Hunger, later become rivals for the leadership of the tribe. The authors, who are husband and wife, are both archaeologists, which is evident in the number of fascinating historical details that season their stories. *People of the Wolf* is the first in a series of more than a dozen books by the duo, each of which focuses on a specific Native American tribe at a certain point in history.

Ragtime, E. L. Doctorow, 1975

Doctorow's masterpiece is an interweaving of history and the lives of three different families in turn-of-the-century America. Mixing real historical figures, like Houdini, Henry Ford, and Sigmund Freud, with fictional characters who seem just as real, Doctorow is a genius at bringing the past to life. It takes your breath away!

Sacajawea, Anna Lee Waldo, 1984

The legendary Sacajawea was a Shoshoni but grew up in a rival tribe. Married to a French fur trader, she eventually became Lewis and Clark's guide on their famous expedition to discover the Northwest Passage. A big, juicy read, it is filled with carefully researched details, from plant life to Native American customs and culture, and is a perennial favorite in the library!

These Is My Words: The Diary of Sarah Agnes Prine, 1881-1901, Nancy Turner, 1998

Based on the actual diaries of Turner's great-grandmother, this novel is a little bit of romance wrapped in a great and moving story. Sarah follows her family on their move westward, eventually settling on a ranch near Tucson. The book's literary style is purposely rough and uneven at first, but gradually becomes more eloquent as Sarah learns to read and write. Independent and spirited, Sarah's life is a mixture of heartache and great happiness. She's a character you'll root for.

Voodoo Dreams: A Novel of Marie Laveau, Jewell Parker Rhodes, 1993

The story of Marie Laveau, who left the bayou to become nineteenth-century New Orleans' most famous voodoo queen, is an entrancing read. Dark, brooding, yet eloquent, Rhodes brings Laveau (an early feminist if there ever was one!) to life, while delving into the dark, superstitious world of voodoo. Rhodes continues Laveau's story in *Voodoo Season*, featuring Laveau's descendent, Marie Levant, a doctor unaware of her voodoo inheritance.

Asia

Empress Orchid, Anchee Min, 2004

This story tells of the extraordinary life of the empress of China, Tzu His or "Orchid," who went from the rank of concubine to the most powerful woman in nineteenth-century China. Min brings unexpected depth and sympathy to this woman that history has traditionally vilified, the last empress of China.

The Impressionist, Hari Kunzru, 2002

Kunzru's many-layered novel of Pran, an Indian boy banished from his lavish home when it is discovered that he is half-British, is a story of someone who reinvents himself to adapt and survive. From nineteenth-century India to Victorian London, *The Impressionist* is a *tour de force.*

Memoirs of a Geisha, Arthur Golden, 1997

A major hit when first published, Golden's first book stunned critics and readers, who found it difficult to believe that a man could write so movingly and realistically from a woman's point of view. Chiyo Sakamoto is sold to a geisha house in Gion where she learns the trade and later becomes the celebrated geisha Sayuri. With such a sumptuous amount of detail and history, you'll want to savor each page. If you thought the movie was great, read the book—you'll love it even more!

Snow Flower and the Secret Fan, Lisa See, 2005

Reading this book is like the delicate unfolding of a fan. Two Chinese women—Lily and Snow Flower—communicate with each other through the secret language of *nu shu,* written on a fan. Exquisitely crafted and richly textured, mystery writer See has triumphed in this, her first historical novel. It's a perfect book for a discussion group read.

Spring Moon, Bette Bao Lord, 1981

The myriad social, economic, and political changes that affected China in the late nineteenth and early twentieth centuries are reflected in the lives of five generations of an aristocratic Mandarin family, including Spring Moon Chang. Think Scarlet O'Hara in Pearl S. Buck's *The Good Earth* in this spellbinding tapestry. Lord initially planned to write her book as nonfiction. Worried that the Chinese government might punish her relatives, she turned her family's story into a novel.

Middle East/Africa

Exodus, Leon Uris, 1958

Uris's classic novel, an international best-seller, is a powerful and passionate epic about the plight of the European Jews, from the turn of the century to the founding of the state of Israel. Uris is one of the best writers of historical fiction. Although he wrote other masterful novels, this is perhaps his most famous. Don't miss the sequel, *The Haj.*

Flight of the Falcon, Wilbur Smith, 1982

Smith is known for his sprawling sagas. *Flight of the Falcon* is the first in his Ballantyne series, featuring a family whose lives and fortunes intertwine with the history of Africa. Set in 1860, the book features unconventional Robyn Ballantyne and her brother Zouga, who both head to Africa to locate their lost missionary father. It's adventure on a grand scale.

And the Award Goes to ...

While mysteries have their Edgars, westerns have their Spurs, and romances have their RITAs, there isn't a separate award for historical fiction. But that doesn't mean this genre isn't deserving of such honors. Many historical fiction novels have won literary awards, including the Pulitzer Prize and the National Book Award. For instance, *Cold Mountain*, by Charles Frazier, won the National Book Award in 1997.

2

Popular Fiction: Books That Fly off the Shelves

In This Chapter:

- ◆ Classics: once-trendy tomes
- ◆ More great reads: all the rage

Are you wondering just what "popular" fiction might include? Can it be those big, splashy books that hit the market just in time for summer beach reading? Or can it also be the books that we have loved that don't quite fit into any other genre? Some of these titles were hard to categorize (Is it literary? Is it historical? Where do you put that darned talented Amy Tan?), but we had to make some difficult decisions! Sweeping sagas, intimate family stories, and everything in between— these books can take you on a gentle ride or whip you around like a roller coaster. They're all here.

Classics

Evergreen, Belva Plain, 1987

In turn-of-the-century New York, Polish immigrant Anna Friedman is hired as a maid for the wealthy Werner family and falls in love with the boss's son. *Evergreen* spent 41 weeks on the *New York Times* bestsellers list and was made into a television miniseries. If you like *Evergreen*, three more books continue the Werner family series.

The Godfather, Mario Puzo, 1969

Do we really have to tell you the plot? Vito Corleone, Mafia don, rises to power but doubts that his sons, Michael and Sonny, will be able to take over the family's empire. *The Godfather* continues with Puzo's *The Sicilian* and *Omerta*. After Puzo's death, Mark Winegardner continued the story with *The Godfather Returns* and *The Godfather's Revenge*, which most fans compared favorably with Puzo's masterpiece.

Hotel, Arthur Hailey, 1965

Plotline and character converge as master storyteller Hailey chronicles five days in New Orleans' St. Gregory Hotel. Owner Warren Trout is concerned with a takeover by a huge hotel chain, while manager Peter McDermott worries about a hotel thief who has been eluding detectives. For each of his books, Hailey used a different industry (banking, airlines, television) as a backdrop and incorporated fascinating, well-researched details into the stories.

If Tomorrow Comes, Sidney Sheldon, 1985

Philadelphia bank employee Tracy Whitney has the perfect life. She is about to wed a wealthy man who is the father of her child, but then her luck runs out. Framed by the Mob for robbery and assault, she goes to prison, where she plots her revenge. Sheldon has perfected the formula for entertaining, sensational, and yes, mindless blockbusters, including *The Other Side of Midnight* and *Stranger in the Mirror*. What the heck, sometimes you just want to have fun!

The Rest of the Story

Sidney Sheldon never won a Pulitzer Prize for his splashy, flashy novels, but the television producer-turned-author sold 300 million copies of his 18 books and wrote more than 200 TV scripts and several Broadway hits.

Kane and Abel, Jeffrey Archer, 1980

Archer's big blockbuster novel features two families at war—those of Will Kane, a Boston banker, and Abel Rosnovski, a Polish immigrant turned hotel magnate. A sequel, *The Prodigal Daughter*, features Abel's daughter as the main character.

Love Story, Erich Segal, 1970

Before Nicholas Sparks or James Robert Waller, there was Erich Segal and his classic love story about Jenny, a poor Radcliffe music student, and Oliver, a wealthy Harvard jock. Even more than three decades after the book was first published, its poignant ending is guaranteed to make you cry. If you don't remember the phrase "Love means never having to say you're sorry," then you're too young!

More Great Reads

The Accidental Tourist, Anne Tyler, 1985

Macon and Sarah separate after their 12-year-old son is killed in a holdup. Macon moves back in with his two brothers and his sister until a pushy dog trainer disrupts his life. Tyler is one of those authors who not only writes masterful prose but can tell a whopping good story as well. You can't go wrong with any of her literary gems (and, yes, this was one of the books that were so hard for us to categorize).

And Then She Found Me, Eleanor Lipman, 1990

The quiet life of meek high school teacher April Epner is turned upside down when her birth mother, over-the-top diva talk show host Bernice Graveman, descends upon her, intent on instant mother-daughter bonding. Lipman manages to make obnoxious Bernice lovable and eventually brings April and Bernice together in an uneasy alliance. Lipman is not as well known as some best-selling authors but deserves a place on any list of great reads.

Big Stone Gap, Adriana Trigiani, 2000

Self-proclaimed as the town spinster, pharmacist Ave Marie Mulligan's life in Big Stone Gap, Virginia, is in a rut until a series of events forever change her. With its warmly endearing characters and quirky small town setting, Big Stone Gap has become such a favorite of readers that Trigiani continued the series with three others (and we hope more). All of Trigiani's books are a laugh-out-loud joy to read.

Blessings, Anna Quindlen, 2002

Young handyman Skip Cuddy finds an abandoned baby in a box at the beautiful estate of crotchety old Mrs. Lydia Blessings. Skip wants to keep the baby, but when Mrs. Blessing finds out about it, she also wants to keep the baby. This story of rescue and redemption will leave you feeling uplifted and totally satisfied.

Chocolat, Joanne Harris, 1999

When the enigmatic Vianne Rocher and her six-year-old daughter Anouk arrive in the small French town of Lansquenet-sous-Tannes and open a chocolate shop, Vianne finds herself in a battle with the town's dour priest for the villagers' attention (or is it for their souls?). Delicious prose and delectable characters make this a tasty treat. And Johnny Depp was pretty yummy in the movie version, too!

Cold Sassy Tree, Olive Ann Burns, 1984

In 1906 Georgia, Will Tweedy lives in the town of Cold Sassy, where his grandfather, E. Rucker Blakeslee, has just married a much younger woman only three weeks after his first wife's death. The characters are quirky but authentic, and the story of Cold Sassy and Will's childhood just flows naturally. Full of warmth and humor, Burns's book is so entertaining you won't want it to end.

The Dogs of Babel, Carolyn Parkhurst, 2003

When Lexy Iverson is found dead at the base of a tree, the police rule it an accident, but her husband Paul wants to know what happened with certainty. Only their dog, a Rhodesian Ridgeback named Lorelei, was witness to Lexy's death. Parkhurst makes Paul's grief achingly real, and the story of his desperation to find the truth is almost painful to read. Sounds fun, huh? But it's worth it.

Eat Cake, Jeanne Ray, 2002

Everything in Ruth's life seems to be falling apart. Her husband loses his job, her estranged father moves in with her family to recover from a fall, and her teenaged daughter is … well, a teenager. But Ruth has an escape from the madness, which is better than yoga and meditation. Ruth bakes and, in baking, she not only finds peace for herself but also a way to save the family. When reading this book, you can almost smell the bundt cake baking.

Five People You Meet in Heaven, Mitch Albom, 2003

Eighty-three-year-old Eddie, a maintenance man at the Ruby Pier Amusement Park, dies while saving a little girl's life. When he arrives in heaven, he meets five people who make him realize that his own life had special meaning. For readers looking for fiction with a message of hope, this sweet book is for you. Albom's parable is his second book, published after his huge nonfiction bestseller, *Tuesdays with Morrie*.

Fried Green Tomatoes at the Whistle Stop Café,
Fannie Flagg, 1987

While visiting her mother in the nursing home, overweight and overwrought Evelyn Couch meets Cleo "Ninny" Threadgood in the waiting room, and her heartwarming and hilarious stories about Idgie and Ruth and the Whistle Stop Café inspire Evelyn to do something more with her life. The multicareered Fannie Flagg is a wonder, and her books are both sweet and tart, like the fine apple pie served at the Whistle Stop Café.

Good Grief, Lolly Winston, 2004

Widowed after only three years of marriage, Sophie Stanton is overwhelmed by despair. When she starts going to work in her bathrobe, she decides to leave everything behind and move to Ashland, Oregon. As she mourns her late husband and her old life, she starts to heal and put the pieces of her life back together again. *Good Grief,* Winston's debut book, touches the reader with its poignant view of grief.

The House on Mango Street, Sandra Cisneros, 1991

In a book inspired by the author's childhood, Esperanza Cordero seeks her own identity and place in the community while growing up in the Hispanic section of Chicago. The story begins when Esperanza is 12, and her family can finally move from an apartment to their own (albeit disappointingly run-down) house. This coming-of-age tale follows Esperanza and her friends as they experience puberty and progress into adulthood. Lyrically spare and written in a youth's voice, Cisneros has carefully chosen each word in this superb novel.

I Capture the Castle, Dodie Smith, 1948

Seventeen-year-old aspiring author Cassandra Mortmain lives in a dilapidated castle with her sister and father. Set in 1930s England, this book has withstood the test of time and become a beloved classic.

An Expert Speaks

"This is one of the most endearing—and dear—novels I have read. *I Capture the Castle* is a coming-of-age book, the story of Cassandra Mortmain, told through her diary. Cassandra lives in the midst of an eccentric family; her father suffers from writer's block, the family as a whole suffers from poverty, and Cassandra suffers from all the agonies of growing up in proximity to a beautiful, embittered sister, a bohemian stepmother, a slightly cracked father, and a clutch of beautiful male neighbors. In short, barring the beautiful men, it reminded me very much of growing up with my father, Robert Bly, who is a poet without a writing block but with a deeply eccentric sense of life and its comforts."

—Eloisa James, author

The Jane Austen Book Club, Karen Joy Fowler, 2004

Five women and one man are connected by their mutual love of the work of Jane Austen. Their group meets once a month to discuss a specific Austen book, and their gatherings begin to change each of their lives. You don't have to be an Austen fan to enjoy this book, but it's even better if you are.

The Kitchen God's Wife, Amy Tan, 1991

Weili Jiang ("Winnie") has kept secrets from her daughter Pearl, just as Pearl has kept her own secrets from Winnie. As Winnie tells Pearl the story of her harrowing life before coming to America, mother and daughter start to heal the rift that separates them. Tan is brilliant at chronicling the universal communication problems between mothers and daughters.

My Sister's Keeper, Jodi Picoult, 2004

Conceived in vitro, teenaged Anna Fitzgerald is perpetually confined to home after being forced over the years to donate bone marrow to her sick older sister. Now her parents are trying to force her to donate a kidney, and she's tired of being spare parts. A perennial favorite with book discussion groups, Picoult handles a difficult topic in each of her books with skill and grace.

The Notebook, Nicholas Sparks, 1996

In a rest home, 80-year-old Noah Calhoun watches his beloved wife Allie struggle with Alzheimer's and reminisces about their love story. From falling in love as teenagers to meeting again three weeks before Allie's wedding to another man, theirs is a love so strong that it can perform miracles. Alternately moving and sentimental, you cannot help but be touched by *The Notebook*.

The No. 1 Ladies' Detective Agency, Alexander McCall Smith, 1998

Mma "Precious" Ramotswe opens the first private detective agency in Botswana and quickly finds herself with clients and mysteries to solve. With Agatha Christie as her role model, Precious finds her knowledge of human nature of more value than forensic science in solving her cases. With its vivid sense of place (and such an exotic place, too) and its wonderfully appealing characters, McCall Smith's book is not just for mystery readers.

Patty Jane's House of Curl, Lorna Landvik, 1995

Follow the hopes, dreams, and sorrows of two wacky Minnesotan sisters, Patty Jane and Harriet, as they face life's challenges in their own unique manner. Former stand-up comic Landvik keeps the laughs coming, along with a spattering of tears, as she creates a winning debut novel about family, friends, food, and the importance of a good hairstyle.

The Secret History, Donna Tartt, 1992

Impoverished Richard Papen arrives at the small Vermont college of Hampden and soon becomes involved with a group of wealthy students and a morally corrupt professor, all of whom share a secret. It's a gripping, literary psychological thriller!

The Secret Life of Bees, Sue Monk Kidd, 2002

In the rural South of the 1960s, 14-year-old Lily Owens runs away from her cold, cruel father. With the help of her beloved housekeeper/nanny Rosaleen, Lily finds a new home and new life in Tiburon, South Carolina, with three beekeeping sisters who knew Lily's late mother. Beautifully written and full of hope, we have yet to find one person who didn't love this book.

The Shadow of the Wind, Carlos Ruiz Zafon, 2004

In 1945 Barcelona, Daniel Sempere is taken to a secret library (called the Cemetery of Forgotten Books), where he is allowed to pick one book for himself. Daniel chooses *The Shadow of the Wind* by Julian Carax and loves it so much that he wants to read more books by the author. Unfortunately, Daniel discovers that someone is destroying every book written by Carax and, if Daniel doesn't stop him, soon Carax's literary legacy will be lost forever. This international best-seller is fascinating, magical, and unforgettable.

Singing in the Comeback Choir, Bebe Moore Campbell, 1998

Like many women, African-American television producer Maxine McCoy has to juggle the personal and the professional sides of her life in Campbell's realistically complex novel of the importance of family. Maxine returns to her childhood home in Philadelphia and the grandmother, Lindy, who raised her. Not only has her grandmother refused to move from her home in a run-down, increasingly dangerous neighborhood, but she has also lost all her joy in life. When Lindy is invited to sing in the choir, Maxine hopes it will encourage her grandmother to embrace life again. What warm and nourishing fiction this is.

The Sparrow, Mary Doria Russell, 1997

Jesuit priest Father Emilio Sandoz is part of a special team to visit Alpha Centauri to discover extraterrestrial life. What he sees there leaves Father Sandoz damaged forever. More than a science fiction tale or a search for God, *The Sparrow* is an absorbing tale that you will think about long after you have finished reading it.

> **An Expert Speaks** _____
>
> *"The Sparrow,* by Mary Doria Russell, with its great characterizations, is a genre-blended delight. This is funny, sad, and thought-provoking—all in one great book."
>
> —Lisa Colcord, librarian

Talk Before Sleep, Elizabeth Berg, 1994

When Ruth Thomas is diagnosed with breast cancer, Ann Stanley and three of Ruth's other friends join together to help take care of her. While we tried not to duplicate Oprah's choices (and it hasn't been easy because Oprah has picked some wonderful books!), we couldn't pass up this one. Berg's writing is lyrical; her characters realistic and big-hearted; and by the end of the book, you are drained of all emotion. However, it's worth all the tears.

The Thirteenth Tale, Diane Setterfield, 2006

Quiet, bookish Margaret Lea is summoned to the house of the famous reclusive writer Vida Winter, who wants Margaret to write her biography. Vida's tale is almost gothic, with tortured heroes and heroines that go mad. *The Thirteenth Tale* is a gem of a book—a page-turner that will keep you riveted.

> **You Can Book on It!** _____
>
> Sure, there were book clubs before Oprah's. Diane Rehm and Charlie Rose were doing book recommendations for years before Oprah decided that she would share her love of reading by recommending some current titles that she enjoyed. From 1996 to 2002, each of her 48 recommendations sold over 650,000 each. When she discontinued her club in 2002, people mourned its demise—but not for long. In 2003, the book club returned with a vengeance ("this time it's personal") and in a surprise move, her choices were the classic books we tried to avoid in college. Her first book was *East of Eden* by John Steinbeck, and it shot to the top of the bestseller list. Only Oprah has the power to make Tolstoy, Faulkner, and Pearl S. Buck hot again. As Oprah has said, "My mission is to make this the biggest book club in the world and get people reading again. Not just reading, but reading great books."

The Time Traveler's Wife, Audrey Niffenegger, 2003

When Henry, a librarian at the Newberry Library in Chicago, experiences stress, his unusual condition, known as Chrono-Displacement Disorder, makes him disappear from this time period and reappear in the past or the future. As you can imagine, this puts a real strain on his marriage to Claire, since she never knows when he will disappear or where he will reappear. But their love is timeless—literally timeless. This brilliantly imaginative book is a tour de force.

Tourist Season, Carl Hiaasen, 1986

Miami tourists start disappearing when an unusual terrorist group targets people whom they believe are ruining Florida. Hiaasen, a columnist for *The Miami Herald* and a fourth-generation Floridian, is a brilliant author, whom some readers find hysterically funny (though some readers just find him to be hysterical). He excels in creating outrageous characters and outlandish plots, but in all, his home state of Florida shines.

Water for Elephants, Sara Gruen, 2006

Veterinary student Jacob Jankowski joins the Benzini Brothers' Most Spectacular Show on Earth, a traveling circus struggling to survive during the Great Depression. There, his veterinary skills prove useful, especially with the star performer, Rosie the elephant, whom Jacob comes to love. With lush details and strong characters, Gruen has re-created the fascinating world of the circus and the unique people who populate it.

A Week in Winter, Marcia Willett, 2002

When independent widow Maudie Todhunter decides to sell the family farmhouse, it stirs up memories and opposition from her family. British author Willett's American debut is filled with the same kind of warmth and charm found in the books of Rosamunde Pilcher and Maeve Binchy.

The Weight of Water, Anita Shreve, 1997

A magazine photographer becomes obsessed by a century-old murder when she is hired to take photos of the place where the murder occurred. The sense of doom grows as the story lines switch from contemporary time with her and her husband, to the time of the murders with the victims. Shreve is always elegantly readable.

Word of Honor, Nelson DeMille, 1985

Fifteen years ago, Ben Tyson was a lieutenant in the U.S. Army, serving in Vietnam. Now he is a regular family man and corporate executive. But his quiet life is turned upside down when a book about a hushed-up army massacre at a French hospital in Hue is published, accusing Ben's platoon of committing the crime. DeMille is a brilliant author and one of the few contemporary writers whose books are read by both men and women.

Chapter 3

Literary Fiction: Books Worthy of Oprah

In This Chapter

◆ Classics: handily highbrow

◆ More great reads: not so hoity-toity!

What's the difference between popular fiction and literary fiction, we hear you ask? According to our very subjective criteria, a book qualifies as literary fiction when …

◆ The writing style is what you remember when you finish the book.

◆ You read a sentence out loud just to hear the beautiful language.

◆ You don't have a sufficient number of superlatives in your vocabulary to recommend it highly enough.

You may not agree with all of our choices, but we loved them (and it *is* our book!).

Classics

The Handmaid's Tale, Margaret Atwood, 1986

In the not-so-distant future, a group of religious zealots have taken over the United States and turned it into The Republic of Gilead. Because Gilead women are not fertile, a whole new social stratum is created that consists of women known as handmaids, who are bred just to have babies. A chilling view of a possible future, Atwood's *Handmaid's Tale* is as brilliant as her other, less didactic books.

The Plot Against America, Philip Roth, 2004

What if the United States never entered World War II and instead negotiated a peace accord with Hitler? In Roth's well-received alternative history, Charles A. Lindbergh wins the presidential election against FDR in 1940, permits Hitler to take over Europe, and initiates anti-Semitic policies against the Jews in the United States. If you have never read Roth (and feel like you're missing the literary boat, so to speak), read *The Plot Against America*.

Rabbit Run, John Updike, 1960

Harry "Rabbit" Angstrom is a former high school basketball star trapped in an unhappy marriage who decides to run away from his discontent. He ends up at his former coach's house and becomes entangled in an affair with a prostitute. *Rabbit Run* is the first book of a four-book series. Harry is a metaphor for the suburban man, and each book chronicles a different decade in Harry's life. Updike has been called one of the greatest novelists of his generation, but it's a lot of angst to handle in one sitting, so pace yourself.

We the Living, Ayn Rand, 1936

In Communist Russia, three idealists—engineer Kira Argounova, her lover, former Russian aristocrat Leo Kovalensky, and her other lover, proletariat Andrei Taganov—struggle to keep their own identities in a totalitarian society.

We Were the Mulvaneys, Joyce Carol Oates, 1996

The Mulvaney family seemed to have it all. Wealthy and socially prominent, the four Mulvaney children grew up on a beautiful farm in upstate New York. But a terrible act of violence against one of the children destroys the family and any happy memories. Oates is a prolific writer of fiction, nonfiction, poetry, and short stories—wait, there's more—children's and teen books, and plays. Is there anything this woman can't write?

An Expert Speaks

"*We the Living* by Ayn Rand: Although much has been said about Rand's ideology, few have recognized her tremendous skill as a writer. And there's no better example of Rand's talent than *We the Living*, her first novel of fiction and her shortest. Set in Communist Russia, the novel is at heart a tragic love story, and since it is fueled rather than overshadowed by Rand's philosophy, it showcases both her exquisite eye for detail and her knack for creating full-bodied characters who brim with vitality and passion … I was so affected after reading it the first time that right then and there I decided to go into publishing."

—Brianna Yamashita, publishing manager

More Great Reads

All the Pretty Horses, Cormac McCarthy, 1992

After his grandfather dies and his mother wants to give up the family ranch, 16-year-old John Grady Cole leaves West Texas with two other boys and rides his horse to Mexico. In a harsh landscape, McCarthy creates a fable of a young man coming of age in 1948. This is the first book in McCarthy's Border Trilogy.

The Amazing Adventures of Kavalier and Clay, Michael Chabon, 2000

In 1939, Sammy Klayman and his Czech cousin, Josef Kavalier, team up to create a newspaper comic-strip hero called The Escapist, loosely based on Houdini, and achieve success beyond their dreams. Chabon skillfully mixes fantasy and reality as he writes about the immigrant experience in New York City and the growing world of comics. What's real and what's imagined? You be the judge.

Atonement, Ian McEwan, 2002

The Tallis children's lives are changed forever when one of them misunderstands an argument they witnessed from a distance. McEwan starts this beautifully realized novel in England in 1935 and continues it through World War II. McEwan writes the most realistic and emotionally wrenching description of the evacuation of Dunkirk that we have ever read.

Bel Canto, Ann Patchett, 2001

American opera star Roxane Coss and Japanese CEO Mr. Hosokawa are among the hostages when political terrorists crash the embassy while Coss is performing. The lines between the hostages and their captors begin to connect as they recognize each other's humanity. Rich in characterizations (even the secondary characters are memorable!), and filled with moral ambiguity, *Bel Canto* will keep you riveted until the last page.

Captain Corelli's Mandolin, Louis de Bernieres, 1994

When Italian and German troops invade the Greek Island of Cephallonia in World War II, Captain Antonio Corelli, the commanding officer, falls in love with Pelagia, the local doctor's independent daughter. That brief description cannot do justice to a book so brilliant, so sly, and so heartrending that, though you know you might break into tears at the next page, you still don't want it to end.

Charms for an Easy Life, Kay Gibbons, 1992

Charlie Kate, her daughter, Sophia, and her granddaughter, Margaret, are three generations of strong-willed Carolina women. Practical and warmhearted describes both the women and Gibbons's writing style.

The Curious Incident of the Dog in the Night-Time, Mark Hadden, 2003

Inspired by his literary hero, Sherlock Holmes, Christopher Boone, an autistic 15-year-old, decides to investigate the strange death of his neighbor's dog, Wellington. In the process, he discovers some clues to his mother's mysterious death two years earlier.

An Expert Speaks

> "*The Curious Incident of the Dog in the Night-Time* is truly a *tour-de-force,* from the first jumbled numbered chapters to the poignant family drama at the heart of this supposed investigation Christopher conducts into who killed Wellington, his neighbor's dog. There are no filters at all between the reader and this first-person narrative, thus no help at all as to how to interpret what Christopher is telling us and what it means. An unforgettable, deeply felt reading experience that will make you hesitate if you ever get the urge to stereotype another human being."
>
> —Jo Manning, author

Empire Falls, Richard Russo, 2001

In the small town of Empire Falls, Maine, Miles Roby's life has taken a bad turn: his wife has left him; his daughter is having trouble at school; and his wastrel father shows up to ask for money. Will these tragedies finally force Miles to make some decisions in his drifting life? Russo's dry humor and realistically nuanced characters are the trademarks of his novels.

Girl in Hyacinth Blue, Susan Vreeland, 1992

An unknown Vermeer painting is at the center of this novel, which tracks the owners of this rare piece of art. Going backward in time, the owners range from a mathematician, to a Nazi looter, to a Jewish family. This story goes all the way back to the creation of the painting. Vreeland has created a jewel of a book, elegantly written and thoroughly compelling.

The God of Small Things, Arundhati Roy, 1997

Gracefully switching backward and forward in time, we learn about siblings Rahel and her twin brother, Estha, who must cope with the accidental drowning of Sophie Mol, their cousin. But was it an accident? Roy's lush, colorful prose and magical realism bring a dreamlike quality to this entrancing story.

Happenstance, Carol Shields, 1994

In one tumultuous week, a husband and wife, Brenda and Jack Bowman, each go through a midlife crisis.

An Expert Speaks

"*Happenstance* follows a 'typical' married suburban couple as they spend a week apart. The book is actually two novels in one—the first half tells the story from the wife's point of view, and the second half tells the same story from the husband's perspective. Both narrators remember the same key events in their courtship, but interpret these moments in entirely different ways. It's a fascinating puzzle of a relationship, and Carol Shields is a master at giving us glimpses of what's really going on beneath the surfaces we see every day. Her characters aren't rich or gorgeous or glamorous, but they are compelling because they remind me that everyone, from my next door neighbor to the staff at my local library, is constantly embroiled in an epic drama all his own. Our psyches are shaped by personal histories that we can never truly share with another human being, and yet somehow, we manage to fall in love and stay together and raise children despite the fact that on the most fundamental levels, we really don't know our partners at all. Every time I read it, I learn something new about storytelling."

—Beth Kendrick, author

The Hours, Michael Cunningham, 1998

Three separate stories, all with a connection to Virginia Woolf, converge in Cunningham's lyrical award-winning novel. Virginia Woolf is in the process of writing her masterpiece, *Mrs. Dalloway*, but contemplates suicide. In 1949, a pregnant Laura Brown prepares for her husband's birthday but really wants to immerse herself in Woolf's book, and, in present-day New York, Clarissa is giving a party for her dear friend, a writer dying of AIDS. Okay, you can tell that this is a very difficult book to describe, but if you read it, you will lose yourself in Cunningham's delicate prose and ingenious plot.

The Kite Runner, Khaled Hosseini, 2003

An unlikely bond is formed between Amir, the son of a well-to-do businessman in Kabul, and Hassan, the son of the businessman's servant, while they grow up in Afghanistan in the 1970s. Amir betrays his friend and is haunted by it all his life, even after Amir and his father escape to America. Heartbreaking, yet redemptive, this beautiful novel gives an insight into a misunderstood culture.

Like Water for Chocolate, Laura Esquival, 1992

Tita, the youngest daughter of the family, has always known that she would have the duty of taking care of her mother, Mama Elena, which meant never marrying and always being at Mama Elena's beck and call. When Pedro, the man she loves, becomes engaged to her sister, Tita, who is not allowed to show her feelings, uses her passionate cooking to express her despair and misery. Magical and romantic, *Like Water for Chocolate* is utterly irresistible. Devour it!

The Lone Ranger and Tonto Fistfight in Heaven, Sherman Alexie, 1993

This series of short stories chronicles modern life on the Spokane Indian reservation. Alexie, a Coeur d'Alene Indian and an author of several books of poetry, uses the same combination of lyricism, power, and brevity found in his critically acclaimed poetry to write realistically about the alcoholism and depression that are part of reservation life. The stories sing.

Love Medicine, Louise Erdrich, 1984

Love Medicine chronicles the stories of two generations of Chippewa families in North Dakota. Erdrich writes of both pain and happiness, and the story, while slow moving, is beautiful in its emotion.

The Lovely Bones, Alice Sebold, 2002

Fourteen-year-old Susie Salmon tells the story of her murder as she watches her family and her killer from heaven. Sound grim? *The Lovely Bones* can be a difficult story to read but is never grisly or gratuitous. And astonishingly, Sebold's elegant prose and compassion leave you with a feeling of hope and peace.

Middlesex, Jeffrey Eugenides, 2002

Calliope Stefanadies, a hermaphrodite, introduces her story by explaining that she was born twice, first as a woman and then as a man. *Middlesex* spans three generations and two continents, as Cal begins with the story of his grandparents, Desdemona and Eleutherios, and their escape from Greece during the Turkish siege of the 1920s. A sprawling epic of a book, *Middlesex* is also an intimate portrait of a person who cannot fit in.

Perfume: The Story of a Murderer, Patrick Suskind, 1986

In eighteenth-century France, Jean-Baptiste Grenouille is born with a perfect sense of smell. As he grows up, he is apprenticed to a perfume maker to learn the craft of making scents. To concoct the perfect scent, Grenouille begins murdering young virgins for their heavenly smell. Suskind has created a frightening, haunted, and soulless murderer who will both repel and fascinate you.

Plainsong, Kent Haruf, 1999

Seven residents of the small town of Holt, Colorado, cross paths and stories in Haruf's novel about what makes a family. Tom Guthrie's wife has left him to cope with two small boys. A pregnant Victoria Roubideaux is kicked out of the house by her mother, but teacher Maggie Jones helps her find a home with Raymond and Ernest McPheron, elderly bachelor brother farmers. Well-crafted and uplifting, *Plainsong* warms the heart.

Possession, A. S. Byatt, 1990

While researching Victorian poet R. H. Ash, contemporary scholar Roland Michell finds two letters from an unknown woman that hint at an affair with Ash. He concludes that the other woman is poetess Christabel LaMotte and, in his search for answers, Michell finds himself in an alliance with beautiful Maud Bailey, not only a scholar of LaMotte but also distantly related to her. An elegant detective story, with a tantalizing premise (some think Byatt based the characters of Ash and LaMotte on Robert Browning and Christina Rossetti), *Possession* dazzles the reader with its sumptuous writing and gothic passions. Byatt even wrote the poetry attributed to the fictitious Ash and LaMotte. P.S.: The movie was very good, too!

Practical Magic, Alice Hoffman, 1995

Their ties to spells and magic unite three generations of Owens women in Hoffman's tale of the bonds of sisterhood. Sally is the practical one, while Gillian is the wild child. Raised by their eccentric aunts, the girls try to avoid their magical talents but ultimately embrace them. This book is lyrical and lovely.

The Prince of Tides, Pat Conroy, 1986

In order to help his catatonic twin sister, the renowned poet Savannah, Tom Wingo leaves his home in South Carolina for Manhattan to work with Savannah's psychiatrist, Susan Lowenstein. *The Prince of Tides* has plenty of dysfunctional family relationships, horrifying emotional secrets, and a convoluted plot, all of which will keep you riveted for the entire 300-plus pages. We know some people liked the movie, but it failed to capture Conroy's passionate writing style.

The Shipping News, Annie Proulx, 1993

In the unforgiving landscape of Newfoundland, Quogue starts a new life with his two children after the death of his faithless wife. Either you love Proulx and her characters, or you want a drink while you're reading her—or maybe both!

Snow Falling on Cedars, David Guterson, 1994

In 1954, fisherman Carl Heine is murdered and another fisherman, Kabuo Myomoto, is accused of the crime. Local reporter Ismael Chambers observes the trial with more than a journalist's dispassionate eye; he is in love with Kabuo's wife. The atmospheric setting of the island of San Pedro off the coast of Washington State is the perfect backdrop for a novel of regret, prejudice, and hatred.

Three Junes, Julia Glass, 2002

Set in three separate summers spanning ten years, *Three Junes* is the tale of three different people—two members of a Scottish family and a young artist— whose lives connect over the years. The first summer features Paul McCloud, a widower who describes how he met his late wife in Greece. The next summer focuses on Fenno McCloud, Paul's gay son, who had moved to New York to blend in better, but must return to Scotland for his father's funeral. And, finally, the last summer centers on Fern Olitsky, the artist Paul met in Greece. This delicate blending of characters and the graceful unfolding of family relationships won the National Book Award.

The Tortilla Curtain, T. Coraghessan Boyle, 1995

A wealthy suburbanite couple in Southern California accidentally meet an illegal immigrant couple from Mexico and experience life-changing events. Contrasting the affluent lifestyle of the Mossbachers with the poverty of the Rincons, Boyle makes you realize that the poor family is living a fuller life than the rich folks. *The Tortilla Curtain* may remind you a bit of the movie *Crash*.

Underworld, Don DeLillo, 1997

Beginning in 1951, on the day the Soviet Union detonated an atomic bomb, DeLillo explores American cultural history through a number of characters, including waste management firm executive Nick Shay; Cotter, a young African American boy from Harlem; Klara Sax, an artist expressing herself in the desert; and controversial comedian Lenny Bruce.

An Expert Speaks

"This magnificent, many-voiced, and soulful symphony of a novel … achieves an extraordinary sensory and psychological intensity and exquisite tenderness as DeLillo interweaves the geopolitical with the personal and explores questions of engagement, empathy, and expression."

—Donna Seaman, editor

Waiting, Ha Jin, 1999

Lin Kong, a military doctor, agrees to his mother's dying wish of an arranged marriage with Shuyu, an unsophisticated older woman with lotus (bound) feet. When Kong falls in love with Manna Wu, he must be separated for 18 years before he can divorce, as dictated by the rules of Communist China. Think *Doctor Zhivago* in Communist China.

White Teeth, Zadie Smith, 2000

In Smith's best-selling debut novel, she mixes cultures in gritty 1970s London. Archie Jones and Samed Iqbal bond during their service in the British Army in World War II and meet up again 30 years later, after marriages, children, and failed dreams. All of the vibrant, oh-so-human characters are brilliantly drawn, and the story is by turns touching, funny, and poignant. It's a window into a different kind of immigrant experience.

And the Award Goes to …

Several of the books in this chapter were awarded the Pulitzer Prize for Fiction:

- *The Shipping News* by E. Annie Proulx (1994)
- *The Hours* by Michael Cunningham (1999)
- *Empire Falls* by Richard Russo (2002)
- *Middlesex* by Jeffrey Eugenides (2003)

Chapter 4

Mystery: Get a Clue

In This Chapter

- ◆ Amateur sleuths: where is Jessica Fletcher when you need her?
- ◆ Private detectives: heirs of Hammett
- ◆ Procedurals: just the facts, ma'am
- ◆ Historical sleuths: crime through time

From Edgar Allen Poe to Sara Paretsky, mysteries have always been popular with readers. Whether you enjoy following the clues with a sophisticated sleuth like Lord Peter Wimsey or walking the mean streets with Philip Marlowe, there's something on this list for you.

Amateur Sleuths

For millions of people, television's Jessica Fletcher is the quintessential amateur sleuth—a sharp-witted, sharp-tongued woman, who seems to stumble into mysteries and murders every week. You've got to wonder why anyone would be her friend, especially since people keep dying around her! While it seems that almost every amateur detective out there solving mysteries is a little old lady, in reality, there exists a huge variety of amateur sleuths—everything from an herb store owner to a forensic anthropologist. There's something for every reader!

Classics

Murder at the Vicarage, Agatha Christie, 1930

When the detestable Colonel Protheroe is found murdered, Miss Jane Marple searches for the killer among the residents of St. Mary Mead. If anyone can claim the title of Queen of Crime, hands down, we think it is Agatha Christie. Christie almost invented the genre with her cleverly constructed plots, and Miss Marple remains the "gold standard" of amateur sleuths.

> ## The Rest of the Story _____
>
> Christie wrote *The Mysterious Affair at Styles* several years after being challenged by her sister Madge, who didn't think Agatha could write a detective novel. Published in 1921, it became the first in her series featuring Belgian police officer turned private detective Hercule Poirot.

The Roman Hat Mystery, Ellery Queen, 1929

When a lawyer is killed while attending a play, Ellery Queen and his father, New York police inspector Richard Queen, investigate and discover that almost everyone had a motive for murdering the man. The pseudonym of cousins Frederick Dannay and Manfred Lee, Ellery Queen is the name of both the detective and the author. Queen inspired a radio show, several movies, a television series, and a mystery magazine, begun in 1941, that's still published.

A Study in Scarlet, Arthur Conan Doyle, 1890

Sherlock Holmes and Dr. John Watson's first case involves a mysterious double murder of two men who are found in a room with the German word for revenge written in blood on the wall. With the help of Watson, Holmes solves perplexing murders and battles his arch-nemesis Professor Moriarty in 4 novels and more than 50 short stories. While Holmes quickly became popular with millions of readers, Conan Doyle came to hate his hero. He even tried to kill him off in *The Memoirs of Sherlock Holmes.* However, public outcry forced him to bring Holmes back to life in his next book.

Whose Body?, Dorothy L. Sayers, 1923

After finding a murdered man in his bathtub, an architect asks Lord Peter Wimsey for help. Considered Christie's literary rival during the 1920s and 1930s, Dorothy L. Sayers refined the classic British mystery with her creation of a more nuanced amateur sleuth in the person of aristocratic Lord Peter Wimsey. Sayers's mysteries have the kind of devilishly clever plots (sometimes a bit too clever!) that mystery readers love. They also have elegant writing, beautifully evoked settings, and complex characters. With Sayers, detective fiction becomes literature.

More Great Reads

Aunt Dimity's Death, Nancy Atherton, 1992

When Lori Shephard travels to England to claim a bequest in a will, she finds out that Aunt Dimity, whom she thought was only an imaginary character in her childhood stories, turns out to have been a very real person, though now a ghost. This Aunt Dimity series contains several books, but we think the first is terrific. It's gentle, sweet, and just a bit romantic.

The Body in the Belfry, Katherine Hall Page, 1990

Minister's wife and caterer Faith Fairchild gets to know her new neighbors when the body of a beautiful blackmailer is found in the church belfry. Humor and food are the two most important ingredients in Page's deliciously entertaining mystery series. Readers who enjoy a classic whodunit will appreciate Page's skill in cooking up tempting traditional mysteries.

Bones, Jan Burke, 1999

Crime writer Irene Kelly isn't quite certain at first that Julia Sayres is another victim of serial killer Nick Parrish, but her suspicions are confirmed when Parrish agrees to take the police and Irene to the gravesite. Burke's books are a little edgier than your basic amateur sleuth novels, definitely not cozy mysteries. *Bones*, not the first book in the series, is one of the best.

Booked to Die, John Dunning, 1992

After quitting the Denver Police Department to open his own bookstore, Cliff Janeway finds himself once again doing detective work when a book scout is found murdered in his store. One of our favorite mysteries, this book is clever and interesting with oodles of details about book collecting.

Bootlegger's Daughter, Margaret Maron, 1992

While running for district judge, attorney Deborah Knott is asked by Gayle Whitehead to find out who murdered Gayle's mom 18 years ago. As the daughter of a famous bootlegger, Deborah understands the region and the small town of Cotton Grove, so she knows who to ask and how to get some answers. Maron's series featuring Knott is set in North Carolina, and she has few rivals when it comes to creating a strong sense of place.

Bubbles Unbound, Sarah Strohmeyer, 2001

Beautician and aspiring journalist Bubbles Yablonsky gets her big break when she stumbles across a murder that could be connected to Lehigh's wealthiest and most powerful family. Strohmeyer's wonderfully outrageous and bawdy sense of humor gives her "Bubbles" books their distinctive flavor, which Strohmeyer has carried over to her recent chick lit/women's fiction novels.

The Cat Who Could Read Backwards, Lillian Jackson Braun, 1966

With a little help from Siamese cat Koko, newspaper journalist Jim "Qwill" Qwilleran investigates the murder of a gallery owner and an art critic. While Qwill starts out with just one cat, YumYum, another Siamese who helps solve murders, soon joins Koko! Braun, also a journalist, began the "Cat Who" series in the 1960s.

Catering to Nobody, Diane Mott Davidson, 1990

When her ex-father-in-law is poisoned at an affair she catered, Gertrude "Goldy" Bear, the owner of Goldilocks Catering, decides to investigate before the police close down her business permanently. This cozy mystery featuring charming "Goldy Bear" is part of an entertaining series. We've tried some of Goldy's recipes in the book—not bad!

 You Can Book on It!

"Cozy" refers to the tone of a mystery and is most often used to describe mysteries in the amateur sleuth subgenre. In a cozy mystery, violence and graphic language are kept to a minimum. The mood of the story is gentle, civilized, and refined. Most of the characters know each other, and the murder takes place in a closed environment, such as a country estate or small town.

Dating Dead Men, Harley Jane Kozak, 2004

Wollstonecraft Shelley (known as Wollie to her friends), a greeting card designer and storeowner, is trying to earn extra money for her struggling card store by dating 60 men in 40 days as part of a research project that could earn her $5,000. She puts everything on hold when she receives a phone call from her mentally ill brother, who claims to have witnessed a murder. This debut novel by actress-turned-writer Kozak is a delightful blend of humor and mystery; it's a hoot.

Death on Demand, Carolyn Hart, 1987

Mystery bookstore owner Annie Laurence must play amateur sleuth when an author is found murdered in her store after a meeting of local mystery writers. With her cleverly constructed plots, we think Hart is the literary heir to Agatha Christie. In addition, Hart fills each of her Annie Laurence books with wonderful references to classic mystery writers and novels.

Fellowship of Fear, Aaron Elkins, 1982

While on a lecture tour in Europe, American anthropology professor Gideon Oliver finds his academic research skills quite handy when he needs to find out who is threatening him. Before there were Patricia Cornwell novels or *CSI*, Elkins, whose own academic background is in anthropology, used science to solve the crimes in his series featuring Gideon "the skeleton detective" Oliver.

Fool's Puzzle, Earlene Fowler, 1994

Benni Harper, a recently widowed rancher's wife and curator of the San Celina Folk Art Museum, investigates when an artist is killed in the museum. While Fowler uses the name of a different quilt pattern in each of her titles, you don't have to know the difference between basting and batting (we don't) to love her crafty stories.

Generous Death, Nancy Pickard, 1984

Wealthy donors to the Port Frederick Civic Foundation are being murdered one by one, and the nasty little notes left beside the bodies are the only clues that Jenny Cain, director of the foundation, has to find the murderer before she becomes the next victim. Jenny is a likable heroine, and Pickard throws in a dash of romance in the form of a police detective, who eventually marries Jenny in a subsequent book in the series.

Nerve, Dick Francis, 1964

Aging jockey Philip Nore turns amateur sleuth to find the murderer of a track photographer. With a background in horse racing, it's not surprising that Francis excels in re-creating this unique milieu in his terrific mysteries. Liz (the Queen of England to you!) loves him—that's good enough for us.

A New Leash on Death, Susan Conant, 1990

Dog's Life columnist Holly Winter becomes a detective when a member of her Thursday night obedience class is strangled with a dog leash. In this first book in the series, Holly is dog-less until she adopts the victim's Alaskan malamute Rowdy, who helps in solving the crime. Conant's books all have some connection to dogs with interesting tidbits about professional dog handling.

One for the Money, Janet Evanovich, 1994

This first book in Evanovich's wildly popular Stephanie Plum series introduces the klutzy heroine; Joe Morelli, her handsome detective lover; Ranger, the enigmatic hunk who wants to be her lover; her gun-toting granny; her boss and sleazy cousin, Vinnie; her pet hamster; and her neighbors, the quirky residents of Trenton, New Jersey's "Burg." Hilarious characters add to the story's charm. Bounty hunting was never so much fun!

The Salaryman's Wife, Sujata Massey, 1998

Japanese-American Rei Shimura earns a living teaching English in Tokyo, but she takes on the job of amateur sleuth when a businessman's wife is murdered. Japanese culture and history play an important part in Massey's novels featuring Shimura. Massey, a reporter for *The Baltimore Sun*, taught English in Japan before completing this book, an Agatha Award winner for best first novel.

Strangled Prose, Joan Hess, 1986

Bookseller Claire Malloy hosts a signing for a local romance author whose latest novel contains secrets someone is willing to kill for. Hess's distinctive sense of humor is refreshingly sharp, and although a few readers may find her a bit too acerbic, others (us included) enjoy her wicked wit, especially Malloy's on-going battles with her teenage daughter.

The Thin Woman, Dorothy Cannell, 1980

Overweight and overwrought, Ellie Simon must not only lose 64 pounds but also convince hired fiancé Bentley Haskell to complete the book he's always wanted to write in order to inherit her uncle's estate. You'll love spunky Ellie in this first book in a charming and humorous series.

Thyme of Death, Susan Wittig Albert, 1992

China Bayles leaves behind the high-powered life of an attorney in Houston to open her own herb shop in Pecan Springs, Texas, but she finds that small towns are not immune to murder. Solving the mystery is only one reason why readers enjoy her books; Albert's characters are so endearing that fans feel like they are old friends. Albert cleverly incorporates herbs in the plot of each of her books in the delightful China Bayles series.

Track of the Cat, Nevada Barr, 1993

Park ranger Anna Pigeon investigates the death of one of her co-workers who was mauled by a mountain lion. The unique settings of each of Barr's books, national parks and monuments such as the Natchez Trace Parkway, the Statue of Liberty, and Ellis Island, are as important to the story as the characters and plots.

Wish You Were Here, Rita Mae Brown and Sneaky Pie Brown, 1990

When people in the small Virginia town of Crozet begin receiving "wish you were here" post cards right before they are murdered, Mary Minor Haristeen, the town's postmistress, investigates the murders with the help of her cat Mrs. Murphy and her Welsh Corgi Tucker. Animals not only help solve crimes, but they also talk to each other in Brown's wonderfully cozy "Mrs. Murphy" series.

The Rest of the Story

Rita Mae Brown is an Emmy-nominated screenwriter, a poet, a renowned social activist, and the author of the classic feminist book, *The Rubyfruit Jungle.* The Mrs. Murphy mysteries are "co-authored" by Brown's cat, Sneaky Pie, a tiger cat Brown adopted from her local Virginia SPCA. In addition to her fiction and Mrs. Murphy mysteries, Brown is the author of the Sister Jane Foxhunting mystery series.

Private Detectives

It's the tough guys and the beautiful babes. It's pulp fiction. When they were first written in the 1930s and 1940s, the classic private eye mysteries were all about *noir.* Modern writers of the genre have honed the characterizations and lightened up the story from the early days of dark alleys and double-crossing broads. But the investigator who could survive the betrayal and break the case wide open still echoes from the old days. Nowadays, the private eye is as often a woman as a man, and she's just as capable of handling matters when the going gets tough.

You Can Book on It!

"Noir" is used to describe mysteries that have a dark, harsh setting, but the protagonist doesn't have to be a private detective.

Classics

The Big Sleep, Raymond Chandler, 1939

When he is hired to investigate a case of blackmail, Philip Marlowe becomes entangled in a web of deceit and murder. With Marlowe, Chandler created a wonderfully complex protagonist: a street-tough, hard-edged realist who is also an idealistic romantic. Chandler's books take the hard-boiled private eye novel to the level of literature. Equally talented at creating a strong sense of place, Chandler's sharp, stylish prose expertly evokes Los Angeles in the 1920s and 1930s.

Fer-de-Lance, Rex Stout, 1934

Nero Wolfe finds that the disappearance of an immigrant ironworker is somehow connected to the mysterious death of a college president. With his Nero Wolfe series, Stout gives readers two detectives: Wolfe and Archie Goodwin, his partner. With few exceptions, Wolfe remains firmly planted in his New York City brownstone, leaving the actual legwork to Goodwin. Stout was a master at blending the traditional detective novel format with the newer hard-boiled private detective style.

An Expert Speaks

"Rex Stout's stories about a detective, Nero Wolfe, and his sidekick, Archie Goodwin, are wonderful reads. I was especially happy when Stout put together some of the recipes Fritz cooked, and Nero and Archie ate, into a cookbook. The idea of being a hermit in the middle of Manhattan, growing orchids on the roof, planning exotic menus, and solving crimes with my brain is my idea of the perfect occupation, almost as good as being a librarian."

—Blanche Woolls, librarian, author, editor

I, the Jury, Mickey Spillane, 1947

In classic pulp fiction style, Mike Hammer is a detective sworn to seek revenge on the murderer of a friend. *I, The Jury* is packed with so much violence and sex that in the 1940s it was one of "those books" that was hidden under a mattress or behind the sofa. Mike Hammer, the tough-talking, hard-drinking private eye, wouldn't hesitate before sleeping with a doll and would only briefly hesitate before shooting her if she betrayed him. Once Spillane started appearing on the books' covers as Hammer, the public couldn't tell where Hammer ended and Spillane began.

The Maltese Falcon, Dashiell Hammett, 1930

San Francisco P.I. Sam Spade wonders if there is some connection between the beautiful Brigid O'Shaughnessy, who needs his help, and the murder of Sam's partner, Miles Archer. Hammett's book was popular, but it became legendary when it was turned into a movie starring the quintessential hard-boiled P.I., Humphrey Bogart. Authors like Ross McDonald, Tony Hillerman, and Raymond Chandler credit Hammett with developing the private detective genre, opening the door for their books.

The Rest of the Story

Hammett based his last book, the witty, sophisticated mystery *The Thin Man*, on his relationship with celebrity playwright Lillian Hellman.

More Great Reads

A Is for Alibi, Sue Grafton, 1982

Is there any mystery reader who doesn't know Kinsey Milhone? In Kinsey's first case, the twice-divorced California detective opens the file on an old case of a divorce lawyer poisoned by his second wife, when the same poison is found in another victim's body. With this book, Grafton wrote a classic hard-boiled private eye novel but changed the gender of the main character, becoming one of the founding mothers of today's independent female private detectives. And yes, you really should start with *A Is for Alibi.*

The Rest of the Story

Grafton began thinking about writing a mystery while going through a bitter divorce. She spent nights imagining how to kill her husband, but instead she channeled these thoughts into writing and began her alphabet series.

Baltimore Blues, Laura Lippman, 1997

Out-of-work journalist Tess Monahan is hired by her friend Rocky to follow his fiancée, but a supposedly simple case of surveillance turns into murder with Rocky as the number-one suspect. Lippman's Tess Monahan books have a strong connection to Baltimore, the series setting—not surprising since Lippman, like Tess, lives in Baltimore and wrote for *The Baltimore Sun.*

Bloody Waters, Carolina Garcia-Aguilera, 1996

Cuban American private eye Guadalupe "Lupe" Solano is hired by the adoptive parents of a terminally ill child to find the child's biological mother, but instead finds a baby-selling racket. Garcia-Aguilera puts her own colorful spin on the traditional dark private eye story, and her use of Cuban culture gives her books a cool twist.

China Trade, S. J. Rozan, 1994

A New York Chinatown museum puts Lydia Chin and her partner Bill Smith on retainer when some priceless porcelain is stolen. In each of the books in her Chin/Smith series, Rozan alternates character viewpoint and creates two different, yet equally entertaining, protagonists. Rozan is one of the few women to have won a Shamus Award, a major mystery writers' award.

You Can Book on It! _____

Ever wonder about the difference between "hard-boiled" and "soft-boiled" detective novels? Hard-boiled novels take a realistically gritty approach to murder, and violence and graphic language can be part of the story. In a soft-boiled mystery, the violence and language are, well, softened.

A Cold Day in Paradise, Steve Hamilton, 1998

Retired cop and former minor league baseball player Alex McKnight leaves his old life behind and moves to the remote town of Paradise, Michigan. However, his past catches up with him when he learns the man who shot him and side-lined his police career is out of jail and stalking him. Hamilton created the classic flawed hero in Alex, but he also gives his series a refreshing twist by using the unusual location of Michigan's Upper Peninsula (the "UP") rather than the mean streets of a big city as the setting for his books.

The Deep Blue Goodbye, John D. MacDonald, 1975

Travis McGee is hired to locate a newly paroled prisoner who has money belonging to someone else. While McGee is technically not a private eye—he lacks the official license—he fits the part with his cynicism and willingness to fight a corrupt system. The Florida-based setting of the series, where McGee lives on his houseboat, *The Busted Flush*, offered mystery readers an interesting alternative to the traditional urban settings found in almost every other P.I. novel of the 1970s.

Devil in a Blue Dress, Walter Mosley, 1990

After being fired from his factory job, Easy Rawlins agrees to find a woman in a blue dress, Daphne Monet, for a shifty mobster. As he begins his search for her and the $30,000 that disappeared with her, Rawlins finds himself deeply involved in the shady side of 1940s L.A. and the men who run it. Mosley's flawed characters and atmospheric settings are perfect for the reader looking for more than just whodunit.

A Drink Before the War, Dennis Lehane, 1994

P.I. partners Patrick Kenzie and Angela Gennaro think it's "easy money" when a Boston politician hires them to track down some stolen documents. Lehane quickly became known as the "new Chandler" after the publication of this book. He published several more titles in his Kenzie and Gennaro series before writing mysteries like *Mystic River*.

The Rest of the Story

Walter Mosley is best known for creating the character Easy Rawlins, a black private detective working in L.A. from the 1940s to the 1960s. Mosley portrays a side of L.A. that few novelists do—the black lower-class. With his cinematic writing style, Mosley has brought a different perspective to the hard-boiled detective novel. Easy does more than solve the mystery or find the girl; he copes with the racism and discrimination of a postwar America. Mosley, who is African American and Jewish, has been nominated for or has won most of the major mystery awards, including the Shamus, the Edgar, and the Dagger.

Edwin of the Iron Shoes, Marcia Muller, 1977

Sharon McCone, staff investigator for All Souls, a legal cooperative, constantly clashes with the San Francisco police. Her latest case is no exception, as she investigates the death of a small-time antique dealer. Muller is credited with creating the strong, female private investigator sleuth who first became popular in the 1970s. While she has written other mysteries, she is best known for feisty, independent Sharon McCone.

Fadeout, Joseph Hansen, 1970

Dave Brandsetter is an insurance agent assigned to investigate an auto-mobile crash where there is no body present. Hansen created one of the first credible and realistic gay series protagonists in the mystery genre, but first and foremost, his Brandsetter books are simply good mysteries.

The Godwulf Manuscript, Robert B. Parker, 1973

Spenser is hired to find a fourteenth-century manuscript that has disappeared from the university's collection. With Spenser, Parker brought the traditional hard-boiled private eye of Chandler and Hammett's era into the second half of the twentieth century. Boston-based Spenser shares some characteristics with Spade and Marlowe, but he isn't the traditional loner. Parker gives Spenser a partner, Hawk, and a romantic interest, Susan Silverman. Spenser's relationship with them gives the series richness and depth.

The Guards, Ken Bruen, 2001

Hard-drinking former police officer Jack Taylor now earns a living as a "finder" in Galway, and Ann Henderson wants Jack to dig up more information about her daughter's supposed "suicide." Bruen takes all the requisite elements of the traditional P.I. novel—an alcoholic ex-cop struggling against a corrupt system—and gives it an intriguing Irish accent.

Indemnity Only, Sara Paretsky, 1982

Victoria Iphigenia "V.I." Warshawski is a wisecracking P.I. *à la* the 1940s hard-boiled detectives. V.I. is hired by banker John Thayer to find his son Peter's missing girlfriend Anita, but when V.I. instead finds Peter's body, her "client" disappears. While the tone of her V.I. Warshawski books is set firmly in the classic private eye tradition, the subject is always some timely social issue, such as unions and illegal immigration, which gives these novels a very modern edge.

The Monkey's Raincoat, Robert Crais, 1992

Wisecracking P.I. Elvis Cole and his partner Joe Pike are hired to find a woman's husband and son. Originally planned as a single title book, Elvis Cole proved so popular that Crais continued creating cases for him to solve. Crais developed his skill with dialog by working as a scriptwriter for such television megahits as *Hill Street Blues* and *Miami Vice.*

Motor City Blue, Loren D. Estleman, 1980

Hard-boiled Detroit P.I. Amos Walker is involved in two cases: finding his old military commander and finding a mobster's missing foster daughter. The versatile Estleman is also the author of a number of award-winning westerns.

The Neon Rain, James Lee Burke, 1987

Atmospheric settings don't get any better than in James Lee Burke's series featuring Cajun detective Dave Robichaux. In this first book of the series, Robichaux is investigating the death of a young prostitute only to run up against the police and the underworld. Robichaux is a classic introspective and damaged hero who tries to right the world's wrongs but becomes increasingly disillusioned. Burke's lyrical writing style makes him Raymond Chandler's unexpected heir.

The Sins of the Fathers, Lawrence Block, 1976

Dark, brooding Matthew Scudder, former cop turned private eye, is asked to investigate the murder of a young woman by her father—not to solve the murder but to find out why. In addition to creating classic tough-guy detective Matthew Scudder, Block pens the lighter burglar/bookstore owner Bernie Rhodenbarr stories and the espionage-flavored Evan Tanner suspense novels. Whatever Block writes is a treat.

The Snatch, Bill Pronzini, 1971

An unnamed San Francisco P.I. becomes involved in delivering the ransom money for the son of a real estate developer. Think of Pronzini's Nameless series as an updated version of Hammett's classic Sam Spade. Pronzini has written books about "Nameless" for over 30 years, but only recently has he let readers know the character's first name is Bill.

*A **Trouble** of Fools,* Linda Barnes, 1987

Red-haired and 6 foot, 1 inch tall, Carlotta Carlyle is brash and bold. A former cabbie and ex-cop turned private eye, Carlotta is approached by Mary Devens, an Irish woman looking for her missing brother who left behind an unexplained $13,000. A simple missing person case turns out to be more than Carlotta expects, when she discovers a gunrunning operation with ties to the IRA. Readers wanting a strong sense of place will enjoy the detailed Boston setting.

Procedurals

If you think amateur sleuths have no business investigating crimes when professionals are trained to do it, then you probably love procedural mystery novels. Procedurals give the readers the "real deal," whether it's the inner workings of a police precinct or forensic details at a morgue. If you want to see how the pros crack a case, these books are for you.

Classics

*The **Blue** Knight,* Joseph Wambaugh, 1972

Bumper Morgan is an old-school cop, putting in 20 years on the force and looking forward to retirement, but with only three days left, he finds more crimes than he has time to solve. Wambaugh drew upon his 10 years in the LAPD to craft authentic characters based on the very real, conflicted officers he knew.

*Cop **Hater,*** Ed McBain, 1956

Detective Steve Carella is on the hunt for a cop killer in the first of McBain's eighty-seventh precinct series. McBain, one of the first writers to show the inner workings of a police precinct, gave the books a timeless quality when he decided not to age his characters in the 30 years of his writing. Without McBain, television shows like *Hill Street Blues* and *NYPD Blue* would not have the stark realism McBain perfected in his series.

The Rest of the Story

Ed McBain was a pseudonym for Salvatore Lombino. As Evan Hunter, Lombino also wrote the classic *The Blackboard Jungle,* based on his first year as a teacher.

More Great Reads

The Black Echo, Michael Connelly, 1992

When LAPD Detective Hieronymous "Harry" Bosch investigates a drug-related death at Mulholland Dam, he recognizes the victim as a former Vietnam soldier with whom he served and doubts that the death was an accident. As Harry looks for the killers, he collides with the FBI and other powerful figures. Connelly was a Pulitzer Prize–winning crime reporter for the *Los Angeles Times*.

The Blessing Way, Tony Hillerman, 1970

When a corpse with a mouthful of sand is found on the Navajo Reservation, Lt. Joe Leaphorn suspects supernatural forces might be involved. Navajo culture and customs are at the core of all of Hillerman's books, giving his readers the chance to experience a different way of life while subtly showing them how much people are ultimately alike. Hillerman brings a welcome diversity to the genre.

Blindsighted, Karin Slaughter, 2001

Sara Linton, a pediatrician and coroner in Grant County, Georgia, must work with her ex-husband, Police Chief Jeffrey Tolliver, and Det. Lena Adams to investigate the grisly murders of young women. Slaughter's debut is bloody, violent, and gruesome, but readers who can stomach the gore will find this a spine-chilling read.

The Blue Hour, T. Jefferson Parker, 1999

Tim Hess, retired cop turned police consultant, is professionally paired—and eventually romantically involved—with Merci Rayborn, an impulsive, ambitious, and beautiful young detective. Together the unlikely pair investigates the murders of a serial killer known as "The Purse Snatcher." Parker's writing style is crisp and vivid, making this suspense-filled novel a cut above the run-of-the-mill contemporary thriller.

The Bone Collector, Jeffrey Deaver, 1997

Quadriplegic former forensic criminologist Lincoln Rhymes is called out of retirement to help capture a serial killer who is recreating turn-of-the-century murders. Lots of forensic and scientific details make this a fascinating read. If you only know Deaver from the movie of the same name (though we love anything Denzel is in), you're missing out.

Chiefs, Stuart Woods, 1981

Three generations of police chiefs in the small rural town of Delano, Georgia, each try to solve a 40-year-old murder that still haunts the town decades later. Woods is the author of several mystery series, including the Stone Barrington series and Holly Barker books, but *Chiefs* is the best book of his career. It's subtle, touching, and filled with dozens of realistically nuanced characters that stay with you long after the last page.

Cover Her Face, P.D. James, 1962

Inspector Adam Dalgliesh of Scotland Yard must find the killer of a beautiful housemaid from among a houseful of suspects. With her elegant prose, James proves that not all police procedurals are hard-hitting and gritty. Her main character is not your basic cop on the street but a gentleman detective—quiet, insightful, cultured, and mannered. Yet, when it comes to catching the killer, Dalgliesh is every bit the equal of his street-tough counterparts. James is a legend in the mystery world. Her polished, literary writing is a joy to read.

Déjà Dead, Kathy Reichs, 1997

Forensic anthropologist Temperance "Tempe" Brennan is sure that the murders and dismemberments of several young women are the work of a serial killer stalking the streets of Montreal. Unable to convince the skeptical police, she decides to investigate on her own. Full of authentic forensic detail, *Déjà Dead* is an auspicious beginning to an engrossing series. Always popular, Reichs's fan base increased with the television series *Bones*.

A Great Deliverance, Elizabeth George, 1988

Unable to work with any other officer, working-class police sergeant Barbara Havers is given another chance to prove herself when she is assigned to work with New Scotland Yard's Detective Inspector Thomas Lynley to investigate a brutal murder in Yorkshire. Lynley is everything Havers isn't—aristocratic, cultured, wealthy, and comfortable in society. After a very rocky start, these two manage to form an effective working partnership. George is one of the few Americans to successfully write British procedurals. She writes so well that some readers have no idea that she's from California.

An Expert Speaks

"In addition to possessing the most important talent a writer can have—the ability to tell a whopping good tale—Miss George is an excellent writer who peoples her novels with complex characters and builds them around intricate plots that inevitably lead the reader astray. I find it especially interesting that her two main characters, Inspector Lynley and his assistant, Barbara Havers, are not only fascinating in their roles as often embattled sleuths, but each has a personal story to deepen their characterization that has been developed through the novels. In case you believe women can only write about 'nice' crime, dip into an Elizabeth George novel and become better informed."

—Leigh Greenwood, author

Knots and Crosses, Ian Rankin, 1987

As he investigates the murders of several girls by the "Edinburgh Strangler," Detective John Rebus begins to realize that he may be the real target. The U.K.'s number-one best-selling crime writer, Rankin has created a memorable character in Rebus, a disillusioned and cynical cop who's all the more compelling for his flaws. Add the atmospheric setting of an Edinburgh that tourists never see, a dark underworld beneath the historic façade, and you'll get lost in this book.

Post Mortem, Patricia Cornwell, 1990

In her first (and we think best book), Cornwell introduces medical examiner Kay Scarpetta, who finds herself in the center of the investigation of the strangler of young women. Gruesome and graphic but utterly compelling, you should read this book in the daylight. Oh, yeah, and lock your door.

The Rules of Prey, John Sanford, 1986

As the only member of the Minneapolis Office of Special Intelligence, Lieutenant Lucas Davenport is called in to help the police capture a serial killer whose murderous spree is terrifying the city. A computer game creator on the side, Lucas must use all his skills to defeat the insane killer. Sanford is a pseudonym of Pulitzer Prize–winning journalist John Case.

The Surgeon, Tess Gerritsen, 2001

In the first of her Jane Rizzoli/Maura Isles series, trauma surgeon Catherine Cordell moves to Boston after barely escaping being killed and mutilated by a serial killer known as "The Surgeon." When several women are murdered in the same manner in Boston, detective Jane Rizzoli must find the killer.

The Rest of the Story

When Gerritsen created the character of Maura Isles, a medical examiner also known as "Queen of the Dead," she got the name from the winner of a charity auction who won the right to be a minor character in one of Gerritsen's books. But Maura Isles so fascinated Gerritsen that she became the star of several books.

The Tin Collectors, Stephen J. Cannell, 2001

Shane Scully, an LAPD sergeant, is called onto the scene of a domestic fight between his ex-partner Ray Molar and his wife, Scully's former girlfriend. When Ray fires, Scully shoots him in self-defense. While awaiting the outcome of his investigation, Scully is transferred to Internal Affairs and uncovers a conspiracy that reaches the top level of city government.

The Rest of the Story

Stephen J. Cannell is more than a talented mystery writer. He is the creator of such classic television shows as *The Rockford Files*, *The A Team*, and *The Commish*. His television background shows in his fast-paced stories and cinematic writing style.

Undercurrents, Ridley Pearson, 1988

With a serial killer and a copycat killer on the loose in Seattle, Detective Lou Boldt, with help from police psychologist Daphne Matthews, follows the clues to the murderers. Pearson is an exceptionally precise writer of police procedures, forensic investigations, and criminal psychology, but he's also gifted at creating fully realized characters.

When the Bough Breaks, Jonathan Kellerman, 1985

Child psychologist Alex Delaware is semi-retired from private practice after a traumatic experience and a mental breakdown. He is called upon to help interrogate seven-year-old Melody, the only witness to a grisly double murder. This is the first book in the very popular Delaware series, and Kellerman, a child psychologist like his character, creates a chilling psychological thriller.

The Rest of the Story

Jonathan Kellerman is married to an equally famous mystery writer, Faye Kellerman, creator of the Rina Lazarus/Peter Decker series. In *Double Homicide*, the Kellermans teamed up to write the stand-alone mystery. Their son, Jesse, is also a mystery writer, publishing his first book, *Sunstroke*, in 2006.

Historical Sleuths

One of the things many readers enjoy most about historical mysteries—other than the wonderfully detailed settings, of course—is that solving the crime depends more on the detective's wits than forensic science (take that, *CSI!*). Rather than simply relying on DNA testing to find a killer, historical sleuths must investigate alibis and motives by using good old-fashioned detective work. So if you like following the clues right along with the detective, try one of these cleverly crafted historical mysteries.

Classics

The Cater Street Hangman, Anne Perry, 1979

Charlotte shocks her upper-class Victorian family when she helps Police Inspector Thomas Pitt investigate the murder of a servant. Few have captured the intricate world of the Victorian era as well as the versatile Perry, who also writes two other mystery series: one featuring Thomas Monk, a Victorian London policeman, and one set during World War I. With each of Perry's meticulously crafted books, the historical setting is as much a part of the story as the characters themselves.

The Crocodile on the Sandbank, Elizabeth Peters, 1975

Unconventional Amelia Peabody pursues her interest in ancient Egypt but winds up exercising her detective skills when she investigates a mummy who walks an excavation at night. Peters, who writes romantic suspense as Barbara Michaels, is an Egyptologist herself, and her academic knowledge shows in the archaeology-rich, entertaining plots of her Peabody books.

A Morbid Taste for Bones, Ellis Peters, 1977

Medieval monk Brother Cadfael becomes involved in murderous events on a pilgrimage from England to Wales. Peters (a pseudonym for Edith Pargeter) has also written a number of historical novels and a contemporary mystery series. She is best known and loved for her Brother Cadfael books, which are still popular, in part due to the PBS series starring Derek Jacobi. When it comes to cleverly constructed plots, accurate historical detail, and nicely nuanced characters, Peters has few equals.

More Great Reads

The Beekeeper's Apprentice, Laurie King, 1994

Teenager Mary Russell stumbles across a retired beekeeper on the Sussex Downs in 1914 but does not realize she has just met the legendary Sherlock Holmes, who will become her mentor in detection. King brilliantly twists the expected Sherlock Holmes formula in her terrifically entertaining Mary Russell series.

A Conspiracy of Paper, David Liss, 2000

Former prizefighter turned detective Benjamin Weaver searches for the murderer of his father in 1719 London. Liss used research material from his doctoral dissertation for the background of this Edgar Award–winning novel.

An Expert Speaks

"A Conspiracy of Paper, a fabulous historical novel, is part of a trilogy about a family of Marranos (supposedly converted Iberian Jews) who flee to Amsterdam during the Spanish Inquisition and make their fortune in the stock market. From there they move to London and continue to prosper—all, that is, save for the family's black sheep, Benjamin Weaver, who becomes a boxer and then a private investigator. The period detail, along with the mystery and the story of the wandering Jews in a hostile climate is enthralling."

—Jo Manning, author

Cut to the Quick, Kate Ross, 1993

While staying at a country home for a wedding, Regency dandy Julian Kestrel discovers a murdered woman in his bed. Dorothy Sayers meets Jane Austen in Ross's deliciously witty series featuring the always-elegant Kestrel.

Jane and the Unpleasantness at Scargrave Manor, Stephanie Barron, 1995

When her friend, the beautiful young Isobel Payne, is accused of murdering her elderly husband, Jane Austen (yes, that Jane Austen!) agrees to investigate. Using Austen's own letters as her primary resource, Barron brilliantly recreates the cool, ironic voice of the real Austen.

The Last Kashmiri Rose, Barbara Cleverly, 2002

In 1922 India, Scotland Yard Commander Joe Sandiland, who is working with the Bengal Police, teams up with the widow of a British officer to investigate the suspicious deaths of several other wives of British officers. Cleverly uses the colorful backdrop of the waning years of the British Raj in her refreshingly different mystery series.

Maisie Dobbs, Jacqueline Winspear, 2003

Maisie Dobbs's first case as a private investigator seems simple—follow a wandering wife—but becomes complicated as she learns more. Each of Winspear's elegantly written, impeccably crafted mysteries explores the costs of WWI, "the war to end all wars."

The Novice's Tale, Margaret Frazer, 1992

When overbearing Lady Ermentrude arrives at St. Frideswide to convince her frail young niece to leave the abbey, Sister Frevisse can't wait until the abrasive noblewoman leaves. But she never wanted her dead. Frazer's series featuring the amateur sleuth Sister Frevisse offers readers a richly detailed look at fifteenth-century England.

The Queen's Man, Sharon Kay Penman, 1996

Justin de Quincy finds himself ensnared in a deadly mix of politics and deception after he agrees to deliver a letter addressed to Queen Eleanor of Aquitaine. We love Penman whether she is writing fascinating historical mysteries, like her Justin de Quincy series, or her vivid, richly detailed historical novels, like *The Sunne in Splendour*.

And the Award Goes to ...

The oldest, and perhaps most prestigious American award given to mysteries is the Edgar. Named after Edgar Allen Poe, the Edgar is awarded by the Mystery Writers of America to authors of mysteries in different categories of the genre, including novels, nonfiction books, screenplays, television scripts, and short stories.

Roman Blood, Steven Saylor, 1991

Roman senator Cicero takes on the case of a man accused of murdering his father, but Cicero will need the help of Gordianus the Finder to discover who the real killer is. If you loved the miniseries *Rome* and *Gladiator*, you'll enjoy Saylor's expertly crafted, history-rich mystery series featuring Gordianus.

Shinju, Laura Joh Rowland, 1994

Seventeenth-century Japanese samurai Sano Ichiro believes the ritual double suicide, or "shinju," of beautiful wealthy Yukiko and artist Noriyoshi is really murder and risks both his career and his life to investigate. Japanese history has provided Rowland with many colorful ways to murder people.

Silver Pigs, Lindsey Davis, 1989

When Roman "informer" Marcus Didius Falco is hired to investigate the disappearance of a senator's niece, the case takes him to the Roman silver mines in Britannia and the missing woman's lovely cousin, Helena Justina. While the Falco series is set in Rome circa 70 A.D., Davis instills each book with the snappy tone of the classic private investigator novels written during the 1930s and 1940s. Imagine Sam Spade in a toga.

To Shield the Queen, Fiona Buckley, 1997

Ursula Blanchard, lady-in-waiting to Elizabeth I, is given the delicate task of protecting Amy Robsart, the wife of Elizabeth's rumored romantic interest Robert Dudley. But when Amy dies in a mysterious accident, Ursula must find out exactly what happened to clear the Queen. History plays an important part in Buckley's books, with historical figures like Elizabeth I and her ill-fated cousin, Mary Stuart, turning up in different plots.

Chapter 5

Suspense: Edge of Your Seat Entertainment

In This Chapter

◆ Suspense and nothing but the suspense: white-knuckle entertainment

◆ Legal thrillers: letter of the law

◆ Espionage: on beyond Bond

◆ Bio/medical thrillers: a healthy way to die

◆ Action and adventure: tales of testosterone

◆ Techno-thrillers: technology run amok

Mystery, suspense, and thriller novels all involve a crime of some kind. The difference between them is in the timing. In a mystery novel, the crime has already taken place or happens early in the book, and the focus of the story is solving the mystery—whodunit, how it was done, or why. In suspense and thriller novels, the crime has not yet taken place. The key to the story is either trying to prevent the crime from happening or escaping from it, all while keeping the reader guessing what's going to transpire next. And the main difference between suspense novels and thrillers is the scope: in a suspense novel, the focus is on a single person or a small group of characters who are in danger from the book's villain. In thrillers, the stakes are higher since not just one or two people are in jeopardy, but instead a whole city, a whole government, or even the whole world.

If you relish a little gore and violence in your reading, this genre is for you. From Mary Higgins Clark's subtle brand of suspense to the much more graphic and intense style of Thomas Harris and James Patterson, you're in for a stomach-clenching adventure. This eclectic assortment of novels is guaranteed to keep you guessing to the very end!

Suspense and Nothing but the Suspense

No gimmicks, no gadgets, these books are just pure suspense!

Classics

Along Came a Spider, James Patterson, 1993

Washington, D.C., cop and psychologist Alex Cross and Secret Service agent Jezzie Flanagan team up to stop a gruesome killer. The best-selling and wildly popular Patterson is known for his short, snappy chapters and compulsively readable plots, so his books are definitely a fast read.

> **The Rest of the Story** _____
>
> In addition to his "Alex Cross" series of suspense novels, Patterson is the author of "The Women's Murder Club" books, which feature four San Francisco women—a cop, a lawyer, a medical examiner, and a reporter—who work together to solve crimes. Patterson has also written and co-authored a number of stand-alone thrillers and even a romance novel!

Where Are the Children?, Mary Higgins Clark, 1983

Nancy Harmon finds herself trapped in a familiar nightmare when her two children from her second marriage disappear, just as her two children from her first marriage did years before. Clark is the queen of this genre, sometimes called "fem jep" (females in jeopardy), and *Where Are the Children?* is one of her best. Twenty-five years after it was first published, *Where Are the Children?* is as popular today as it was in 1983.

More Great Reads

Absolute Power, David Baldacci, 1996

Can the president of the United States really get away with murder? That's the premise for this debut novel, which features a cat burglar who is a witness when the president gets into a drunken fight with his mistress, the wife of a wealthy political campaign contributor, and accidentally kills her. When it comes to crafting tense, adrenaline-fueled thrillers, Baldacci sets a new standard and then just gets better with every book.

The Da Vinci Code, Dan Brown, 2003

Harvard professor of symbology Robert Langdon becomes the prime suspect in the murder of a Louvre museum curator, and only by teaming up with French cryptologist Sophie Nevue can he solve the baffling cipher found next to the body and find the real killer. If you haven't read it, you're probably the only one, but if you're new to *The Da Vinci Code,* plan on blocking out time to read it. Yes, Brown's version of the origins of the Catholic Church has annoyed more than one person, to say the least. And yes, if you stop to think too much about the plot, it all seems to fall apart. But the point is that most readers don't stop turning the pages once they start this utterly riveting book. And that is the definition of a "good" read!

The Rest of the Story

> Brown introduced Langdon in an earlier book, *Angels and Demons,* in which the Harvard professor teams up with a young woman when her physicist father is found murdered at the Vatican. The "Illuminati," a shadowy religious group, is suspect.

The Eight, Katherine Neville, 1989

Computer expert Catherine Velis finds herself caught up in the search for the mystical Montglane Service, a chess set owned by Charlemagne, which holds the key to great power. Neville moves in time between Catherine's story set in the 1970s during the OPEC oil embargo and 1790s France during the revolution when the chess set was broken up in an effort to keep it out of the hands of Napoleon. We call this the thinking man's *The Da Vinci Code. The Eight* quickly became a favorite with readers for its blend of action, intrigue, history, and chess!

The Rest of the Story

When OPEC began its oil embargo in the 1970s, Katherine Neville worked as an international consultant to the Algerian government. This experience provided the inspiration for *The Eight*.

Fast Forward, Judy Mercer, 1995

Ariel Gold wakes up one morning and looks in the mirror, only to realize she has no idea whose face is looking back at her. Mercer keeps the tension high while Ariel sorts through clues to her identity. As the series progresses, both Ariel and the reader gradually learn more about her past.

Fatal Gift, H. Michael Frase, 1996

Kasey Riteman, former steakhouse waitress, pretends to be a clairvoyant in order to lead the police to the killer without revealing that she was actually a witness to the crime. Frase adds a dash of romance to the standard Mary Higgins Clark formula, and the result is a riveting suspense novel with a romantic ending.

The Girl Next Door, Patricia MacDonald, 2004

Nina Avery never believed her father murdered her mother 15 years earlier, but when Nina moves back to her old hometown with her father and another murdered body turns up, Nina begins to wonder if she might have been wrong. If Mary Higgins Clark doesn't write fast enough for you, try MacDonald's subtle suspense.

The Kill Clause, Gregg Andrew Hurwitz, 2003

After his daughter is murdered, U.S deputy marshal Tim "Troubleshooter" Rackley accepts an invitation to join a group of vigilantes who target criminals. If you like your suspense dark and gritty, Hurwitz is the author for you.

The Killing Floor, Lee Child, 1997

Ex-military policeman Jack Reacher investigates the murder of his U.S. Treasury official brother in the small Georgia town of Margrave and in the process uncovers a conspiracy that stretches beyond the town's borders. Child, a former television writer, knows how to ratchet up the tension in his suspenseful Jack Reacher series.

Labyrinth, Kate Mosse, 2006

While working on an archaeological dig in France, Alice Tanner stumbles across two skeletons and a ring engraved with a labyrinth design that turns out to be the key to the Holy Grail. Mosse deftly weaves together two stories. The first is that of modern-day Alice Tanner and her adventures. The second tells of Alais Pelletier, who lived in the same area in the 1200s and was entrusted with keeping the ring and three books safe during the French crusade against the Cathars. Think *The Da Vinci Code* but with two strong female protagonists.

Night of Reunion, Michael Allegretto, 1990

Psychopathic killer Christine Helmstrum has unfinished business with Alex Whitaker as she begins playing a deadly game of revenge with his family. *Fatal Attraction* is just a warm-up compared to this nerve-jangling suspense tale.

Paranoia, Joseph Finder, 2004

After he is caught manipulating Wyatt Telecom funds to finance a co-worker's retirement party, 20-something Adam Cassidy is given two choices—go to jail or spy on their biggest competitor, Trion Systems. Finder uses the cutthroat world of billion-dollar corporate finance as the foundation for his story, but anyone who has ever worked in a cubicle will relate to Adam's dilemma.

The Patriots Club, Christopher Reich, 2005

New York City investment banker Thomas Bolden needs all of his old "street skills" after he is kidnapped, and later escapes, from a centuries-old secret society of powerful businessmen, lawyers, and politicians. Reich worked in Swiss banks for nearly a decade, and many of his thrillers, like *The Patriot's Club* and his debut book, *Numbered Account,* have a connection to the world of high finance.

See Jane Run, Joy Fielding, 1991

A woman's deepest instincts tell her something is terribly wrong when she wakes up with $10,000 in her pockets, blood on her clothes, and no knowledge of her own name. While Fielding has written other novels in several different genres, including women's fiction, we voted *See Jane Run* as her best.

The Survivor's Club, Lisa Gardner, 2002

Three women band together to help each other heal after they have all been raped by the same man, but when the rapist is killed by a sniper's bullet, they all become suspects. Like many suspense writers, Gardner got her start as a writer in romance fiction, which shows in her expertly crafted characters, but she's no slouch when it comes to creating white-knuckle plots either.

Tell No One, Harlan Coben, 2001

David and Elizabeth have the perfect marriage, but their security is shattered when Elizabeth is abducted and murdered. Eight years later David receives an e-mail using a phrase that only Elizabeth knew, making him wonder whether she is dead or alive. In addition to writing page-turning suspenseful thrillers, Coben is the author of a terrific mystery series featuring sports agent/sleuth Myron Bolitar.

The Templar Legacy, Steve Berry, 2006

Cotton Malone, a former Department of Justice operative turned bookseller, is reluctantly brought back into "the business" when a book with links to the centuries-old missing treasure of the Knights Templar turns up. Action, adventure, history, conspiracies, and, of course, many international settings are the key ingredients of Berry's irresistible thrillers.

The Rest of the Story

If the first time you heard about the Knights Templar was in Steve Berry's *The Templar Legacy* or Dan Brown's best-selling suspense novel *The Da Vinci Code* (or one of its now numerous literary clones), you'll be surprised to know that it is an actual religious order. Originally founded in the Middle Ages during the Crusades to protect European pilgrims going to the holy city of Jerusalem, the Knights also became the protectors of the popes. Eventually, they grew too powerful and became the scourge of the papacy.

Term Limits, Vince Flynn, 1997

Originally a self-published novel, *Term Limits* launched Flynn's literary career, which continues to grow with each book in his series featuring CIA counterterrorism specialist Mitch Rapp. In *Term Limits*, Rapp must stop U.S. Congressman Michael O'Rourke when O'Rourke becomes involved with a shadowy group of assassins who are murdering other politicians. High-powered Washington politics, high-tech security, and riveting suspense give Flynn's political thrillers their distinctive edge.

Legal Thrillers

What readers love most about a good legal thriller (other than the chance to see a lawyer in trouble) is the "inside look" at the law it provides. The best legal thriller writers find clever ways to skillfully incorporate fascinating details about the inner workings of the courts or a legal firm into a wonderfully suspenseful plot. So even if you think Shakespeare was right when he wrote "first, kill all the lawyers," we're sure you won't object to any of our recommendations.

After Dark, Philip Margolin, 1995

While working for eccentric lawyer Matthew Reynolds, Tracy Cavanaugh is given the case of defending Portland prosecutor Abbie Giffe, who has been charged with the bombing murder of her ex-husband, an Oregon Supreme Court Judge. Margolin adds plenty of suspense and a psychological edge to his legal thrillers, making them particularly addictive.

The Case of the Velvet Claws, Earle Stanley Gardner, 1933

A woman caught up in a blackmail scheme needs Perry Mason's help when her husband is murdered. Gardner, a California attorney who started out writing for the pulp magazines of the 1920s and 1930s, was one of the first authors to popularize the idea of the law as a setting for a mystery novel. For five decades, Gardner featured Perry Mason in more than 80 books, and in the process, became one of the most successful mystery authors of the twentieth century. While the Perry Mason books are not quite the fast-paced legal thrillers readers are used to today, Gardner's books have their own timeless appeal.

Compelling Evidence, Steve Martini, 1992

California attorney Paul Madriani loses his job when his boss Ben Potter discovers Paul having an affair with his wife, Talia, but Paul agrees to defend his old lover when Talia becomes the prime suspect in Ben's murder. Martini was a newspaper reporter before becoming an attorney, and his books have a snappy journalistic writing style.

The Defense, D. W. Buffa, 1997

Defense attorney Joseph Antonelli's reputation as having never lost a case is about to be tarnished when he defends a man accused of rape. Before he turned to writing legal thrillers, Buffa was a university professor, a special assistant to a U.S. senator, and author of several nonfiction books on politics.

Degree of Guilt, Richard North Patterson, 1993

Christopher Paget defends his ex-wife, television journalist Mary Carelli, when she is charged with the murder of a famous novelist, Mark Ransome. Though Patterson's books are usually the length of *War and Peace*, he really knows how to keep the reader enthralled to the very end with a riveting mix of murder, mayhem, and cracking good courtroom dramatics. In addition, each of Patterson's books centers on some contemporary issue, such as political reform, abortion, or gun control. The events are so timely you almost feel as if you're reading a newspaper.

Everywhere That Mary Went, Lisa Scottoline, 1993

Mary DiNunzio is on the partner track at a prestigious Philadelphia law firm when a dangerous stalker threatens to derail her career plans. Scottoline, a Philadelphia lawyer herself, loved reading legal thrillers. When she noticed that no women were writing this kind of suspense novel, she decided to give the "writing thing" a try and in her first book created an all-female law firm, Rosato and Associates. Scottoline is now the author of more than a dozen legal thrillers, many of which feature members of Rosato and Associates.

The Firm, John Grisham, 1991

Law school graduate Mitchell McDeere discovers his new employers at a Memphis law firm have ties to organized crime. *The Firm* is actually the second book attorney Grisham wrote, following *A Time to Kill*, but this book catapulted him to fame and fortune, and it's easy to understand why. *The Firm* is the very definition of page-turning suspense. While most of Grisham's books follow a formula—fast-paced plots that usually feature an idealistic protagonist battling corruption within the legal or political system—readers can't get enough of it.

Hard Evidence, John T. Lescroat, 1992

San Francisco Assistant District Attorney Dismas Hardy is assigned the case of prosecuting May Shinn for the murder of her billionaire Silicon Valley businessman boyfriend. May produces a watertight alibi before the trial, and Dismas loses his job. He's then hired by the next person the police charge with the crime—Andrew Fowler, the judge in the first trial and Dismas's ex-father-in-law. This third book in Lescroat's Dismas series is an excellent introduction to his entertaining legal thrillers.

Hostile Witness, William Lashner, 1995

Philadelphia attorney Victor Carl is given a once-in-a-lifetime career opportunity when he is invited to become part of the legal team defending a local politician and his aide, who are charged with murder. Unlike some legal thriller writers, Lashner shows the gritty and realistic side of the law: the power struggles, the deal cutting, and the compromises attorneys face.

Motion to Suppress, Perri O'Shaughnessy, 1997

After losing both her job and her husband, San Francisco attorney Nina Reilly moves to Lake Tahoe, where her first case involves defending a woman charged with the murder of her ex-husband. *Motion to Suppress* is the first book in the Nina Reilly series.

The Rest of the Story

Perri O'Shaughnessy is the pseudonym for two sisters—Mary, a writer, and Pamela, an attorney. Perri is a combination of both their first names as well as a special homage to Perry Mason, the classic lawyer/sleuth.

Presumed Innocent, Scott Turow, 1987

Chief Deputy Prosecuting Attorney Rusty Sabich is put in charge of investigating the murder of a co-worker and former lover. Before Grisham's *The Firm*, Turow's *Presumed Innocent* really started the whole demand for legal thrillers in the 1990s. With its crackerjack plot that explores the complexities of the law (and what a twist of an ending!), some surprisingly nuanced characters, and accurate representations of courtroom procedures, this book set the standard for legal thrillers that followed.

Primary Justice, William Bernhardt, 1991

Hot shot Tulsa attorney Benjamin Kincaid's first case at his new law firm involves helping Jonathan and Bertha Adams adopt Emily, an abandoned child. But when Jonathan's mutilated corpse is found, Ben begins his own investigation into the murder. Lawyers and all sorts of skullduggery abound in this first book in Bernhardt's series featuring Ben Kincaid.

Shadow of a Doubt,
William J. Coughlin, 1991

Lawyer and recovering alcoholic Charley Sloan finds himself helping defend the stepdaughter of a woman he once loved when the girl is charged with murder. As both an attorney and former federal judge, Coughlin brings lots of real-world experience into his gripping legal thrillers.

The Tenth Justice, Brad Meltzer, 1997

When Ben Addison, a brand-new clerk for one of the U.S. Supreme Court justices, is tricked into giving out one of the court's decisions before it is officially announced, he finds himself anonymously blackmailed into providing more of the court's decisions until, with a little help from his friends, he tries to stop the blackmailer. Meltzer also writes for the comic book series *Justice League* and is a co-creator of the short-lived but well-received television series *Jack and Bobby.*

Bio/Medical Thrillers

Bio/medical thrillers are so popular with readers because they play off the fact that the people we should trust the most, like doctors, could be the very ones who are purposely trying to kill us. It's hard enough to stop a serial killer like Hannibal Lector, but how do we fight an airborne microbe that could easily wipe out thousands of people? Whether it's a doctor gone bad or a devastating virus cooked up in a lab, the novels that follow will make you think twice (and maybe three times) before you open a letter, get on a bus, or (heaven forbid) enter the hospital for a minor procedure.

Bad Medicine, Eileen Dreyer, 1995

Trauma nurse Molly Burke investigates a strange increase in suicide deaths among lawyers. Dreyer got her literary start in romance fiction as Kathleen Korbel before she began writing her own thrilling brand of medical suspense novels. Not only does Dreyer have 20 years' experience in the field of medicine, including 16 years in trauma nursing, but she also trained in forensic nursing and death investigation, so her books are as realistic as they can get (as opposed to the way *CSI* does things).

The Blood Artist, Chuck Hogan, 1998

Center for Disease Control virologists Peter Maryk and Stephen Pease thought they had successfully controlled a deadly virus in Africa, but a few years later, the virus resurfaces in America, and now Peter must find the cure to help Stephen. Unlike some authors who can churn out a book in a year or even less, Hogan takes time to write his books, and it shows in his carefully crafted thrillers.

Coma, Robin Cook, 1977

Medical student Susan Wheeler discovers that some doctors at Memorial Hospital are harvesting parts from patients and then putting the victims into comas. Cook is often credited with creating the medical thriller subgenre and decades later still continues to dominate this category of suspense novels. Each of Cook's medical thrillers centers around one particular hot topic, such as genetic engineering or drug research, and no one is better at expertly plumbing our fears of hospitals and death.

The Rest of the Story

Robin Cook was a surgeon before he wrote his first book, *The Year of the Intern*, in which he told about his experiences in medical school. The book didn't sell all that well, so Cook studied what makes a best-selling book and came up with the idea of *Coma*, which became an instant hit, jump-starting his career as a novelist.

Critical Judgment, Michael Palmer, 1996

Emergency room physician Abby Dolan thinks there may be a connection between the town's biggest employer and the mysterious disease infecting several of her patients. After training at Boston City and Massachusetts General Hospitals, Palmer spent 20 years practicing internal and emergency medicine. After reading Robin Cook's classic *Coma*, Palmer was inspired to write his own first medical thriller. That first manuscript was never published, but it did lead him to write *The Sisterhood*, which came out in 1982.

The First Horseman, John Case, 1998

Journalist Frank Daly and virologist Anne Adair team up to stop a group of terrorists who may have gained control of a deadly form of influenza. Case is the pseudonym for the husband and wife writing team of Jim and Carolyn Hougan. As a source of inspiration for this chilling thriller, they use the great influenza epidemic of 1918, which killed millions of people around the world.

The Fourth Procedure, Stanley Pottinger, 1995

Congressman Jack MacLeod and organ transplant pioneer Dr. Rachel Redpath both become involved when the strangely mutilated bodies of anti-abortionists begin turning up in the Washington, D.C., medical examiner's office. Pottinger mixes current politics into his outrageously thrilling book.

Harvest, Tess Gerritsen, 1996

Boston Bayside Hospital surgical resident Abby DiMatteo risks her career and her life when she investigates an organ-harvesting scheme. Former internist Gerritsen wrote romantic suspense for Harlequin before penning her first medical thriller, *Harvest*, which was inspired by a chance dinner conversation Gerritsen had with an ex-cop who was currently running a security firm that protected American businessmen in Russia.

Isolation Ward, Joshua Spanogle, 2006

When a renegade virus strikes Baltimore, Centers for Disease Control officer Dr. Nathaniel McCormack investigates and follows the virus's dangerous trail to a "university" in the Silicon Valley. With the gritty, graphic, and totally unputdownable *Isolation Ward*, Spanogle proves a welcome addition to the bio/medical thriller subgenre.

Espionage

Readers love espionage and spy fiction for many different reasons. The potent combination of danger and intrigue enthralls some readers. For others, the colorful, exotic locales, beautiful femme fatales, wonderfully over-the-top villains, and heroes who take a licking and keep on ticking are elements that count. Still others love spy novels written by those who bring their own insider's knowledge to the story. For whatever reasons you enjoy espionage fiction, we have some terrific titles to recommend!

A Coffin for Dimitrios, Eric Ambler, 1939

An English writer tries to trace the trail of a Greek spy found dead in Istanbul. Ambler, who began his writing career in advertising, is credited with not only modernizing the spy novel but also realistically writing about the bleak and definitely nonglamorous world of twentieth-century espionage.

Above Suspicion, Helen MacInnes, 1941

While "vacationing" in Europe in 1939, Oxford professor Richard Miles and his wife Frances are actually searching for a British agent who may already have been captured by the Nazis. MacInnes was the first woman to successfully crack the "good old boys" school of espionage fiction, and her addictively entertaining, superbly suspenseful novels usually feature an amateur who somehow becomes caught up in the dangerous world of professional spying.

AKA Jane, Maureen Tan, 1997

British MI-5 agent Jane Nichols becomes a mystery writer, but she may have to return to her former job when she spots an old nemesis while in Atlanta. With Jane, Tan creates a strong heroine in a genre not known for them.

The Bourne Identity, Robert Ludlum, 1980

After being shot in the head and falling overboard during a storm at sea, a man is rescued by a Greek fisherman. Unfortunately, the man who's been shot has no memory. The victim's only clue is a Swiss bank account under the name Jason Bourne and the instructions that he must find the professional assassin named Carlos. *The Bourne Identity* is the first book of a trilogy featuring conflicted hero Jason Bourne. Ludlum takes all the ingredients of a stock thriller—megalomaniac villains, political conspiracies, secret organizations, Byzantine plots, and reluctant heroes forced into saving the world—and spins the whole thing, if not into literature, at least into literary gold.

> **The Rest of the Story**
>
> Ludlum's first novel, *The Scarlatti Inheritance* (1971), was rejected 10 times before it was finally published. It became an instant best-seller, the first of many for Ludlum.

The Brotherhood of the Rose, David Morrell, 1984

Adopted and raised as brothers, Chris Kilmoonie and Saul Grisman have been trained as assassins from their youth, but when their father turns against them, the two discover that they are not the only killers he created. Now, the two must work together to stop their father and his other assassins. Morrell is a versatile author who also wrote *First Blood*, on which the Rambo series was based.

Casino Royale, Ian Fleming, 1954

British spy James Bond attempts to smash the evil Soviet murder organization SMERSH by beating their nefarious banker, Le Chiffre, in a high-stakes game of baccarat. Fleming created one of the most famous fictional spies of all time with James Bond. While the plots can be cartoonish and the characters less than nuanced, Fleming's stylish 007 books are top-drawer escapist fiction. If you only know Bond, James Bond, through the movies, you might be surprised at how entertaining the books are.

Charlie M., Brian Freemantle, 1977

Middle-aged, rough-around-the-edges MI6 agent Charlie Muffin reluctantly takes charge of things when a high-level KGB agent hints that he wants to defect to Great Britain. Freemantle wrote more than a dozen well-researched and grittily realistic adventures for Charlie Muffin.

The Company: A Novel of the CIA, Robert Littell, 2002

The careers of four fictional spies are the focus of this long, lushly detailed account that integrates major espionage events into the plot. *The Company* is practically a history of espionage work in the last half of the twentieth century.

The Cutout, Francine Mathews, 2001

CIA analyst Caroline Carmichael thought her husband had been killed but discovers that he might be alive and involved in the kidnapping of the vice president. A former analyst for the CIA, Mathews writes not only vividly realistic spy novels, like *The Cutout* and *Blown*, but also an excellent small-town police procedural series set in Nantucket. Writing as Stephanie Barron, Mathews penned a historical mystery series featuring Jane Austen.

Eye of the Needle, Ken Follett, 1978

One woman tries to stop "The Needle," a Nazi agent who is attempting to escape from England with the secret of D-Day. Follett has written historical fiction and contemporary suspense but also has published four excellent historical espionage novels.

Gentleman's Game, Greg Rucka, 2004

Tara Chace, a British Secret Intelligence Service Special Ops agent, assassinates the Saudi Arabian mastermind behind a series of terrorist attacks that have killed hundreds of British citizens. Unfortunately, Tara accidentally kills a Saudi prince at the same time. Rucka based his gritty, suspenseful novel on the award-winning "Queen and Country" graphic novel series.

The Ipcress File, Len Deighton, 1964

Harry Palmer, an agent for a secret British intelligence group, looks into the disappearance of a biochemist. Deighton is often credited with helping transform the spy genre from its early action-adventure stories into novels that focus on the complex politics and real-world compromises of espionage work.

The Kill Artist, Daniel Silva, 2000

Art restorer and former Mossad agent Gabriel Allon is pulled back into the game with the offer of finding the terrorist who murdered his family. Former CNN reporter Silva brings the world of espionage fiction into the twenty-first century with this complex and gripping series.

Masquerade, Gayle Lynds, 1996

When Liz Sandsborough wakes up with amnesia, she's told that she is a top CIA agent, but later she discovers that she's really Sarah Walker and that the same people who told her she is Liz are now trying to kill her. In addition to writing her own espionage novels, Lynds has co-authored three books with Robert Ludlum.

Night Soldiers, Alan Furst, 1988

After his brother is murdered in Bulgaria, Khristo Stoianev escapes to Moscow where he becomes an agent for the NKVD. But when Khristo thinks his new employers have betrayed him, he turns against them. Furst is known both for expertly evoking the shadowy world of espionage during the mid-twentieth century and for his richly nuanced, complex characters.

The Quiller Memorandum, Adam Hall, 1965

British agent Quiller goes in search of a dangerous group of neo-Nazis in Berlin. Hall, one of author Elleston Trevor's pseudonyms, wrote 18 different books starring Quiller, a shadowy executive who works for "the Bureau," a secret government agency.

The Spy Who Came in from the Cold, John Le Carré, 1964

British agent Alex Leamas is given one last assignment before he can retire—to play an agent defecting to East Germany. Le Carré, pseudonym for David John Moore Cornwell, worked for British Intelligence. His carefully written novels brilliantly explore the moral ambiguity and conflicted loyalties of modern-day espionage. With Le Carré, spy fiction becomes literature.

The Unexpected Mrs. Pollifax, Dorothy Gilman, 1966

Bored with her garden club, sixtyish widow Emily Pollifax applies for a job with the CIA and is politely rejected but then is mistakenly given a job as a courier. While Gilman's gently humorous series featuring the intrepid Mrs. Pollifax has many of the requisite elements of a spy novel, including the exotic locations and danger-filled plots, Gilman adds her own unique, cozy twist to the subgenre through her creation of a heroine whose age and inexperience in espionage give the books their endearing charm.

Techno-thrillers

As the name implies, techno-thrillers are really all about technology, whether in the form of computers, electronic gadgets, or high-tech weapons. Sure, the stories are fast-paced and packed with plenty of action and adventure, but if the author doesn't incorporate high-tech toys in the plot, as far as techno-thriller readers are concerned, it's just another book.

Choosers of the Slain, James H. Cobb, 1996

Amanda Lee Garrett, Commander of the USS *Cunningham*, must stop Argentina when the country tries to take over a portion of Antarctica. Cobb gives the typically male-dominated techno-thriller genre one of its first—and best—female protagonists, proving that an abundance of testosterone is not required for a leader to be strong.

Deep Sound Channel, Joe Buff, 2000

When World War III breaks out in 2011, Lieutenant Commander Jeffrey Fuller takes a team of U.S. Navy SEALs on the submarine USS *Challenger* to destroy a biological weapons lab being built by the Germans and South Africans. Buff successfully blends old-fashioned sea battles with cutting-edge technology to create the kind of techno-thriller that readers love.

Flight of the Intruder, Stephen Coonts, 1986

Lieutenant Jake "Cool Hand" Grafton has led a number of successful air raids into North Vietnam, but anger at a friend's unnecessary death pushes Jake to take one last mission. It's a realistic look at war through the eyes of an average naval pilot, who is tired of the pointless battles, wasted lives, and incompetent leadership.

The Rest of the Story

Flight of the Intruder, Coonts's first book, was rejected by 34 publishers before the Naval Academy Press accepted it. The same publisher gave Tom Clancy his start with *The Hunt for Red October.*

Flight of the Old Dog, Dale Brown, 1987

Aerial warfare strike expert Patrick McLanahan leads a crew of engineers flying "Old Dog Zero One" on a mission to bomb a ground-based laser installation in Siberia. Former U.S. Air Force captain Brown knows his technology and weapons and translates this knowledge into his thrilling weapons and warfare books.

The Hunt for Red October, Tom Clancy, 1984

When Soviet officer Marko Ramius disappears with the USSR's most valuable submarine, the Tycoon class nuclear *Red October,* both the United States and the Soviets begin a desperate search in the Atlantic Ocean for Ramius, believing that he's out to destroy the world. CIA agent Jack Ryan is the only one who thinks Ramius is really trying to defect to the West. Clancy pretty much invented the techno-thriller.

> ### The Rest of the Story _____
>
> *The Hunt for Red October* was the first novel ever published by the Naval Institute Press during its more than 100 years of publishing history.

Nimitz Class, Patrick Robinson, 1997

When the Nimitz Class aircraft carrier *Thomas Jefferson* vanishes in a nuclear blast, Lieutenant Commander Bill Baldridge investigates. Robinson's writing career began with nonfiction books, about such varied topics as thoroughbred horses, the Falklands War, and a 1987 rowing scandal in England. With the publication of *Nimitz Class,* Robinson became a rival for Tom Clancy's techno-thriller crown.

Pandora's Clock, John J. Nance, 1995

Captain James Holland can't land his packed-to-the-gills airplane after he discovers that one of the passengers is infected with a deadly virus. If you think flying today is scary, imagine sitting next to the guy with a lethal disease! Nance is a lieutenant colonel in the U.S. Air Force.

Red Phoenix, Larry K. Bond, 1990

When war breaks out between North Korea and South Korea, the United States finds itself fighting the Soviets. A former naval officer and computer game designer, Bond got his literary start collaborating with Clancy on the novel *Red Storm Rising.*

Action and Adventure

In the best action and adventure novels, the protagonist—whether an individual or a small group of people—triumphs over seemingly insurmountable odds to accomplish some kind of heroic mission. Although men have traditionally held the starring role in classic adventure tales, women are gaining on them. Writers such as James Rollins and the team of Douglas Preston and Lincoln Child have created clever, strong female characters who prove they can save the world equally as well as any man.

Blue Ice, Hammond Innes, 1948

A search party of Norwegians and Englishmen are looking for George Farnell, who is rumored to have discovered some unusual mineral deposits in the glaciers of Norway. While not as well known as some adventure authors, Innes, an assured and skilled writer, is able to evoke the chilly fjords and mountains while keeping you on the edge of your seat. For 60 years, Innes has been writing the kind of classic adventure stories that never go out of style.

The Guns of Navarone, Alistair MacLean, 1957

A small band of British commandos must infiltrate a Nazi-held Greek island and destroy the Guns of Navarone. If we could bring one author back into vogue, it would have to be Alistair MacLean. MacLean wrote terrific old-fashioned adventure novels featuring tough, determined heroes and plots packed with plenty of intrigue and danger that were popular with readers for decades and inspired several classic adventure films.

Hawke, Ted Bell, 2003

Billionaire businessman and descendant of a pirate, Alex Hawke has been given a highly secret assignment for the government involving a submarine with nuclear warheads and some very cranky Cubans intent on deposing Castro. Ian Fleming would be proud.

Ice Station, Matthew J. Reilly, 1999

Lieutenant Shane "Scarecrow" Schofield leads a team of U.S. Marines to the Antarctic when a mysterious metallic object is found deep beneath the ice. Lots of action and a huge amount of testosterone fuel this nonstop adventure thriller, the first in a series to star tough-as-nails Scarecrow.

The Lieutenants, W.E.B. Griffin, 1982

After being captured by the Nazis, Lt. Robert Bellmon is given evidence of a Soviet massacre of Poles by a German officer who helps him escape. *The Lieutenants* is first in a nine-book Brotherhood of War series, which stretches from World War II to the Vietnam War. Having served in the military, Griffin knows how to write about war, and with 36 books in 6 different series, fans of blood-and-guts military adventures will be in heaven.

The Lions of Lucerne, Brad Thor, 2003

After Secret Service agent and former Navy SEAL Scot Harvath fails to protect the president of the United States from being kidnapped, he is determined to right his wrong but finds himself caught up in a powerful political conspiracy. With exotic locations, a seemingly indestructible hero, and a plot stuffed with so many twists and turns you need a map just to figure out where you are, Thor is the literary heir to Robert Ludlum.

Map of Bones, James Rollins, 2005

Rollins's thriller opens in a church in Germany when a group of masked commandos steal the bones of the Magi, killing almost everyone before they leave. Grayson Pierce, top agent in the Department of Defense's covert Sigma Force, teams up with Rachel Verona, a *carabinieri* corps lieutenant, to investigate. The plots of Rollins's thrillers are often outlandish, and his characters can be over-the-top, but he still manages to keep you believing the story. We think *Map of Bones* is better than *The Da Vinci Code!*

Night of the Fox, Jack Higgins, 1987

Three imposters join forces to rescue an American, who has all the details about D-Day, when he washes ashore on the German-held island of Jersey. Higgins is the most famous pseudonym of author Harry Patterson. While Higgins has written a variety of adventure and suspense novels, we think his best works are those set during World War II, such as *Night of the Fox* and the classic *The Eagle Has Landed.*

The Ninth Buddha, Daniel Easterman, 1989

Christopher Wylam travels from India to Outer Mongolia to Tibet to find his kidnapped 10-year-old son, who is believed to be the reincarnation of the Buddha. Lots of cliffhangers and a blend of metaphysics, politics, and religion make this thriller a page-turning read, guaranteed to keep you up late.

Raise the Titanic, Clive Cussler, 1976

Dirk Pitt races the Soviets for a rare cache of byzanium believed to be somewhere on the sunken *Titanic. Raise the Titanic* is the fourth in Cussler's series featuring Pitt, and we think it is one of the author's best. By this book, Cussler had established the pattern of the Pitt books: take an exotic location, add an intriguing historical event or treasure to the plot, throw in some high-tech gadgets, and mix in plenty of nonstop action and adventure seasoned with a pinch of romance. In recent years, Cussler has partnered with his son Dirk (hmm, where did he get that name?) to continue Pitt's adventures, and Cussler, with a little help from other literary contributors, is the creator of both the Kurt Austin series and the Oregon Files books.

The Rest of the Story

Not only does Cussler share his series character Dirk Pitt's love of classic cars, but he is also involved in underwater research. Cussler established NUMA (National Underwater and Marine Agency), a nonprofit organization that researches and recovers shipwrecks. He has written about these explorations in several nonfiction titles, including *The Seahunters: True Adventures with Famous Shipwrecks.*

Riptide, Douglas Preston and Lincoln Child, 1998

Thirty years ago, Dr. Malin Hatch lost his brother to a booby trap on their family's island off the coast of Maine while searching for the buried treasure of a seventeenth-century pirate. Now a group of treasure hunters have convinced him to let them search the island using their high-tech gear in the hopes of finally finding the legendary treasure of Red Ned Ockham. Preston and Child are two of our favorite authors because they pack the plot of *Riptide* with plenty of juicy information about code cracking, good old-fashioned pirate lore, and cutting-edge twentieth-century technology.

Rogue Warrior II: The Red Cell, Richard Marcinko, 1994

Former Navy SEAL Marcinko began his writing career with his autobiography, *Rogue Warrior,* but switched to fiction to continue his story for "security" reasons. In *Red Cell,* Marcinko casts himself as the hero and uses his special knowledge to thwart terrorists trying to smuggle nuclear weapons to the North Koreans.

The Rose of Tibet, Lionel Davidson, 1962

Charles Houston travels to Tibet to get information about his brother who died in an avalanche, but there he discovers that his brother may not be dead after all. Reminiscent of the adventure films of the 1950s (think *King Solomon's Mines* meets *Lost Horizon*), this book is a classic thriller with plenty of danger, betrayals, and a she-devil abbess (yes, we said she-devil abbess!).

Vulcan's Forge, Jack B. Du Brul, 1998

Forty years ago, the Russians sank a ship carrying an A-bomb in an attempt to create their very own thermonuclear volcano, but now, a rogue KGB agent is trying to sell it to North Korea. Mine engineer and geological consultant Philip Mercer becomes entangled in the complex scheme when he is enlisted to save a friend's missing daughter. Du Brul makes science sexy. Readers can count on his stories to have plenty of thrilling twists and turns.

And the Award Goes to...

The first conference dedicated solely to thrillers was held in Phoenix, Arizona, in 2004. That conference became the inspiration for the founding of International Thriller Writers, an organization dedicated to the thriller genre. The first "official" Thrillerfest was held in Phoenix in 2006, and as part of that conference, awards were given out, including the first Thrillermaster Award for Lifetime Achievement, which was bestowed on best-selling author Clive Cussler. The 2007 recipient was James Patterson.

Chapter 6

Romance: Reading to Your Heart's Desire

In This Chapter

- ◆ Historical romances: the passionate past
- ◆ Regencies: Jane Austen's legacy
- ◆ Contemporary romances: love in the here and now
- ◆ Romantic suspense: kiss me, kill me
- ◆ Paranormal, futuristic, and time-travel romances: vampires and werewolves and E.T.'s, oh my!

Have you read a romance lately? With romances making up 54.9 percent of all mass-market paperbacks sold, it's evident that many people have. Although all romance novels have, by definition, a romantic relationship between two people and a happily (or hopefully)-ever-after ending, each book is unique. We've listed our favorites by type: historical, Regency, contemporary, romantic suspense, and paranormal. So if you're a romance reader, we hope you find some great books you may have missed. And you say you've never read a romance before? Then try one. You just might like it!

Historical Romances

What makes a historical romance a romance and not historical fiction? It's a fine line, but when you read a historical romance, the story's primary focus deals with the relationship between the hero and the heroine, and the history is simply a backdrop.

Classics

Flowers from the Storm, Laura Kinsale, 1992

When the powerful, rich, debauched Christian, Duke of Jervaulx, is put into an asylum after he has a stroke and can no longer talk, the only person who believes he will speak again is the quiet Quaker, Maddy Timms. With its sensitive, innocent heroine, whose love redeems the damaged hero and an emotionally complex, richly nuanced story, this is romance at its very best.

The Gamble, LaVryle Spencer, 1987

Prim and proper milliner Agatha Downing finds herself engaged in a battle against alcohol when Scott Gandy opens a saloon in 1880s Kansas. Spencer's keen historical details and flesh-and-blood characters make this tale of two mulish people a winner.

Roselynde, Roberta Gellis, 1978

Queen Eleanor of Aquitaine appoints Simon Lemagne to be the warden of the estates of independent Alinor Devaux, who would rather stay the "lord" of her own castle and never marry. As Alinor comes to know the honor-bound Simon, she begins to change her mind. Gellis is known for her rich historical details and strong heroines.

Skye O'Malley, Bertrice Small, 1980

Beautiful Skye O'Malley matches wits and wiles with Queen Elizabeth I and wins. While there are many, many men (trust us, many!) in Skye's tempestuous, passion-filled life, she only has one true love, Lord Niall Burke. This book spawned 11 more featuring Skye and her progeny, and even today it is one of Small's most popular books, with its fiery heroine, sensual heroes, and steamy sex scenes.

The Wolf and the Dove, Kathleen Woodiwiss, 1974

Norman warrior Wulfgar arrives in Darkenwald to claim the land and its residents for King William, but Saxon princess Aislinn is determined that her enemy will never win. Woodiwiss is credited with starting the sensual historical romance subgenre in 1972, with her first book, *The Flame and the Flower*.

An Expert Speaks

"The Wolf and the Dove is definitely my favorite book. I have three copies. One is held together by a rubber band. I could get another, I'm sure, but there's something comforting in taking that old copy out once a year and re-reading it—especially when the weather is bad or I'm feeling down. The style is representative of good old fashioned historical romance at its finest. Politically incorrect. Lots of description and history. Broad canvas for a plot. Fabulous characters. It was one of the books that inspired me to become a writer."

—Jill Marie Landis, author

More Great Reads

The Bartered Bride, Mary Jo Putney, 2002

When wealthy American merchant Gavin Elliot sees Englishwoman Alexandra Warren being sold into slavery by pirates on the island of Maduri, he wants to rescue her, but he must successfully complete a series of dangerous tasks to win her freedom. Exotic locales, superbly crafted characters, and a compelling story make *The Bartered Bride* an unforgettable read. Trust us, we know. In fact, we stayed up all night to finish it.

The Book of True Desires, Betina Krahn, 2006

In order to get the funding she needs for her own expedition, Cordelia O'Keefe must first track down the legendary Gift of the Jaguar. Her tycoon grandfather insists on sending his stuffy but gorgeous British butler, Hartford Goodnight, on the trip as his official representative (think Clive Owen as Jeeves). Few have Krahn's gift for creating humorous yet sexy historicals.

Bridal Season, Connie Brockway, 2001

While fleeing from her occasional partner in crime, actress Letty Potts finds herself in Little Bidewell, where she is mistaken for Lady Agatha Whyte, London's most famous wedding planner, by everyone except the local magistrate, the very proper Elliot March. A charming and sexy hero, a feisty, spirited heroine, and a dash of humor are all ingredients in this enchanting tale.

The Bride and the Beast, Teresa Mederios, 2000

The Scottish village of Ballybliss is plagued by a "dragon," who is demanding food, drink, and gold. Instead, the citizens try offering the only (yes, the only) virgin in the village, stubborn, plump, sarcastic Gwendolyn Wilder. Gwen discovers the dragon is really the son of the murdered laird of the village, who's bent on revenge. Plenty of sassy humor and fairy-talelike charm fill this story.

The Charm School, Susan Wiggs, 1999

Frumpy Boston spinster Isadora Peabody blackmails dashing sea captain Ryan Calhoun into allowing her passage on his clipper ship, the *Silver Swan*, hoping that he will hire her as an interpreter. In this neat twist on *Pygmalion*, the sailors play Prof. Henry Higgins to Isadora's Liza Doolittle.

Dangerous Deceptions, Lynn Kerstan, 2004

Both impoverished viscount Jarrett and actress Kate Falshaw have been recruited by the mysterious "Black Phoenix" organization to infiltrate Paradise, society's most exclusive resort. In order for their mission to succeed, the two must engage in a very public affair. Danger, deception, and desire brilliantly blend together in Kerstan's irresistible romance.

Devil's Bride, Stephanie Laurens, 1998

Caught in a compromising position with governess Honoria Wetherby, "Devil" Cynster surprises everyone in society when he offers to marry her, but the unconventional woman has a taste for adventure and isn't about to settle down with Devil. The first of Laurens's sexy, scintillating "Cynster" series.

High Country Bride, Linda Lael Miller, 2002

The first McKettrick son to marry and produce a child will inherit the family ranch, so Rafe McKettrick decides to beat his brothers to the altar by getting himself a mail-order bride. Rafe expects his good looks will win the love of his new bride, but he didn't count on independent, feisty Emmeline Harding being immune to his charms. It's *Kiss Me Kate*, western-style.

In the Thrill of the Night, Candice Hern, 2006

When widow Marianne Nesbitt decides to take a lover, her old friend and disreputable rake Adam Cazenove offers to help her make a list of potential candidates. The more time Adam spends with Marianne, the more convinced he becomes that he's the only one for her. Elegant, witty, and sexy, this is the first in the "Merry Widows" series.

A Lady's Guide to Rakes, Kathryn Caskie, 2005

Merredith Merriweather is almost through with her "guide" to rakes for young ladies, but her study won't be complete until she's researched London's most notorious, but supposedly reformed rake, Alexander Lamont, Lord Lansing. It's wickedly funny.

Lord of Vengeance, Tina St. John, 1999

As an ultimate act of revenge against Baron Luther d'Bussy, the man who killed his parents, Gunnar Rutledge kidnaps d'Bussy's daughter, Raina. The more time

Gunnar spends with Raina, the more he realizes that he has been captured by her love. St. John puts a fresh spin on a classic plotline.

Man of My Dreams, Johanna Lindsey, 1992

Megan Penworthy is determined to marry a duke so she'll be accepted by society, but the only man she really wants is stable master and horse trainer Ambrose St. James. Ambrose, of course, is a duke in disguise. This is the first in the "Sherring Cross" series.

Miss Wonderful, Loretta Chase, 2004

To prove that he's not just a worthless fop, Alistair Carsington agrees to help his friend, Lord Gordmer, by convincing Gordmer's neighbors to let the noble-man build a canal through their land. Alistair finds everyone in Derbyshire friendly and helpful, with the exception of straight-laced Mirabel Oldridge, who'll do everything in her power to keep Alistair from succeeding. Charming, realistically quirky characters and sparkling, witty dialogue make this a good read.

Moon in the Water, Elizabeth Grayson, 2004

James Rossiter offers riverboat pilot Chase Hardesty his finest steamboat if Chase agrees to marry his stepdaughter. Chase eventually accepts, but he didn't expect his new wife to insist on accompanying him on his first voyage or the two of them to fall in love. The combination of superbly crafted characters and a quietly powerful story is simply mesmerizing.

Much Ado About You, Eloisa James, 2005

Tess Essex thinks wealthy, socially connected Garret Langham, the Earl of Mayne, would be the perfect choice for a suitable husband, but she can't quite forget the much less acceptable Lucius Felton and his tempting kisses. This story is elegantly sensual.

The Orchid Hunter, Jill Marie Landis, 2000

Joya Penn has grown up wild on the island of Matarenga, off the coast of Africa, with her father, a reclusive orchid hunter. When importer and amateur orchid hunter Trevor Mandeville arrives on the island, he proclaims Joya to be the exact twin of his adopted sister, Janelle. In fact, she *is* Janelle's twin, and Joya accompanies Trevor back to England to find out more about her heritage. Culture clash was never so much fun.

The Outsider, Penelope Williamson, 1996

Amish widow Rachel Yoder is still grieving over her husband's murder, but the struggle to raise her son and run her sheep ranch keep her occupied. When a wounded stranger appears one cold winter night, Rachel finds that she can't turn him away, even after she discovers that he's a gunfighter. Beautifully poignant, it's a romance you'll treasure.

The Promise of Jenny Jones, Maggie Osborne, 1997

Jenny Jones, a muleskinner about to be executed in a Mexican prison, agrees to switch places with the terminally ill Senorita Margarita Sanders. As a part of the exchange, Jenny agrees to take Margarita's six-year-old daughter, Graciela, to relatives in California. This task won't be an easy one, since Graciela's uncle has shown up to claim his niece. This book conveys both the grit and the honor of the Old West and will stay with you long after you finish reading it.

The Rogue's Return, Jo Beverley, 2006

Simon St. Bride is ready to leave Canada and return to his family's estate in England when he becomes involved in a duel to protect the honor of Jane Otterburn, whom he's then forced to marry. Simon's bride has a secret, which threatens to destroy their fragile new relationship. Filled with unexpected love and a dark secret, *The Rogue's Return* is a rewarding read.

Saving Grace, Julie Garwood, 1993

Newly widowed 16-year-old Johanna, finally free from her abusive husband, is determined never to marry again. But because King John suspects Johanna knows something that could ruin him, he arranges a marriage to one of his loyal henchmen. Joanna foils the king's plot by marrying unrefined Scottish laird Gabriel McBain instead.

Seduction, Amanda Quick, 1990

Sophy Dorring, innocent country girl and budding feminist, agrees to a marriage of convenience with dark, brooding Julian, Earl of Ravenwood, despite the rumors that he had some part in his first wife's mysterious death. *Seduction*, combines a dangerous, lusciously sexy hero and a sharp-witted, sharp-tongued heroine who is more than his equal. It is simply irresistible.

The Rest of the Story

Amanda Quick is a pseudonym of the amazingly versatile *New York Times* best-selling author Jayne Ann Krentz. Whether she's writing historical romances as Quick, contemporary romances as Krentz, or futuristics as Jayne Castle, she proves that danger and desire are always a winning combination.

Sleeping Beauty, Judith Ivory, 1998

Returning home from a successful African expedition, explorer James Stoker is the toast of London. But when he meets older, wiser, infamous courtesan Coco Wild, he's willing to throw everything away for a chance at love. The book is full of sumptuous prose and lusciously sensual love scenes.

Slightly Married, Mary Balogh, 2002

To fulfill a final request from a dying friend, Colonel Lord Aiden Bedwyn must tell the man's sister, Eve Morris, of his death. When he discovers she's in danger of losing her family estate, Aiden proposes a marriage of convenience. This is an appealing tale of an honorable hero and an independent heroine.

Some Enchanted Evening, Christina Dodd, 2004

When revolutionaries threaten her home in Beaumontagne, Princess Clarice Lilly and her two sisters are sent to England, where Clarice is forced to earn their way by selling cosmetics. Although Robert Mackenzie isn't sure about Clarice's claims of royal blood or assassins on her trail, he does need her skills for his own plan of revenge. Here's a sexy fairy tale for adults!

Stealing the Bride, Elizabeth Boyle, 2003

Heiress Diana Fordham is tired of waiting for the Marquis of Templeton to realize they belong together. She arranges to elope with a notorious fortune hunter, certain that it will push "Temple" into coming after her. Boyle's light, witty style creates a book that's delightful fun.

Suddenly You, Lisa Kleypas, 2001

Spinster author Amanda Briars decides to hire a "professional" man to be her first lover, but when arrogant, sinfully sexy Jack Devlin arrives at her door, she mistakes him for the man she "rented." Much to her horror, she discovers that her passionate dream lover is none other than her new publisher. This scorchingly sexy Victorian romance is filled with lots of humor.

The Texan's Wager, Jodi Thomas, 2002

Imprisoned for assaulting a man trying to steal their wagon, Bailee Moore and her two female companions' only ticket out of jail is to agree to a marriage "lottery" set up by the tricky sheriff of Cedar Point, Texas. When she is "bought" by taciturn farmer Carter McCoy, Bailee finds herself falling in love with her new husband.

Texas Destiny, Lorraine Heath, 1997

When a broken leg prevents Dallas Leigh from meeting his mail-order bride, Amelia Carson, at the train station, he sends his brother, Houston, in his place. But on the journey back to his family's ranch, Houston, whose face has been disfigured during a Civil War battle, begins to fall in love with Amelia. It's subtle, poignant, and beautifully written.

To Tame a Texan, Georgina Gentry, 2003

The only way suffragist Lynnie McBride can get to Dodge City for a women's rights meeting is to disguise herself and go on a trail drive led by Ace Durango. If Ace finds out who she really is, he's more than likely to send her right back home. This classic battle of the sexes features a strong-willed heroine and an equally stubborn hero.

A Wanted Man, Susan Kay Law, 2004

Escaping her pampered life, heiress Laura Hamilton heads west for adventure, but being caught in a shootout is more excitement than she bargained for. Fortunately, gunslinger Sam Duncan is there to save her, and appoints himself her bodyguard, but his motives are not as pure as they seem. Realistically flawed, three-dimensional characters make this book hard to put down.

Whitney, My Love, Judith McNaught, 1985

Recently returned home from Paris, Whitney Stone believes her best chance at true love is with her friend Paul, but she is bargained away by her bankrupt father into marrying Clayton Westmoreland, the Duke of Claymore, instead. A strong but vulnerable heroine clashes with a really yummy "bad boy" hero.

The Widow's Kiss, Jane Feather, 2000

After the suspicious death of Lady Guinevere Mallory's fourth husband (three we can understand, but four?), King Henry VIII sends Hugh of Beaucaire, who has a personal interest in the widow's recently inherited estate, to investigate. Hugh finds himself becoming intrigued and enthralled by Guinevere.

The Windflower, Tom and Sharon Curtis, 1984

While on her way to England, American Merry Patricia Wilding is mistakenly kidnapped by a band of pirates led by callous Captain Rand Morgan and his gorgeous half-brother Devon Crandall. With a classic romance and pirates, how can you go wrong?

A Woman Scorned, Liz Carlyle, 2000

In order to investigate the suspicious death of his brother, Lord Mercer, Captain
Cole Amherst becomes the tutor to his brother's two young children to get
closer to their mother, whom he suspects of murder. The more he gets to know
her, the less convinced he is that she's an unrepentant adulteress and killer.
Carlyle twists classic conventions by creating a heroine with a scandalous,
wicked reputation, making the hero the innocent one.

Regencies

If you love *all* the film versions of *Pride and Prejudice* and believe the Regency
era to be the most romantic and elegant ever, you were meant to read Regency
fiction. Inspired by Jane Austen's classics, the traditional Regency novel immor-
talizes the early nineteenth century, when England battled Napoleon and the
Prince Regent ruled England because King George, his father, was just a teeny bit
insane. With vividly detailed descriptions of the clothes, customs, and manners
of that time, Regency romances celebrate the delicate dance of love in a most
witty, wonderful way.

Classics

The Grand Sophy, Georgette Heyer, 1950

While staying with her aunt in London, outspoken Sophy Stanton-Lacy
decides to meddle in everyone's affairs, including those of her cousin Charles,
who's engaged to a woman she thinks is too straightlaced for him. Convincing
Charles won't be easy, especially when, in the midst of sorting out everyone
else's love lives, Sophy unexpectedly finds romance.

Minerva, Marion Chesney, 1982

While enduring a season in London to secure her family's financial future, Minerva Armitage crosses paths with the elegant and exalted Lord Sylvester Comfrey. *Minerva* is the first in a six-book series featuring the Armitage sisters. Chesney quickly became known and loved by Regency readers for the many cleverly interconnected series she created, such as her "Traveling Matchmaker" and "Poor Relations" series.

More Great Reads

Deirdre and Don Juan, Jo Beverley, 1993

Mark Juan Carlos Renfrew's next choice for a wife is the very quiet and plain Deirdre Stowe, but much to Mark's surprise, rather than being flattered by his offer, Deirdre is annoyed with "Don Juan's" proposal since she plans on marrying someone else.

The Errant Earl, Amanda McCabe, 2002

Julia Barclay is worried that once her stepbrother, Marcus Hadley, returns home, the first thing he will do is kick out all of her actor friends who have been living with her. So Julia convinces her friends to take on new roles as household "servants." A quirky cast of characters adds a winning touch of theatrical drama to this delightfully humorous story.

The Famous Heroine, Mary Balogh, 1996

After the annoyingly foppish Lord Francis Keller helps untangle Cora Downes from one too many social disasters, Cora finds her reputation is so compromised that she has no choice but to marry him. This richly poignant story is yet light and frothy.

A Grand Design, Emma Jensen, 2000

When Draco Llywelyn St. Clair Wright hires the Scottish firm of Buchanan and Buchanan to restore and renovate his London townhouse, he has no idea that Catherine Buchanan is the real architect designing his new home. Jensen's superbly written Regencies are rich in droll humor and captivating characters.

Knave's Wager, Loretta Chase, 1990

Lilith Davenant can't believe that Julian Wyndhurst, Marquess of Brandon, could really be in love with her. She discovers she's right when she learns Julian's only romantic interest in her is a wager the nobleman made with his friends over whether he could successfully seduce her. Now Lilith is determined to turn the romantic tables on Julian by seducing him instead!

Lord Will and Her Grace, Sophia Nash, 2005

Foppish dandy William Barclay wagers Sophie Somerset that he can teach her how to attract an aristocratic husband before she can show him how to find a suitable lady. Sophie doesn't realize her new tutor is a rake determined to seduce her. With a cunning sense of wit, Nash fashions a wickedly entertaining romance.

Marry in Haste, Lynn Kerstan, 1998

The first time Miss Diana Whitney meets Colonel Alex Valliant, she mistakes him for a burglar and hits him on the head with a frying pan. Now, to avoid being forced into an unwanted marriage, Diana finds herself accepting a marriage proposal from Alex instead. If Shakespeare dabbled in Regency romances, the result would be something like Kerstan's novels.

Miss Westlake's Windfall, Barbara Metzger, 2001

When Ada Westlake finds a small fortune hidden in her family's orchard, she turns to her very good friend and wealthy neighbor, Charles Ashford, for help in returning the ill-gotten booty to its rightful owner. Light and amusing, the book is absolutely splendid.

Miss Whittier Makes a List, Carla Kelley, 1994

American Hannah Whittier has come up with a list of qualifications of her ideal man, but she never expected the perfect candidate would be Daniel Spark, the brusque British captain who rescues her when she is shipwrecked. This book vividly details shipboard life during the War of 1812 and gives readers a brilliantly nuanced hero and heroine.

My Lady Gamester, Cara King, 2005

Atalanta James is determined to exact revenge against the men who used her father's gambling addiction to bankrupt her family. That includes Richard Stanton, who has no idea his own father was one of the men who personally profited from the card game that ruined Atalanta's life. Readers won't be gambling if they choose this author's charming debut.

Moonlight and Mischief, Rhonda Woodward, 2004

Mariah Thorncroft is tired of fortune hunters, so when Nicholas Morley invites her to a house party, she decides that while she is staying at his estate, she's going to ignore him completely. Much to her surprise, Mariah finds it isn't as easy to banish Nicholas from her thoughts as she thought it would be.

The Nobody, Diane Farr, 1999

While walking home one evening after overhearing another lady call her a "nobody," Caitlin Campbell bumps into a handsome stranger who steals a kiss from her. When Caitlin is later introduced to Viscount Kilverton, she's surprised to discover that not only is he the same man who kissed her, but he also seems quite interested in continuing what he started. It's superb!

The Scandalous Widow, Evelyn Richardson, 2004

The widowed Lady Catherine Granville's in-laws want Lucian, the Marquess of Charlmont, to talk Catherine out of her new career as the owner of a Select Academy for Genteel Young Ladies. When Lucian arranges a meeting with Catherine, he finds he already knows her from nearly a decade earlier when he broke her trust by running off with an actress.

Seducing Mr. Heywood, Jo Manning, 2002

When widowed Lady Sophia Rowley arrives in Yorkshire to claim her two sons, she discovers the local vicar, Charles Heywood, is already their legal guardian. Since she's stuck in the countryside, Sophia decides she might as well spend time with the handsome Charles, but the more time the two spend together, the more difficult it is to determine exactly who's seducing whom.

A Singular Lady, Megan Frampton, 2005

In order to pay off her family's debts, Titania Stanhope must marry for money. Her carefully thought-out plans take an unexpected turn when she meets the irresistibly charming, but seemingly impoverished, Edwin Worthington. Frampton's debut will wow you with its classic storyline and tart wit.

Utterly Devoted, Regina Scott, 2002

In order to earn a much-needed estate from his brother, Jareth Darby must reform his rakish ways by apologizing to every woman he has romantically wronged. Jareth has successfully gotten 11 women on his list to forgive him, but when he reaches number 12, Eloise Watkin, he discovers it won't be quite as easy to get her to accept his apology. Readers will root for the spunky Eloise as she teaches Jareth a much-deserved lesson in love. It's great fun!

The Vampire Viscount, Karen Harbaugh, 1999

In order to save her mother and sister from a life of poverty, Leonore Farleigh agrees to a marriage of convenience with Nicholas Viscount St. Vire. The union becomes very inconvenient when she discovers she is married to a vampire! Harbaugh was among the first to add a paranormal element to the traditional Regency, giving The Vampire Viscount its deliciously dark edge.

Contemporary Romances

They can be sweet. They can be sexy. They can be poignant. They can be sassy. Contemporary romances come in all different flavors, but the one common ingredient throughout is the joy that finding love in today's hectic world brings.

Classics

The Color of Love, Sandra Kitt, 1995

In New York City, African American artist Leah Downey is attracted to white cop Jason Horn. When Jason asks Leah out, she accepts, despite objections from friends and family. Can their newfound love overcome the obstacles that are thrown in their path? Kitt, a groundbreaking author in the romance genre, was the first to write about an African-American couple for Harlequin books. With *The Color of Love*, Kitt tackles the controversial topic of interracial romance with her usual elegance and grace.

It Had to Be You, Susan Elizabeth Phillips, 1994

Phoebe Somerville has returned to Chicago for the reading of her father's will, never expecting that she would even be mentioned. Much to her surprise, Phoebe inherits her father's football team, the Chicago Stars. But there's a catch. In order for her to be able to keep the team, the Chicago Stars must win the American Football Conference championship. Unfortunately, they don't have a chance of winning unless Phoebe learns to get along with stubborn, irascible, and irritatingly sexy head coach Dan Calebow. The book is an amusing, sexy, smart, and completely satisfying read.

> **An Expert Speaks**
>
> "Susan Elizabeth Phillips' book *It Had to Be You*, the first in her series about the Chicago Stars Football team, is a great read: funny, sincere, and insightful. The perfect romance book."
>
> —Judi McCoy, author

A Rose for Maggie, Kathleen Korbel, 1991

Allison Henley is a single mother struggling to raise Maggie, who has Down's syndrome, and doesn't think there's room in her life for romance. Then she meets reclusive author Joe Burgett, who is determined to prove her wrong. You'll need boxes of tissues while you read this book, but it's worth every tear.

Sarah's Child, Linda Howard, 1985

Two years after a horrendous accident took the life of Rome Matthews's beloved wife and two little boys, he remarries, choosing his wife's best friend, Sarah Harper, as his bride. Sarah knows that Rome is still in love with his late wife, but she loves him and is willing to settle for a marriage of convenience, although she begins to hope for more.

An Expert Speaks

"My favorite contemporary romance is *Sarah's Child* by Linda Howard. The quality of the writing is superb. The story of a man whose pain at the loss of his wife and children is so pervasive and tormenting that it affects adversely his second wife and the child she bears him. But her patience, love, caring and understanding bring the great man to his knees and into her arms. It might well have been entitled *The Power of Love.*"

—Gwen Forster, author

More Great Reads

Bet Me, Jennifer Crusie, 2004

When Min Dobbs overhears handsome stranger Calvin Morrisey betting Min's former fiancé David Fisk that Cal can bed her within a month, Min decides to turn the tables on Cal by using Cal as her date for a friend's wedding and then dumping him! All of Crusie's books are filled with delectably sexy, sharply humorous, splendidly sassy writing.

Blame It on Chocolate, Jennifer Greene, 2006

If she hadn't been sampling the new brand of chocolate she was developing for Bernard's Chocolate, Lucy Fitzhenry never would have indulged in one amazing night of passion with her boss, Nick Bernard. Two months later, Lucy discovers she has a more permanent "reminder" of their sexy fling. Much humor and plenty of sizzle make this a delightfully entertaining book.

Born in Fire, Nora Roberts, 1994

Strong-willed and independent glass artist Maggie Concannon reluctantly agrees to let Rogan Sweeny exhibit her art in his Dublin gallery, but their already rocky business relationship really becomes complicated when she finds herself attracted to the sexy and sophisticated Irishman. Filled with plenty of Celtic flavor, *Born in Fire* is the first in a trilogy featuring three sisters.

And the Award Goes to ...

To be inducted into the Romance Writers of America Hall of Fame, an author needs to win at least three RITAs in a single category. Only nine writers (Nora Roberts, Jo Beverley, Justine Dare, Jennifer Greene [Alison Hart], Kathleen Korbel [Eileen Dreyer], Francine Rivers, LaVyrle Spencer, Jodi Thomas, and Cheryl Zach) have been awarded this honor. Of these, only Roberts has been honored in three categories: Long Contemporary Romance, Romance Suspense, and Contemporary Single Title Romance.

Charming Grace, Deborah Smith, 2004

Hollywood's most popular action star, Stone Senterra, has arrived in Dahlonega, Georgia, with plans of making a movie based on deceased Georgia Bureau of Investigation Agent Harp Vance. Harp's widow, Grace Bagshaw Vance, will do anything to stop Stone from filming.

A Crazy Kind of Love, Maureen Child, 2004

Michaela "Mike" Marconi, the plumber in the family's construction business, has picked out the perfect location for her "dream" home. But scientist Lucas Gallagher has beaten her to the punch by purchasing the land and beginning construction of his own "dream" home. Not one to be deterred by such a small obstacle, Mike proceeds to tell Lucas how to build it.

Dreaming of You, Francis Ray, 2006

Brandon Grayson is so determined to be the one Grayson brother not married off by their matchmaking mother that he decides to become celibate. But when a leaky pipe forces Brandon to stay at his friend Faith McBride's hotel, abstinence suddenly seems like a bad idea. It's a sweet, sexy, and fun read.

Good Girls Do, Cathie Linz, 2006

Julia Wright loves her serene life and her job working at the library in peaceful little Serenity Falls, but Julia's small, quiet world is about to be shaken up when her wacky family show up for a visit and bad-boy biker Luke Maguire roars back into town. This romance is filled with love and laughter.

Hidden, Tara Taylor Quinn, 2005

For her own safety, and that of her unborn child, Kate Whitehead leaves her violent husband and moves to San Diego, living under the name Tricia Campbell. "Tricia" accepts firefighter Scott McCall's offer of a place to stay, and they gradually become something of a family. But when Tricia hears that her former husband is suspected of murdering her best friend, Tricia's new life slowly starts to unravel.

Hot Dish, Connie Brockway, 2006

Just as Jenn Lind is poised to become television's next big star, she finds herself coerced into returning to her hometown of Fawn Creek, Minnesota, to be grand marshal in the town's sesquicentennial parade. Once there, Jenn finds she has to share her grand marshal duties with sexy sculptor Steve Jaax, and that a 20-year-old sculpture of her has turned up, which everyone in town seems to desperately want. Plenty of quirky characters and lots of tart humor give Brockway's book its unique charm.

How to Trap a Tycoon, Elizabeth Bevarly, 2000

Sociology graduate student and teaching assistant Dorsey MacGuinness is doing everything she can to keep her alter ego, Lauren Grable-Monroe, author of the best-selling *How to Trap a Tycoon,* a secret. Dorsey gathers data for her graduate thesis by working at Drake's, an exclusive men's club. Adam Darien, publisher of *Men's Life* magazine and a regular at Drake's, is determined to discover the real identity of the elusive Ms. Grable-Monroe.

Jude's Law, Lori Foster, 2006

Jude Jamison, former prizefighter turned movie star, moves to the small town of Stillbrook, Ohio, to escape his life of fame and scandal. Once there, Jude finds himself falling in love with curvy art dealer May Price, who initially wants nothing to do with him. Unfortunately, May needs his help dealing with her brother's gambling debts.

The Last Good Man, Kathleen Eagle, 2000

Savannah Stephens was a lingerie supermodel until she got breast cancer and had a mastectomy. She takes her six-year-old daughter, Claudia, back to Wyoming, where Clay Keogh, rancher and old friend, has designs to marry her. There are obstacles—his ex-wife, Savannah's coming to terms with her body, and the fact that Claudia looks just like his half-brother, Native American activist Kole Catches Crow.

Love in Bloom's, Judith Arnold, 2002

When her formidable grandmother appoints her the new president of Bloom's, the family's famous delicatessen, newly minted divorce lawyer Julia Bloom wants to say no, but she just can't refuse. Now Julia finds herself desperately trying to modernize the family business, tune out the irritating family members trying to tell her how to run the place better, and keep annoying, yet oh-so-sexy, business reporter Ron Joffe from writing the article he desperately wants to write. Warm and witty, this story is as delicious as a bagel fresh from the oven.

Nerd in Shining Armor, Vicki Lewis Thompson, 2003

Genevive Terrance was looking forward to an overnight "business" trip with her handsome boss, Nick Brogan. Then Nick bails out of their plane, leaving Genevive and computer geek Jack Farley to die in the inevitable crash. Jack manages to land on a deserted tropical island, and now Genevive finds herself with a nerd who is proving to be surprisingly resourceful and sexy. The always entertaining Thompson's first "Nerd" book was chosen by television personality Kelly Ripa for her book club.

On Angel Wings, Roz Denny Fox, 2006

Pilot Mick Callen, a member of Montana's Angel Fleet, has a lot of experience rescuing stranded rock climbers. But his latest mission is different. After airlifting injured Hana Egan, Mick falls in love with her. Here is a beautifully poignant romance.

The Secret, Shirley Hailstock, 2006

Searching for her biological family, Stephanie Hunter uses a friend to introduce her to the powerful Clayton family and eventually lands an interior design job. Unfortunately, this puts her in close proximity to hunky architect Owen Clayton.

Sweet Nothings, Catherine Anderson, 2002

After stealing a badly beaten racehorse from her ex-husband, Molly Wells shows up at Jake Coulter's Lazy J Ranch hoping his gift as a "horse whisperer" can help. Jake convinces Molly to stay at the ranch as his cook/housekeeper. One day, Molly's past—and her ex—catch up with her.

Truly, Madly Yours, Rachel Gibson, 1999

To inherit the $3 million her stepfather has left her, Delaney Shaw must live in Truly, Idaho, for one year. Nick Allegrezza, who seduced and then dumped her 10 years earlier, also has a chance at a share of the estate, and he's willing to do whatever it takes to get it.

When You Dance with the Devil, Gwen Forster, 2006

Thank the Lord Boarding House is the perfect place for people wanting to start over. Ready for a new beginning, Sara Jolene Tilman moves there. A 35-year-old who's lived under the thumb of a controlling mother, Sara's anxious to finally lose her virgin status. Richard Peterson is a 45-year-old, self-made, successful businessman. The woman he loves has married someone else, and all Richard wants is some peace, quiet … and celibacy.

Romantic Suspense

Danger and desire are the two main ingredients in the gothic and romantic suspense subgenre. While the heroine may not be exactly sure she can trust the hero, one thing readers can rely on is that by the end of the book, kissing—and sometimes steamy sex—will be involved. Both romantic suspense and gothics are about heroines in danger, and both borrow elements from the mystery and romance genres. The key differences between the two are time and place. Gothics are almost always set in the past, while romantic suspense is usually set in the present day. Most gothics are set in some isolated location, such as a mansion, castle, or estate, while romantic suspense novels can be set anywhere. The best of these novels create a synthesis of romance and mystery that readers can't resist.

Classics

Emerald, Phyllis Whitney, 1983

Journalist Carol Hamilton finds danger and romance in Palm Springs when she tries to discover why her great-aunt, film star Monica Arlen, mysteriously gave up her career years ago. For nearly four decades Whitney reigned as America's undisputed queen of romantic suspense and gothic fiction as she turned out wonderfully addictive tales of danger, deception, and desire.

Mistress of Mellyn, Victoria Holt, 1960

After taking a job with a mysterious family in Cornwall, a young governess discovers that the mother of her young charge was murdered and that everyone thinks her new employer is the killer. While Holt, one of the pseudonyms for popular and prolific author Eleanor Hibbert, didn't invent the gothic subgenre, she, perhaps more than any other author, helped popularize it with readers in the 1960s and 1970s. Even today, every one of her books is still a classic.

Nine Coaches Waiting, Mary Stewart, 1958

The Château Valmy is too luxurious and beautiful to be true. In fact, beneath these trappings of fabulous old wealth is a dark, dangerous secret, one that threatens the very life of young British nanny Linda Martin and Philippe, her nine-year-old charge. Stewart's flair for edge-of-your-seat suspense, as well as her incredibly detailed settings (check out the sights, sounds, and smells of Paris) make this book, like her other extraordinary works, a delectable read.

Rebecca, Daphne du Maurier, 1938

The second Mrs. DeWinter discovers that although her husband's first wife, Rebecca, is dead, her legacy lingers on at Manderley. Du Maurier wrote a number of novels, including historical fiction and suspense, but she's best known and loved for the timeless *Rebecca.* Could there be a better first line than "Last night, I dreamt I went to Manderley again"?

More Great Reads

After Midnight, Merline Lovelace, 2003

Col. Jessica Blackwell is reluctant to return to her hometown, where she and her family were pariahs, but being a good military officer, she obeys the relocation order. As luck would have it, people start getting murdered soon after Jessica moves to town, and all clues point to the colonel. Jessica finds the only one who believes she isn't guilty is Sheriff Steve Paxton. This taut suspense has honorable characters.

Amber Beach, Elizabeth Lowell, 1997

Honor Donovan needs Jake Mallory's help when Honor's brother, and a fortune in amber, disappear somewhere near Puget Sound. Lowell uses the intriguing true story of the legendary eighteenth-century Russian room made completely of amber as the Maguffin in *Amber Beach.*

Angels Fall, Nora Roberts, 2006

Former chef Reece Gilmore only intended to stay in the tiny town of Angels Fall, Wyoming, long enough to earn money to fix her broken-down car. After taking a job as a cook in a diner, Reece settles into her new life. When she witnesses a murder, the only person who believes her story is a reclusive mystery writer, "Brody."

Black Ice, Anne Stuart, 2005

After accepting a job at a remote chateau, translator Chloe Underwood becomes tangled up with covert operative Bastien Toussaint. Stuart is a legend in the romance world and has written everything from historical romances to paranormals to Regencies. Stuart's heroes are deliciously dark and tortured.

The Cove, Catherine Coulter, 1996

After escaping from an asylum, Sally St. John Brainerd returns to the small town of Cove and her aunt Amabel, but when Sally suspects something is going on, the only one who believes her is private investigator James Quinlan. Coulter began her writing career in historical romances but successfully transitioned into contemporary romantic thrillers.

Dark Desires, Eve Silver, 2005

Darcie Finch begins to understand why her new employer, Dr. Damien Cole, has trouble keeping servants and staff, when she sees him leaving his laboratory stained with blood. Wonderfully atmospheric settings give an ominous sense of danger.

Flirting with Danger, Suzanne Enoch, 2005

When cat burglar Samantha Jellicoe breaks into the home of incredibly wealthy Richard Addison, she accidentally sets off a bomb left there by someone else. Samantha inadvertently saves Richard during the blast, but there's still the question of who's trying to kill him. The light banter and fast-moving plot will remind you of *To Catch a Thief* or the *Thin Man* mysteries.

French Silk, Sandra Brown, 1992

Claire Laurent owns French Silk, an exclusive mail-order lingerie business in New Orleans. When a televangelist is murdered, Claire becomes a suspect. Despite her lies, District Attorney Robert Cassidy is drawn to the enigmatic businesswoman. But is she guilty? Steamy, sultry, and sexy, *French Silk* was one of the books that catapulted Brown to fame and the bestseller list. Think Victoria's Secret meets John Grisham (but with beaucoup more sex!).

> ### The Rest of the Story _____
>
> Sandra Brown began writing for both Harlequin and Bantam Loveswept under a variety of pseudonyms. Twenty years and 60 books later, she commands a cool $4 million per book.

Home Before Midnight, Virginia Kantra, 2006

When a best-selling true crime author's wife is found murdered, the suspicion falls on his pretty assistant, Bailey Wells. Detective Steve Burke is almost positive Bailey is innocent, especially when the killer strikes again. Kantra is a rising star in romantic suspense.

Kiss and Tell, Cherry Adair, 2000

While staying in her grandmother's old cabin in the woods, Marnie Wright stumbles into former covert agent Jake Dolan and becomes a target of the same men who are trying to kill him. When it comes to mixing riveting suspense and sizzling sexy romance, Adair has few rivals.

The Mistress of Trevelyan, Jennifer St. Giles, 2004

Despite rumors about the mysterious death of Benedict Trevelyan's first wife, Ann Lovell accepts the job of tutor to his two sons. Ann's determined to bring some joy and light back into her students' lives, but she quickly finds herself caught up in secrets that haunt Trevelyan Manor and her brooding employer. Think Victoria Holt, but with sizzling sex.

Mr. Perfect, Linda Howard, 2001

When Jaine Bright and her three friends came up with a list of qualities their "perfect man" must have, Jaine never thought the list would attract a killer or that she would need the help of sexy police detective Sam Donovan. Edgy and spine-tingling, the book has a nice touch of sharp humor.

Nothing to Fear, Karen Rose, 2005

Strong-willed Dana Dupinsky, a woman who'll do anything to protect the clients of the women's shelter she directs, and hot security expert Ethan Buchanan, who's searching for his kidnapped godson, are pitted against a ruthless killer. Rose is known for her dark, intense, utterly riveting novels.

You Can Book on It! _____

A wide range of sensuality exists in the Gothic and Romantic Suspense genre. There's everything from the sweetly romantic tales of Mary Stewart and Victoria Holt to today's brand of scorchingly sexy novels by Sandra Brown and Linda Howard.

Picture Me Dead, Heather Graham, 2003

Despite the fact that the police believe her friend's death was accidental, Ashley Montague, a rookie cop who's now a forensics artist, continues to look into the case on her own. Ashley soon finds there may be a connection to a previous, ritualistic murder. Detective Jake Dilessio is investigating the killings, too, and he's afraid that Ashley will be the next victim.

Sharp Edges, Jayne Ann Krentz, 1998

Museum curator Eugenia Swift and private investigator Cyrus Chandler Colfax are reluctant partners in the search for the killer of a collector of art glass. When it comes to snappy dialogue, sharply defined characters, and sizzling sexual chemistry, few are better.

Shattered Silk, Barbara Michaels, 1986

After her marriage falls apart, Karen Nevitt starts over again by house-sitting for her aunt in Georgetown. A behest of antique clothing inspires her to open a vintage clothing store, but Karen's hopes for a new business and a second chance at love are threatened by both a ghostly intruder and a murder.

The Rest of the Story _____

Barbara Michaels is one of the pseudonyms for the versatile Barbara Mertz, who also writes as Elizabeth Peters, famous for her Amelia Peabody historical mysteries. If you like her romantic suspense novels as Barbara Michaels, you will also enjoy her early works as Elizabeth Peters, especially our favorites, *The Jackal's Head* and *Summer of the Dragon*.

Slow Burn, Julie Garwood, 2005

After Kate Mackenna narrowly escapes two separate suspicious explosions, her best friend, Jordan Buchanan, sends her cop brother Dylan to keep an eye on her. Kate and Dylan have already shared one night of passion, but now, if the two are to have any chance at a long-term relationship, Dylan must find exactly who wants her dead. It's a ripping good suspense novel.

The Ugly Duckling, Iris Johansen, 1996

After surviving the brutal attack that killed both her husband and her child, Nell Carter is transformed through plastic surgery into a beautiful woman whose sole goal is to find the person responsible for killing her family and make him pay for it. This is a great tale of female empowerment and the ultimate revenge.

The Unsung Hero, Suzanne Brockmann, 2000

Recovering Navy SEAL Lt. Tom Paoletti thinks he sees the notorious terrorist known as "The Merchant," but the only one who can help him is his uncle's neighbor, Kelly Ashton. Brockmann wrote contemporary series romances for Harlequin and Silhouette before she began her popular Navy "SEAL TEAM 10" series. When it comes to gritty action, nail-biting suspense, and sexy Navy SEALs, Brockmann delivers.

Walking After Midnight, Karen Robards, 1995

While cleaning up at the funeral home late one night, Summer McAfee finds that one of the "customers" is still breathing. The "body" turns out to be the very much alive, former police officer Steve Calhoun, who must kidnap Summer to keep her safe from the men who put him into the funeral home and now want to finish the job. If you like your romantic suspense with a sexy, humorous edge, you'll enjoy *Walking After Midnight*.

Paranormal, Futuristic, and Time-Travel Romances

Paranormal romance fiction encompasses a wide range of subgenres, including futuristics, time travels, werewolves, vampires, witches, ghosts, second sight, fairies ... just about anything not of this world that gives a good romance a little mystical punch. And when it comes to the ultimate in bad-boy heroes, nothing can match a vampire or a werewolf. So we've compiled a variety of titles that we think are some of the best in paranormal romance fiction.

Classics

A Knight in Shining Armor, Jude Deveraux, 1989

After Dougless Montgomery's fiancé and his bratty daughter abandon her in a remote medieval English church, Dougless begins crying over the sixteenth-century tomb of Nicholas Stafford, wishing for her very own knight in shining armor. Her tears summon Nicholas from 1564, and the knight now has a chance to not only help Dougless but also rewrite his own history. This is one of our all-time favorites.

Outlander, Diana Gabaldon, 1991

In Scotland on a second honeymoon, war nurse Claire Randall walks into an ancient circle of stones and finds that she has been transported from 1945 back to 1743, where she meets and falls in love with Scottish warrior James Fraser. First in a series, *Outlander* delivers an addictive mix of history, romance, adventure ... and a yummy man in a kilt. This rare book crosses genres and genders.

Sweet Starfire, Jayne Castle, 1986

Ethereal Cidra Rainforest, raised by one race but actually a member of the savage wolf race, must team up with handsome fortune hunter Teague Severance on a deadly quest where they will battle human and alien danger (as well as their own desire!).

More Great Reads

Beyond the Highland Mist, Karen Marie Moning, 1999

Adrienne de Simone is whisked back in time from the twentieth century to 1513 Scotland, where she is supposed to wed Hawk, a sexy Scottish warrior. But first, Hawk has to convince Adrienne they belong together. Think *Taming of the Shrew*, in kilts, with angry fairies.

Bitten and Smitten, Michelle Rowen, 2006

After her date bites her and turns her into a vampire, Sarah Dearly is saved by tortured and tormented vampire Thierry de Bennicour, who reluctantly agrees to help Sarah adapt to her new way of life. Readers will love the sharp bite of humor and sexy flavor of Rowen's debut.

Blue Moon, Lori Handeland, 2004

No-nonsense police officer Jessie McQuade didn't believe in werewolves, but when normally shy wolves begin killing residents of her small town, she agrees to work with Will Cadotte, a professor of Native American mythology, to stop the deadly attacks.

Breath of Magic, Teresa Medeiros, 1996

After being accused of witchcraft, Arian Whitewood escapes seventeenth-century New England through the means of a magical amulet and finds herself in twentieth-century New York in the office of billionaire businessman Tristan Lennox, who is seeking proof that magic really exists. Medeiros was one of the first to write in the paranormal subgenre, and the results are witty and fun.

The Bride Finder, Susan Carroll, 1998

Clairvoyant Anatole St. Leger finally bows to fate and asks the Bride Finder to locate the one woman who's his destiny. He's paired with sensible, levelheaded Madeline Bretton. A dark, brooding hero meets his match in the form of the sharp-witted and sharp-tongued Madeline. Think *Beauty and the Beast* (but without the dancing candlesticks).

Christmas Knight, Christina Skye, 1998

Hope O'Hara needs a lot of help to complete the renovations necessary to turn the ancient Glenbrae House into the inn she has always dreamed of owning. Hope never expected that help would come from the former owner of Glenbrae House, thirteenth-century knight Ronan Macleod. Skye's time travel is magical, mystical, and marvelous.

Dark Lover, J. R. Ward, 2005

Beth Randall has no idea she is half vampire but is rapidly approaching the "transition," when she will definitely know. The only person who can help her understand her new heritage is the leader of the Black Dagger Brotherhood. Ward puts her own distinctive stamp on the vampire subgenre with her dark, edgy, and sinfully sensuous "Black Dagger Brotherhood" series.

Dark Prince, Christine Feehan, 1999

While staying in the Carpathian Mountains, psychic Raven Whitney telepathically hears the mournful cries of wounded Prince Mikhail Dubrinksy, who eventually becomes her life mate. Feehan pretty much rules the paranormal romance subgenre, with four continuing series, including her "Dark" series, featuring those tortured, tormented, yet oh-so-sexy Carpathians.

Date Me, Baby, One More Time, Stephanie Rowe, 2006

In order to break the curse that's killed four generations of men in his family, pretzel king Derek LaValle must find the Goblet of Eternal Youth and kill its guardian, Justine Bennett. You've got to love a book in which the heroine's best friend is a pretzel-loving dragon!

A Hunger Like No Other, Kresley Cole, 2006

Lachlain, king of the Lykae (think werewolves) Clan, has just escaped from the vampire horde, only to discover the one woman the fates have decreed to be his true mate is none other than Emmaline Troy, a half-vampire, half-Valkyrie. This book is brilliantly intense, sexy, and dark.

I Dream of You, Judi McCoy, 2001

Maddy Winston's fiancé has just dumped her, and her family's computer chip manufacturing company is on the rocks, so she escapes to her grandmother's bed and breakfast in the Florida Keys. While on the beach, she finds a bejeweled bottle housing a handsome genie who wants to grant her every wish. A clever twist on the Aladdin story, McCoy's fun, frothy, fiction is perfect beach reading (but keep an eye out for a bottle!)

Imagine, Jill Barnett, 1995

San Francisco attorney Maddie Smith finds her South Seas dream vacation taking an unexpected detour when the ship blows up, leaving Maddie stranded on a desert island with escaped convict Hank Wyatt, three orphans, and a genie in a bottle. Humor is Barnett's trademark, as evidenced by this laughter-laced treat.

Knight of a Trillion Stars, Dara Joy, 1995

Deana Jones comes home after a simply rotten day to find sexy alien Lorgin ta'al Krue waiting for her in her living room (that happens all the time!). Joy's debut novel added lots of sharp humor and plenty of sizzle to the paranormal romance subgenre.

Naked in Death, J. D. Robb, 1995

In futuristic New York City, Police Lieutenant Eve Dallas becomes involved with Roarke, an Irish billionaire and a prime suspect in the murder of a high-priced call girl who turns out to be the granddaughter of a senator. Robb, also known as Nora Roberts, can basically write anything (and we'll read it!).

Night Pleasures, Sherrilyn Kenyon, 2002

All Amanda Devereaux wants is a regular life, yet somehow she manages to find herself caught up in a deadly battle between Dark-Hunter Kyrian of Thrace and the Daimons, vampires who kill humans. Kenyon writes historical romances as Kinley MacGregor.

Prince of Wolves, Susan Krinard, 1994

Joelle Randall is determined to face her demons and visit the site of her parents' plane crash, but the only guide she can find to lead her through the Canadian Rockies is Luke Gevaudan, one of the last survivors of an ancient race of werewolves. Lyrical and intense, Krinard's debut became the first in a series featuring her distinctive brand of werewolf heroes.

The Reluctant Miss Van Helsing, Minda Webber, 2006

When reluctant vampire slayer Jane Van Helsing tries to get over her fears by seducing and "staking" Neil Asher, the Earl of Wolverton, she ends up marrying the sexy vampire instead! Webber adds a charming dash of humor to the all too often dark and angsty vampire subgenre.

The Smoke Thief, Shana Abe, 2005

Halfling drakon (dragon) Clarissa Rue Hawthorne flees her village for a new life as a jewel thief in London, but Christoff, the Marquess of Langford and the leader of the shape-shifting drakons, is determined to find the thief and catch "him."

Tiger Eye, Marjorie M. Liu, 2005

When Dela Reese opens the antique puzzle box she's just bought, she meets a 2,000-year-old, shape-shifting warrior and also unleashes a whole lot of magical trouble for both of them. Liu, new to the paranormal romance world, is quickly becoming a brand name for her delightfully inventive books.

The Very Thought of You, Lynn Kurland, 1998

Transported from present-day Scotland to medieval England, former CEO Alexander Smith becomes involved in Margaret of Falconberg's efforts to save her family's estate from an evil suitor. Kurland brings a sweetly romantic (that means not a lot of sex) element to the often dark, sensual paranormal romances.

You Slay Me, Katie MacAlister, 2004

While on a "simple" job in Paris, Aisling Grey discovers the new owner of the statue she's delivering has been murdered. When she tries to solve the crime, Aisling quickly becomes tangled up with smoldering Drake Vireo, who just happens to be a dragon (yep, you read right, a dragon).

7

Chick Lit and Women's Fiction: A Woman's Story Is Never Done

In This Chapter

- ◆ Chick lit: looking for Mr. Right Now
- ◆ Women's fiction: by women, for women
- ◆ Glitz and glamour: fashion, furs, and fame

Have you been to a bookstore lately? Did you notice dozens of oversized paperback books with covers emblazoned with shoes, martini glasses, or chic little black dresses? This chapter lets you peek inside these shiny covers.

Chick Lit

Welcome to the world of chick lit, a trend launched with the 1999 publication of *Bridget Jones's Diary*. Chick lit features young heroines, usually in their 20s and early 30s, struggling to find love, professional success, happiness—or all three! A chick lit man is more "Mr. Right Now" than "Mr. Right." Generally light in tone with lots of humor, chick lit might also have a more serious undertone. So strap on your Manolos and join us!

Classics

Bridget Jones's Diary, Helen Fielding, 1998

Helen Fielding was at the right time and right place when she created Bridget Jones, a 30-something London "singleton" whose struggle to stop smoking and lose weight is overshadowed by her search for the perfect man. Ironic and endearing by turns, this book is *the* template for all future "chick lit" novels. Nearly a decade later, it's still a fabulous read.

The Girls' Guide to Hunting and Fishing, Melissa Banks, 2000

Banks's first book is a series of seven interconnected stories, all but one of them featuring Jane Rosenal, a young woman searching for the elusive Mr. Right and the happiness that is supposed to follow. We meet Jane at 14, a sardonic teenager, and follow her through the crucial moments of her love life. Part coming-of-age story and part chick lit, think of this witty debut novel as a literary *Bridget Jones's Diary.*

More Great Reads

Always the Bridesmaid, Whitney Lyles, 2004

As the bridesmaid (or "bride slave" as she calls it) in four of her friends' weddings, kindergarten teacher Cate wonders just exactly when it will be her turn. Anyone who has ever been part of a wedding will love the hysterically funny descriptions of wedding showers, rehearsals, and the brides-to-be.

American Idle, Alesia Holliday, 2004

Jules Vernon discovers her job as a production coordinator of a popular show is more than ultra competitive contestants and cranky co-workers when she meets sexy set carpenter Sam Blake. This hilarious parody of *American Idol* will keep you laughing.

Animal Husbandry, Laura Zigman, 1997

After talk show producer Jane Goodall is inexplicably dumped by her co-worker, she develops her own theory—"Old Cow/New Cow"—to explain men. The theory seems to work perfectly with every man except her new roommate, Eddie Alden.

Bergdorf Blondes, Plum Sykes, 2003

After one of her Park Avenue Princess friends turns up with an engagement ring, "Moi," the narrator of this frothy literary confection, and her best friend, Julie Bergdorf, begin their own hunt for P.H.s (perspective husbands). It's a cross between *People Magazine* and *Lifestyles of the Rich and Famous.*

Bookends, Jane Green, 2003

Catherine, Simon, Josh, and Portia were all best friends in college until a messy fight cut Portia out of the group. Now 10 years later, Portia returns to once again upset their worlds. Green's characters are fun and funny.

Boy Meets Girl, Meg Cabot, 2004

Told in the form of e-mails and all the tech ways we now communicate, Kate MacKenzie finds herself caught in the middle when her evil boss wants her to fire an older and beloved employee, Ida Lopez. When Ida sues the company, Mitch Hertzog, a handsome (of course) lawyer takes on the case—and Kate.

The Rest of the Story

> Meg Cabot, best known for her *Princess Diaries* series, has written under other pseudonyms—Patricia Cabot (historical romances) and Jeny Carroll (supernatural teen novels).

Calendar Girl, Naomi Neale, 2005

Tired of her dead-end job and dead-end love life, Nan Cloutier decides to stop whining and do something about it. So when sexy Colm Iverson walks into her life, Nan doesn't intend to let him go. Neale gives Nan plenty of problems, both in work and her personal life, and it's a treat to watch her overcome them.

Charmed and Dangerous, Candace Havens, 2005

White witch (those are the good ones) Bronwyn works for the British government protecting the prime minister, but her latest assignment is to magically guard a sexy sheik. This engaging chick lit book has a cute twist of the supernatural.

Confessions of a Shopaholic, Sophie Kinsella, 2001

When her out-of-control shopping catches up with her, Rebecca Bloomwood struggles to put herself on a budget while at the same time trying to catch the interest of dreamy Luke Brandon. Think of Rebecca as Bridget Jones's financially challenged younger sister. There are more books in the Shopaholic series—you can charge them on your credit card!

The Devil Wears Prada, Lauren Weisberger, 2004

Andrea Sachs has just gotten the job most women would kill for: assistant to Amanda Priestly, the chic, fabulously famous editor of *Runway* magazine. However, once Andrea gets to know her boss, all she wants to do is quit.

The Rest of the Story

Before writing *The Devil Wears Prada*, Weisberger worked as a personal assistant for Anna Wintour, the famously difficult editor-in-chief of the American edition of *Vogue*. Weisberger's deliciously gossipy book is considered a *roman à clef* of her own experiences in the magazine biz. Those who are only familiar with the movie version, a *tour de force* in its own right, will find that the literary version of Miranda Priestly is an even more ruthless character than the one portrayed by Meryl Streep.

Do Me, Do My Roots, Eileen Rendahl, 2005

Two years after her husband's death, Emily Simon is finally ready to start dating again, but the really important people in her life are still her two sisters, Leah and Claudia. Anyone struggling to put her life back together will identify.

The Dominant Blonde, Alisa Kwitney, 2002

When Lydia Gold's fiancé Abe—and $3 million of her family's fortune—disappear while scuba diving on their tropical vacation, Lydia turns to scuba instructor Liam MacNally for help in tracking him down. Smart, savvy, sexy, and sassy, *The Dominant Blonde* is the essence of chick lit.

Fashionably Late, Beth Kendrick, 2006

After quitting her boring job and dumping her equally boring boyfriend, Becca Davis heads for L.A. to realize her dream of becoming a fashion designer. With her gift for sharp dialogue and memorable heroines, Kendricks is a top author in this genre.

The Frog Prince, Jane Porter, 2005

Shortly after their honeymoon, Holly Bishop's new Prince Charming turned into a toad. Now Holly has moved to San Francisco for a new job and another crack at kissing some frogs.

Good in Bed, Jennifer Weiner, 2001

Philadelphia journalist Cannie Shapiro is stunned when she reads a magazine article on the joys of loving a "larger" woman written by her ex-boyfriend, Bruce. The article prompts Cannie to take a good look at her life and what she wants. Weiner communicates the angst of being a size 14 in a size 00 world.

The Good, the Bad, and the Ugly Men I've Dated,
Shane Bolks, 2005

Just as Rory Egglehoff finally realizes her goal of dating her high school crush, Hunter Chase, she starts changing so much she threatens to ruin any chance she might have with him. Bolks has created a lovable heroine, a *Star Wars*-quoting, self-proclaimed geek who never imagined that this cool guy would want her.

L.A. Woman, Cathy Yardley, 2002

Sarah Walker dumps her fiancé after he refuses to commit, but now in order to financially survive, Sarah must share her apartment with Martika, who wants to introduce Sarah to a whole different world of men. The story is told with a fresh, sassy voice.

The Little Lady Agency, Hester Browne, 2006

When an unexpected merger costs Melissa Romney Jones her job, she reinvents herself as "Honey" and uses her inherent organizational skills to open "The Little Lady Agency" which helps the clueless men of London with their lives. Browne's sparkling debut and endearing heroine quickly made fans.

See Jane Date, Melissa Senate, 2001

After telling everyone about her fabulous boyfriend, who exists only in her imagination, Jane Gregg finds herself madly dating in the hopes of finding someone she can take to her cousin's wedding. *See Jane Date* was the first book in Harlequin's Red Dress Ink imprint, which helped popularize chick lit.

Something Borrowed, Emily Giffin, 2004

Rachel always thought she was a good friend to Darcy until she finds herself falling in love with Dex, Darcy's fiancé, right before the wedding. Darcy is potentially unlikable, but Giffin cleverly turns her into an appealing heroine.

The Sweet Spot, Kayla Perrin, 2006

Sports reporter Zoe Andrews will do anything to secure the good copy she needs to boost her career, including humiliating sexy Oakland Raider Kahari Brown on national television. With her African-American hero and heroine, Perrin brings a much-needed multicultural element to this genre.

32AA, Michelle Cunnah, 2003

Passed over for a much-deserved promotion and dumped by her boyfriend for his buxom mistress, Emma Taylor's ready to write off men forever, but we know she's gonna meet someone ....

Time Off for Good Behavior, Lani Diane Rich, 2004

Wanda Lane's life could be better. She's lost her job, just come out of a five-day coma, and received death threats from her ex-husband. Fortunately for Wanda, lawyer Walter Briggs wants to help. Wanda's realistic edge will make readers empathize.

True Love (and Other Lies), Whitney Gaskell, 2004

American travel writer Claire Spencer's new transatlantic romance with London-based American attorney Jack is complicated not only by distance but also by the identity of Jack's soon-to-be ex. Is Clare's new romance worth losing her best friend?

Watermelon, Marian Keyes, 1998

Claire gives birth to her first child the same day her husband walks out on her. She returns to her family in Dublin, where with their help, she begins rebuilding her life. James reappears, but where does he fit in now? Complex characters and bracing Irish wit make this a captivating read.

The Rest of the Story

Marian Keyes refers to herself as an "accidental novelist." She never dreamed of becoming a writer, instead focusing on a more practical career path by studying law and accounting. She wrote her first short story in 1993. When Keyes submitted several of her stories to her publisher, she told them she was working on a novel, too. The publisher asked to see it, and the frantically written *Watermelon* became her first book. Since then, Keyes has written six more novels, which have sold a total of 10 million copies and have been published in 31 different languages. Not bad for someone who didn't want to be a writer!

Women's Fiction

What is women's fiction? Women's fiction is books written by women about women for women. While romance can play an important part in the books, it's not required. What these novels share is a focus on the many roles and relationships in a woman's life—friend, mother, daughter, grandmother, granddaughter, sister, wife, ex-wife, lover ... Women's fiction isn't a one-size-fits-all genre. It can be hilariously funny, heart-wrenchingly tragic, flamboyantly soap opera-ish, thoughtfully introspective, mysterious, glitzy and glamoury, and even a little otherworldly. But one thing holds true—there's something here for every woman.

Classics

Beaches, Iris Ranier Dart, 1985

When brassy Cee Cee Bloom and cautious Bertie White meet one summer beneath the boardwalk in Atlantic City, a friendship is born that lasts for decades and survives life's joys, sorrows, triumphs, and tragedies. If you loved *Beaches* (and cried your way through the movie), you should read the sequel, *I'll Be There*.

Divine Secrets of the Ya-Ya Sisterhood, Rebecca Wells, 1996

When Siddalee Walker tells a reporter that her mother Vivi was abusive, it tears their relationship apart until her mother's lifelong friends, The Ya-Yas, step in to bring them back together. Alternating between present day and Vivi's Louisiana childhood, Wells writes a poignant and funny tale of mothers and daughters and the ties that bind them.

Once in a Lifetime, Danielle Steel, 1983

Twice married and twice widowed best-selling novelist Daphne Fields has one more chance at love and happiness, but first she must choose between hunky Justin Wakefield and sensitive Matthew Dane. Roman à clef, anyone?

You Can Book on It!

Danielle Steel has authored 67 books since 1981, all of them best-sellers. Twenty-one were adapted for television. The French government named Steel a Chevalier of the Distinguished Order of Arts and Letters for her "lifetime contribution to world culture." She even has a perfume named for her!

The Shell Seekers, Rosamunde Pilcher, 1987

Sixty-something Penelope Keeling must decide whether to listen to her children and sell a suddenly valuable painting by her father or keep it for the memories it contains. Pilcher was a popular author in England, but *The Shell Seekers* brought her fame and a place at the top of the bestseller list in the United States.

Waiting to Exhale, Terry McMillan, 1992

Four African American women—Savannah, Gloria, Robin, and Bernadine—are all waiting for the right man to come along so they can finally "exhale." They discover that it is their strong friendship that truly sustains them. The movie of the same name actually managed to capture the essence of the book, a rare feat.

A Woman of Substance, Barbara Taylor Bradford, 1979

In 1904, pregnant servant Emma Harte begins her life's journey to riches and revenge against the Fairlie family when she opens her first store, which will eventually become a retail empire. Legendary Bradford wrote several sequels to *A Woman of Substance*, continuing the dynasty founded by Emma Harte.

More Great Reads

The Cotton Queen, Pamela Morsi, 2006

Babs Hoffman, a former Cotton Queen runner-up, is the mother of Laney, who does the exact opposite of everything her mother says until Laney finally understands what her mother has had to overcome, including widowhood and rape. Morsi's sensitive exploration of the complex relationship between a mother and a daughter has many memorable moments, from poignant to downright funny.

The Dirty Girls Social Club, Alisa Valdes-Rodriguez, 2003

Since they met in college ten years earlier, six Latina friends meet every six months to catch up. Each woman brings a unique view of the Latina experience and has a distinct voice, as you come to know and care for them. Valdes-Rodriguez was hailed as the Latina Terry McMillan because, like McMillan, her characters and their stories transcend race and speak to all.

The First Wives Club, Olivia Goldsmith, 1992

After their husbands dump them for younger and blonder models, three friends—Annie, Elise, and Brenda—form their own club with the purpose of evening the score with their ex-husbands. *The First Wives Club* is flavored with Goldsmith's wonderfully acerbic sense of wit, and watching the women's husbands get their comeuppance is just part of the fun in this amusing book.

Flight Lessons, Patricia Gaffney, 2002

After discovering her boss in bed with her boyfriend, Anna Catalano decides it's time to go home again. Set against the background of the family's Italian restaurant in Maryland, the characters in *Flight Lessons* are extraordinary, especially Anna, whose journey on the long, hard road from blame to forgiveness is one that readers will find utterly compelling.

Follow the Stars Home, Luanne Rice, 2000

Given the choice between two brothers—quiet, reliable Dr. Alan Robbins and edgy, unreliable Tim—guess which one Dianne picks. Tim proves untrustworthy when he abandons Dianne after they find out that their baby will be born with genetic abnormalities. With the help of Alan, Dianne begins raising her disabled daughter and putting her life slowly back together. Rice creates realistically flawed families, whose lives are changed by the healing power of love. Tissues? Oh, you betcha!

Magic Hour, Kristin Hannah, 2006

When her career as a child psychologist is destroyed by the press, Julia Cates returns to her hometown of Rain Valley, Washington, where she receives a new sense of purpose helping with an unusual case of a feral child. Have plenty of tissues handy; few authors do heartbreaking, emotionally wrenching, yet thoroughly satisfying, women's fiction better.

The Ocean Between Us, Susan Wiggs, 2004

After 20 years of marriage, Grace is tired of being the perfect wife and mother, but when she begins changing her life, it creates "an ocean" between her and her husband, Navy Captain Steve Bennett. When an accident on Steve's ship leaves him lost at sea, Grace must rethink her choices. Wiggs got her start writing historical and contemporary romances and brings the same rich characterization to her excellent women's fiction.

A Piece of Heaven, Barbara Samuel, 2003

Luna McGraw's 15-year-old daughter, who hasn't lived with her for 8 years, is coming home, and the stress and anticipation make Luna, a recovering alcoholic, long for a drink of liquid comfort. Thomas Coyote, a twice-divorced adobe maker, becomes Luna's touchstone as she learns to accept that her daughter prefers her stepmother. Samuel's flawed, loving characters, who try to be the best they can, will put a grip on your heart.

The Queen Bee of Mimosa Branch, Haywood Smith, 2002

Southern belle Lynn Breedlove Scott discovers that Emily Post doesn't cover what to do when her husband takes their money and runs off with a stripper. She heads back to Mimosa Branch, Georgia, to recover and regroup at her parents' house. Replete with quirky family members, eccentric friends, and life lessons, Smith's book is like cool lemonade on a hot summer day.

The Rose Revived, Katie Fforde, 1995

May Sargent, Sally Bliss, and Harriet Devonshire meet when they all apply for jobs with Quality Cleaners. When their new employer tries to cheat them out of their hard-earned wages, they open their own house-cleaning company. Set in England, *The Rose Revived* gives women's fiction a charming British accent!

A Simple Gift, Karyn Witmer, 2006

Avery Montgomery had no idea that her wayward daughter, Fiona, had returned home, until she saw her working at the local grocery store. Avery desperately wants to bring the family back together, but when she discovers that her husband had known about Fiona's return for months and didn't tell her, the rift between them seems impossible to bridge. Witmer writes with quiet grace about how difficult it is to keep a family together but how it's worth the struggle.

Since You're Leaving Anyway, Take Out the Trash, Dixie Cash, 2004

When the richest woman in Salt Lick, Texas, is murdered, Debbie Sue Overstreet, the owner of the town's most popular beauty salon, decides the $50,000 reward sure would come in handy, but the only problem is she'll have to work with her ex, Sheriff Buddy Overstreet, on the investigation. Cash is the pseudonym for two sisters, and their debut novel is laugh-out-loud funny. We think this is one of the best book titles since *Get Your Tongue Out of My Mouth, I'm Kissing You Goodbye.*

6 Rainier Dr., Debbie Macomber, 2006

Justine and Seth Gunderson's marriage hits the skids after their restaurant is torched by an arsonist. This book explores their marital problems as well as the lives of other people in Cedar Cove. Macomber's warm, homey style resonates throughout.

The Summer I Dared, Barbara Delinsky, 2004

After surviving a boating accident off the coast of Maine, Julia, Noah, and Kim are inextricably bound together when they find their lives changed by the experience. Delinsky got her start writing romances but found her voice in women's fiction.

Sweetgrass, Mary Alice Monroe, 2005

Mary June Blakely finds herself the head of the family when her domineering husband, Preston Blakely, suffers a severe stroke. She has to deal with the return of their estranged son, Morgan, as well as her failing marriage, which was on the brink of collapse before Preston's stroke. With Preston incapacitated, his sister, Adele, is trying to force them to sell Sweetgrass, the plantation that's been in the family for eight generations. In moving metaphors and sweeping, evocative descriptions of the low country, Monroe has crafted a spellbinding story that you don't want to end.

Glitz and Glamour

What do you think of when we say big shoulder pads, big hair, and cat fights? No, it's not the Miss America pageant, it's glitz-and-glamour books, huge blockbuster beach reads and best-sellers that were especially popular during the 1980s but may be making a comeback. We hope so, because we still have suits in our closet with linebacker-size shoulder pads!

Classics

Deceptions, Judith Michael, 1983

Sabrina, Lady Longworth, and her identical twin, Stephanie, married with children, are so dissatisfied with their lives that they decide to switch places. They revel in their "new" lives until something happens that changes everything. With their debut novel, Michael, a husband and wife writing team, created a sexy, scandal-rich book that still has the power to enthrall the reader. Trust us, the twist is a good one—so good, in fact, that you'll want to read the sequel, *A Tangled Web*.

Hollywood Wives, Jackie Collins, 1983

Jackie Collins knows exactly who her readers are and what they want. She consistently delivers the goods in her books—designer labels, name-dropping, gossipy scandal, and tons of sex. *Hollywood Wives* has all the classic glitz and glamour ingredients: in this case, three Tinseltown couples at various stages of success. She even throws in a serial killer.

Lace, Shirley Conran, 1982

Cinematic superstar Lili wants to know which of the four women, Kate, Pagan, Maxine, or Jordan, who she has called to her Paris hotel, is her mother. With what is perhaps the most memorable opening line that we've read, Conran immediately hooks the reader and reels her in.

The Rich Shall Inherit, Elizabeth Adler, 1989

The search for a missing heiress to the estate of wealthy Poppy Mallory has been narrowed down to five possible candidates, and as journalist Mike Preston investigates each one, he learns more about Poppy's own mysterious origins. Adler's early books—*Peach, Leonie,* and *Fortune Is a Woman*—all deserve to be on every must-read list for fans of soap opera fiction. Somewhere in the 1990s, Adler wandered into romantic suspense, then women's fiction, and she has never returned to her roots. Elizabeth, all is forgiven; please come home.

Scruples, Judith Krantz, 1978

The rich and chic are soon flocking to Billy Winthrop Ikehorn Orsini's high-fashion boutique in Beverly Hills, where their most lavish dreams and wildest fantasies can be realized. With tons of descriptions of high fashion, exotic locales, and luxury lifestyles, Krantz's book is the epitome of glitz and glamour.

The Two Mrs. Grenvilles, Dominic Dunne, 1985

During World War II, Ann Arden, a showgirl, marries Billy Grenville, the scion of New York's most aristocratic family. The two seem like the ideal couple, until one rainy night in 1955, when Ann shoots her husband. Dunne, a gossip columnist (a.k.a. "legal correspondent") for *Vanity Fair,* first made his name with his insider's view of the rich, powerful, and decadent.

Valley of the Dolls, Jacqueline Susann, 1966

This is the tawdry tale of three women drawn to the glitter of Hollywood and the dream of fame, only to discover the emptiness that lies beneath the tinsel. The drugs and sex fueling the story, shocking for its time, now seem almost tame. Susann opened the door that Collins, Gould, and "new kids" like Bagshawe are now sashaying through.

More Great Reads

Adored, Tilly Bagshawe, 2005

Sexy, smart, strong-willed Siena McMahon, granddaughter of Hollywood legend Duke McMahon, charts her path to success by becoming a supermodel and then the silver screen's latest leading lady. If anyone can bring back the big, juicy, beach-read books of the 1980s (the literary equivalents of *Dallas* and *Dynasty*), it's British-born, LA transplant Bagshawe.

Too Damn Rich, Judith Gould, 1995

Burghley's, the world's oldest and most respected auction house, is the backdrop for this story of three vibrant, stunningly beautiful (aren't they always!) women who become caught up in a race for wealth, power, and social position. While not as well known as Krantz or Collins, when it comes to crafting wickedly fun novels, Gould is more than their equal.

Chapter 8

Westerns: Giddy-Up and Read!

In This Chapter

- ◆ Classics: old, but not old hat
- ◆ More great reads: dusty trails to you

Westerns are well loved. Some of these books have been in and out of print for an amazing length of time. For instance, Owen Wister's *The Virginian*, one of the books that established the genre, was first published in 1902. Zane Grey wrote *Riders of the Purple Sage* in 1912. Alfred Bertram Guthrie's *The Big Sky* has been around for more than 50 years. For the reader who likes a world where it's easy to tell the good guys from the bad and where justice almost always prevails, westerns are the perfect genre.

Classics

The Big Sky, Alfred Bertram Guthrie, 1947

This Pulitzer Prize winner provides a glimpse into the Montana wilderness and the pioneers who settled there. The focus is on three characters—Boone Caudill, a young man driven from his Kentucky home by an abusive father; Jim Deakins, a frontiersman and trader; and Dick Summers, also a frontiersman. Then there's the daughter of a Blackfoot chief, who captures the hearts of two of the travelers. This is the first of Guthrie's six *Big Sky* novels.

Hondo, Louis L'Amour, 1953

Hondo Lane, a loner riding west through the Arizona desert, loses his horse to Apaches and so stops by an isolated cabin to see if the owner has a horse for sale. The owner of the cabin turns out to be a strong pioneer woman raising her small son in Apache territory. L'Amour's stellar descriptions of people and places make this a hard-to-put-down western adventure.

And the Award Goes to ...

Louis L'Amour's book *Down the Long Hills* was awarded the Western Writers of America's Golden Spur Award as well as the Theodore Roosevelt Rough Rider Award. Two of his works, *Hondo* and *Flint,* are on the 25 Best Westerns of All Time list. In 1983, the U.S. Congress gave him the National Gold Medal, following that with the Medal of Freedom in 1984. L'Amour has sold more than 100 million books.

Lonesome Dove, Larry McMurty, 1985

You don't have to like Westerns to love this 1986 winner of the Pulitzer Prize for fiction. Retired Texas Rangers Augustus "Gus" McCrae and Woodrow F. Call might be co-owners of the Hat Creek Cattle Company, a small ranch in Lonesome Dove, Texas, but they couldn't be more different. McCrae, a happy fellow who's lucky with the female sex, sees work as something to be done only when absolutely necessary. Call is an inflexible, easily annoyed workaholic. There's also a colorful cast of secondary characters who alone would make a fantastic story, but throw in an adventure-filled cattle drive from the Rio Grande to Montana, and you have the perfect epic.

An Expert Speaks

"Lonesome Dove is my favorite western, and probably my favorite book of all time ... The story line was great, and there were enough characters for anyone to like or identify with ... From the hard times at the Hat Creek Ranch, the hard luck and death on the trail, until reaching the final destination, I never lost interest. It was a hard book to put down ..."

—Fred Wann, rodeo rider, cowboy, avid reader

The Ox-Bow Incident, Walter Van Tilburg Clark, 1940

As two drifters pass through town, they learn that a local farmer has just been murdered and three of his cattle are missing. The drifters join a posse to find the men responsible for the crime, and when the posse finds three men who have the stolen cattle, they want justice, and they want it now. The absence of law and order, the danger of group-think, the real meaning of justice—all are explored in this masterpiece.

Riders of the Purple Sage, Zane Grey, 1912

Lassiter, the hero, is a gunman with a grudge against the Mormons because his true love married one of their leaders instead of him. The heroine, Jane Witherspoon, a Mormon spinster who's known for her good deeds to the less fortunate "Gentiles," has inherited a ranch with a spring from her father. Eager for her property, the leaders of the church want her to marry one of their polygamous elders. Jane's refusal causes the elders to turn on her with a vengeance, and Lassiter becomes her champion. *Rainbow Trail* continues the tale of Jane and Lassiter.

 The Rest of the Story _____

> Zane Grey, whose real name was Pearl Zane Grey, the son of a farmer/preacher and a Quaker mother, practiced dentistry before turning to writing. Because of Grey's severe dyslexia, his wife had to edit his manuscripts to make them readable.

Shane, Jack Schaefer, 1949

It's 1889 Wyoming, and a ruthless cattle baron is crushing the local homesteaders. An enigmatic cowboy named Shane appears and helps these downtrodden pioneers in their fight. Against the advice of his father, a young boy is drawn to the stranger, but he can't get over his hero worship any more than Shane can put down roots.

Somewhere They Die, L. P. Holmes, 1955

Riley Haslam, who thinks he's been given a job as a ranch hand for powerful Syl Overdeck, soon finds that he's actually supposed to be a hired gun. Moreover, Overdeck isn't the only bully in town; his rival, Hugh Racklyn, is just as evil and land hungry. It's up to Haslam to take down both of these villains—with or without the help of the townspeople.

The Violent Land, Wayne D. Overholser, 1954

In this coming-of-age story, 18-year-old Dan Nathan is torn between loyalties to his greedy employer and the families who lost their lands to this wealthy rancher. And more conflict is in store for Dan as he falls for a woman with a bad reputation. Maturity comes fast but hard in *The Violent Land.*

The Virginian: A Horseman of the Plains, Owen Wister, 1902

Set in the vast openness of the Wyoming Territory and featuring a loner called "the Virginian," the schoolmarm he loves, a villain (the Virginian's best friend turned bad), and a gang of rustlers, this book established the western novel genre.

More Great Reads

The Buffalo Soldiers, John Prebble, 1959

The Tenth Nubian Horse Soldiers, a troop of African American recruits, have been given the order to help the Comanche hunt buffalo for food. Their leader, Lieutenant Byrne, an Irishman who fought for the North in the Civil War, has trouble establishing relationships with his troops. But the soldiers are brave and loyal, even when Byrne leads them on a potential suicide mission.

Comanche Captives, Fred Grove, 1962

While much has been written about the Cherokee Nation and the Trail of Tears, most people don't realize that other Native Americans went through similar forced marches. In this book, the army has ordered Lieutenant Baldwin, his sergeant, and his platoon to relocate 300 Comanche captives. The problem is, their path goes directly through Indian Territory, where many Comanches are roaming free—and armed.

The Court-Martial of George Armstrong Custer,
Douglas C. Jones, 1972

This book is based on the premise that instead of being killed during the Battle of Little Big Horn, General Custer was merely wounded and, once recuperated, is put on trial for his actions. Is he guilty or not? You decide.

Cripple Creek Bonanza, Chet Cunningham, 1996

The 1891 Gold Rush turns the citizens of Cripple Creek, Colorado, into instant millionaires. The way they deal with their newfound wealth and the effect this affluence has on their town make for a very entertaining story.

The Day the Cowboys Quit, Elmer Kelton, 1971

The ill-fated Canadian River Cowboy Strike of 1883 began when the cattle barons refused to let the working cowboys own their own herds. Hugh Hitchcock isn't sure whether to side with the boss he admires or the cowboys he supervises. It's a question of loyalty as Kelton skillfully recounts this true event.

And the Award Goes to ...

Many may argue that Zane Grey, Louis L'Amour, or Larry McMurty is the king of the Western genre. However, we'd add the lesser-known Elmer Kelton to the list. Kelton has won seven Spurs—more than any other writer—and was awarded the first Lone Star Award for Lifetime Achievement.

Destry Rides Again, Max Brand, 1930

Revenge is a strong motivator for Harrison Destry, who's just finished serving six years in prison. The problem is, he was innocent, and his conviction came after a friend turned on him. Now Destry's goal in life is to find the 12 people on the jury that found him guilty and mete out his own justice.

The Rest of the Story

Max Brand, an amazingly prolific writer whose real name was Frederick Faust, also wrote the Dr. Kildare series.

From Where the Sun Now Stands, Will Henry, 2000

In 1877, Chief Joseph of the Nez Perce was forced to lead his people from their Oregon reservation to Montana, a journey of more than a thousand miles. Henry masterfully recounts this event with excellent characterizations and descriptions.

Gold in California, Todhunter Ballard, 1965

Austin Garner and his family head across the country to join the California Gold Rush. But the losses they sustain on the trail begin to outweigh any treasure they might find when they make their final destination.

The Rest of the Story

The title of Will Henry's book *From Where the Sun Now Stands* is from Chief Joseph's famous surrender speech: "I am tired of fighting. Our chiefs are killed. Looking Glass is dead. Toohulhulsote is dead. The old men are all dead. It is the young men who say yes or no. He who led the young men is dead. It is cold and we have no blankets. The little children are freezing to death. My people, some of them, have run away to the hills and have no blankets, no food. No one knows where they are—perhaps freezing to death. I want to have time to look for my children and see how many I can find. Maybe I shall find them among the dead. Hear me, my chiefs. I am tired. My heart is sick and sad. From where the sun now stands, I will fight no more forever."

The Gunfighter's Apprentice, Jerry S. Drake, 2006

When a shopkeeper kills a nefarious gang leader's brother in self-defense, his father knows it won't be long before someone comes gunning for him. To teach his son how to defend himself, the shopkeeper's father hires a reclusive gunslinger. Both the gunfighter and the shopkeeper learn important lessons in Drake's impressive debut.

A Hanging in Sweetwater, Stephen Overholser, 1974

When 15-year-old Boomer Jones runs away from home, he has no idea that he's going to be caught up in a range war between the powerful ranchers and vulnerable homesteaders.

I Should Be Extremely Happy in Your Company So Wild, Brian Hall, 2003

This superb tale of the Lewis and Clark expedition is told from several viewpoints—Lewis, Clark, Sacagawea, and Toussaint Charbonneau, Sacagawea's fur trader husband. The contrast between Lewis and Clark is particularly interesting. It's a must read.

The Kincaids, Matt Braun, 1976

Set between 1871 and 1924, this sweeping family saga takes place during the settlement of Oklahoma and Kansas. Buffalo hunter Jake Kincaid becomes a wealthy man after winning a card game. The story of Kincaid and his offspring is set against the advent of the railroad, the discovery of oil, the mistreatment of the Native Americans, and finally, the issue of Prohibition.

Little Big Man, Thomas Berger, 1964

This is the memoir of 111-year-old Jack Crabb, the sole white survivor at the Battle of Little Big Horn. Kidnapped by the Cheyenne, the tribe adopts Jack and gives him the name "Little Big Man." He leaves his Native American family for a while to live with the white population, but finds he can't stand his own kind and moves back with the tribe. Jack's wife and child are killed when Custer attacks their village. Ironically, Jack later joins Custer at Little Big Horn. From its quirky hero to the grand span of history it covers, this compelling novel is great entertainment.

> **You Can Book on It!**
>
> Westerns can be far from politically correct, in that they often reflect the mores and prejudices of the times in which they were written.

Mattie, Judy Alter, 1997

This story, based on the life of the first female doctor in Nebraska, is told as the reminiscences of the 80-year-old woman herself. She recalls the trials and tribulations of practicing medicine in the days when it wasn't considered a proper profession for the "fairer sex." If you love television's *Dr. Quinn, Medicine Woman*, you'll enjoy this book.

Moontrap, Don Berry, 1991

Oregon mountain man Webb is having a hard time with the encroachment of "civilization." Webb's friend, Johnson Monday, and his wife, Mary, a Native American, are awaiting the birth of their first child. The childbirth is difficult, and Mary becomes withdrawn. The bigoted town preacher rails against mixed marriages, and between that and the hanging of Native Americans in town, Mary decides life isn't worth living. She smothers the baby and then commits suicide. Webb murders the hate-mongering preacher and heads for the mountains. Monday, who has been implicated as an accomplice, joins the posse. Prejudice comes to the Old West in this gripping tale of paradise lost.

The Nameless Breed, Will C. Brown, 1960

The Republic of Texas is battling for its independence as Brazos McCloud searches for his father, who is a captive of the Cherokee. Brown peppers this story with rich details from Texas history as he describes McCloud's efforts to free his dad.

Nickajack, Robert J. Conley, 1992

The Cherokee nation, once a proud and prospering people, has been brutally torn from their homeland and forced on a death march across the country by Andrew Jackson's infamous "Indian Removal Act." Now in their final destination of Oklahoma, one of them, Nickajack, is tried for a murder he didn't commit, becoming a symbol for the Cherokees themselves.

Panther in the Sky, James Alexander Thom, 1989

Shawnee Chief Tecumseh (1768–1813) was born under a shooting star, a fitting portent for the fearless leader who would unite several tribes to fight the white man. Alexander's well-researched, richly detailed account of the legendary military genius follows Tecumseh from childhood to his death.

Prophet Annie: Being the Recently Discovered Memoir of Annie Pinkerton Boone Newcastle Dearborn, Prophet and Seer, Ellen Recknor, 2000

Annie Pinkerton Boone Newcastle was 17 when she was widowed after a mule kicked her gandy dancer (railroad laborer) husband in the head. Now it's 1881, and 22-year-old Annie is once again a widow, having married Jonas, a man 54 years her elder who didn't survive their wedding night. The problem is, Jonas' ghost now inhabits her body. It's a rollicking, off-beat western novel.

The Shootist, Glendon Swarthout, 1974

It's 1901, and John B. Books, legendary gunfighter, finds out he has prostate cancer and not long to live. He checks into a boarding house in El Paso to await the inevitable but then decides he wants to go out in a gunfight. Books's widowed landlady and her rebellious teenage son enrich this moving story of a man who truly wants to die with his boots on.

The Rest of the Story

John Wayne played the part of John Bernard Books in the 1976 film version of *The Shootist,* which was his last movie. In the movie, Books is dying of prostate cancer. Wayne, too, was a victim of cancer—he had lost his left lung and two ribs to lung cancer in 1964 and died of stomach cancer in 1979.

St. Agnes' Stand, Tom Eidson, 1994

Nat Swanson is on the lam for shooting a gang member. In New Mexico territory, Nat runs across three nuns and seven orphans who are being attacked by Apaches. Elder nun Sister Agnes is convinced that Nat's the answer to her prayers. However, they're trapped, Nat has taken a bullet to the leg, and the posse that's chasing him draws closer. This incredible tale is not to be missed!

Stone Song: A Novel of the Life of Crazy Horse,
Win Blevins, 1995

Crazy Horse, an outsider in his own tribe because of his light hair and rumors that he was part white, often lived a lonely life. This novel explores how he became the great warrior and military genius who led his people to victory at Little Big Horn. It presents a fascinating character study.

Summer of Pearls, Mike Blakely, 2000

In addition to gold and silver rushes, the West also experienced pearl rushes. Octogenarian Ben Crowell recalls finding a perfect pearl in Texas when he was 14 years old and the ensuing pearl rush sparked by his discovery. Humor, adventure, and even an old mystery make for an excellent read.

Trail of the Spanish Bit, Don Coldsmith, 1980

Set earlier in time than most westerns, this is the story of conquistador Juan Garcia. Because the Native Americans who discover him think that he might be a god, Garcia must undergo life-threatening rituals to prove his strength and bravery. The book is a different, interesting take on the Old West.

The Trail to Ogallala, Benjamin Capps, 1964

This is a realistic account of a cattle drive along the Chisholm Trail to Ogallala, Nebraska. Trail boss Billy Scott loses his position when the man who hired him dies and the widow replaces Billy with Colonel Kittredge. When the colonel dies in a stampede, Billy is given another chance to prove his worth.

True Grit, Charles Portis, 1968

After a drunken Tom Chaney shoots and kills Frank Ross, 14-year-old Mattie Ross wants Chaney dead. For the "executioner," she wheedles the help of Rooster Cogburn, a U.S. marshal with a reputation for heartlessness and a quick trigger finger. Two unforgettable characters mete out frontier justice.

The Undertaker's Wife, Loren D. Estleman, 2005

When a major financier shoots himself in the head, a group of powerful men try to avoid financial panic by hiring retired undertaker Richard Connable to doctor the corpse so no one will know the man committed suicide. While Richard's gone, his wife, lonely and introspective, feels that she's about to die, and reminisces about their life together.

The Wolf Is My Brother, Chad Oliver, 1967

Although both Colonel Bill Curtis of the Twelfth Cavalry and Comanche Chief Fox Claw are honorable leaders, the men find themselves on opposite sides. Here is a lesson that not all things in the Old West were good versus evil.

9

Science Fiction: Out of This World Reading

In This Chapter

◆ Classics: before the Space Age

◆ More great reads: Star Trek, Star Wars, and beyond

In his 1931 book *Living Philosophies*, Albert Einstein wrote, "The most beautiful experience we can have is the mysterious—the fundamental emotion which stands at the cradle of true art and true science." The combination of art and science is the *raison d'etre* for science fiction. As opposed to fantasy, science fiction emphasizes science in its tales that range from space travel to time travel, from future societies to ancient ones.

Classics

A Canticle for Leibowitz, Walter M. Miller, 1959

A holy artifact has been excavated, one written by St. Leibowitz herself. The Brothers of St. Leibowitz are thrilled to have the ancient piece of paper containing the holy words: "Pound pastrami, can kraut, six bagels—bring home for Emma." So little survived the nuclear holocaust that this humble grocery list is deemed sacred. Written in three sections—"Fiat Homo" ("Let There Be Man"), "Fiat Lux" ("Let There Be Light"), and "Fiat Voluntas Tua" ("Thy Will Be Done")—this book serves as a cautionary tale about the abuse of nuclear technology.

Childhood's End, Arthur C. Clarke, 1953 (revised 1990)

An armada of enormous spaceships arrives on Earth and hovers over all the major cities (a concept the movie *Independence Day* obviously borrowed). The aliens state they have come to serve mankind and will allow humans to run their own affairs *except* they forbid them to engage in any form of warfare. The Overlords, as they are known, refuse to reveal themselves, saying mankind is not yet ready and make their contacts through UN Secretary General Rikki Stormgren. After 50 years, all the ships save one vanish. The last ship lands, and the Overlords reveal themselves, but what is their true purpose?

The Foundation Series, Isaac Asimov, 1951, 1952, 1953, 1982, 1986

For 12,000 years the planet Trantor ruled a galactic empire encompassing all the star systems in the Milky Way galaxy. Scientist Hari Seldon has developed a new field of study, psychohistory, through which he can predict the future by analyzing social trends in large populations. Using his new science, Seldon predicts the coming collapse of the empire and the resulting 30,000 years of dark ages and barbarism until a second empire rises from the ashes. Seldon resolves to reduce the interregnum to a single millennium by establishing two Foundations to preserve science and knowledge. And so he established the first Foundation on the inconsequential and resource-poor planet of Terminus on the periphery of the galaxy. Within 50 years, the nearby star systems break away from the empire and threaten the Foundation. Seldon's actual plan is then revealed: the first Foundation itself will become the new empire. Through a series of crises, predicted by psychohistory, the Foundation becomes the dominant power in that part of the galaxy. However, not even psychohistory can foretell the unexpected rise of a mutant with psychic powers, the Mule …. All in all, it's an epic well worth the read.

Arguably the most acclaimed science fiction series in the history of the genre, the original three books, *Foundation, Foundation and Empire,* and *Second Foundation,* were collected together and published as the *Foundation Trilogy.* In 1966, the trilogy won the Hugo for Best All-Time Series, besting the expected winner, *The Lord of the Rings.* Thirty years after the last of the trilogy appeared, Asimov returned to the Foundation universe and produced the fourth and fifth volumes, *Foundation's Edge* (the 1983 Hugo winner) and *Foundation and Earth.*

The Rest of the Story

Foundation and Earth brought the Foundation series to the halfway point to the second empire, but Asimov didn't know how to continue the tale. Hints in *Foundation and Earth* suggested that nonhuman aliens might invade from another galaxy, but we will never know. To the disappointment of many fans, Asimov turned instead to writing a series of prequel novels (e.g., *Prelude to Foundation*) that recount Hari Seldon's adventures before he established the two foundations.

Journey to the Center of the Earth, Jules Verne, 1864

German professor Otto Lindenbrock and his nephew, Axel, discover an ancient coded message in an Icelandic text. Decoding the message, they discover directions to the center of the earth. They immediately travel to Iceland, hire a guide, and proceed into the mouth of the volcano specified in the message. The three have incredible adventures, including encounters with prehistoric beasts. Although the science has not withstood the test of time, the story, told from Axel's point of view, is still a rousing read.

Lest Darkness Fall, L. Sprague De Camp, 1941

Based on the 1939 short story "Unknown," Martin Padway, a twentieth-century Ph.D. candidate, goes back to the sixth century to prevent the fall of the Roman Empire. Full of tantalizing bits of historical detail and many humorous moments, this spellbinding book is hard to put down—even after darkness falls.

The Martian Chronicles, Ray Bradbury, 1950

This collection of short stories tells of the first journeys to Mars and the resulting colonization of the red planet. The first four stories describe the first four expeditions to Mars. The connections between the stories are thin, but they all rely on the psychic abilities of the Martians. "Ylla," the story of the first expedition, tells of a young Martian wife whose jealous husband kills the astronaut. In "The Earth Men" the members of the second expedition are confined to an insane asylum for thinking they are from another planet. The members of the third expedition are easily killed when they are misled into believing that Mars is Heaven. The fourth expedition discovers that the Martians have all died after succumbing to chicken pox. What happens next is quintessential Bradbury.

Mission of Gravity, Hal (Harry Stubbs) Clement, 1954

The planet Mesklin is an enormous oblate spheroid, so flattened by its rapid rotation that the gravity at the poles is over 200 times the equatorial pull, dropping to a "mere" 3g at the equator. Into this gravitational maelstrom a scientific probe has gone astray. To recover the presumably priceless data, the human scientists in orbit convince a group of natives (20-inch-long centipede sailors, actually) to retrieve the data for them. The Mesklinite leader has his own motives for undertaking the difficult journey. The leader and his crew have many adventures as they travel through previously unknown lands, but the primary protagonist is the planet Mesklin itself and the scientific principles that manifest themselves.

The Stars My Destination, Alfred Bester, 1956

A future-age version of *The Count of Monte Cristo.* Gully Foyle is the sole survivor of the wreck of the spaceship *Nomad,* now drifting in space. He becomes enraged when another ship, the *Vorga,* passes by without rescuing him. Summoning resources he didn't know he had, he manages to avoid an imminent death and vows vengeance on the *Vorga.* His initial attack against the *Vorga* is foiled, and he's captured and imprisoned in an underground cell. While incarcerated, he learns of a valuable treasure that was aboard the *Nomad.* After escaping, he relocates the *Nomad* and, with the immense treasure, reinvents himself as a rich dandy, Fourmyle of Ceres. In the course of his revenge, he learns he has a hidden ability. Bester's dark vision of the future anticipates the cyberpunk subgenre with powerful megacorporations, cybernetic enhancements to the body, and one additional twist—everyone can teleport.

An Expert Speaks

In *The Simpson's* episode titled "Lisa's Substitute" (the nineteenth episode in the second season), Martin Prince is running for fourth grade class president against Bart. Here's an excerpt from Martin's campaign speech:

Martin: As your president, I would demand a science-fiction library, featuring an ABC of the overlords of the genre: Asimov, Bester, Clarke!

Kid: What about Ray Bradbury?

Martin: (dismissively) I'm aware of his work.

Stranger in a Strange Land, Robert Heinlein, 1961 (revised 1991)

Valentine Michael Smith, born on Mars, is the sole survivor of the first expedition to that planet. Raised by Martians, he lacks understanding of humans, their emotions, and their societal rules. Returned to Earth, he's imprisoned by the government in a hospital until certain rights of inheritance can be sorted out. With the help of a nurse and the use of some of his "Martian" powers, he escapes. *Stranger in a Strange Land,* the 1962 Hugo winner, became a cult favorite and popularized the term "grok."

The Time Machine, H. G. Wells, 1895

The Time Traveler, as he's known throughout the novel, demonstrates to his skeptical friends that time is the fourth dimension by using a small model. After constructing a full-sized version that can accommodate a passenger, he immediately embarks on a journey through time. He arrives in the year 802,701 A.D., where he discovers the diminutive Eloi leading a pastoral life. The Eloi are remarkably uninterested in the Time Traveler. However, after exploring the nearby area, he returns and discovers that his Time Machine is missing. Alas, the cannibalistic Morlocks have taken the Time Machine, and the Time Traveler must struggle against them lest he be stuck in their time forever … or be their next meal.

More Great Reads

The Alien Years, Robert Silverberg, 1998

Silverberg chronicles one family as they live through a 50-year alien occupation that encompasses the entire planet. The Entities, as the invaders are called, have pulled the plug on all electricity and power on Earth, giving a whole new meaning to the term "Dark Ages." Civilization collapses rapidly, and people decide to either coexist with the aliens by flying low under the radar or, in a handful of cases, staging insurrections—all unsuccessful. The Carmichael family becomes a metaphor for humankind as they deal with the unwelcome visitors. This exciting saga was based on Silverberg's short story, "The Pardoner's Tale."

The Black Sun, Jack Williamson, 1997

Aboard the ninety-ninth and final starship from Project Starseed to leave earth is a crew that includes the project director, a criminal on the lam, and a computer genius who has stowed away. They land on a dark planet composed of ice, rock, and frozen gas, yet one of the people on board is communicating with something alive in this hostile place that can't possibly support life. This thrilling outer space adventure features superb details and characters so real they seem to leap from the page.

The Boat of a Million Years, Poul Anderson, 1989

This short story collection tells of a small group of people—a wife, a sailor, a Native American, and so on—who are normal in every way save one: they are immortal. Nothing obvious caused their immortality, but they do not age (although they can be killed). They try to hide this fact of immortality from their suspicious families and neighbors. In the first story, we meet Hanno, a sailor from Phoenicia on a trip to Britain about the year 300 B.C. Hanno is the common bond that links these stories together. We meet each immortal as he comes to realize his condition and then takes the initial steps to hide his true nature. Can immortality be a curse? Anderson's novel, both a Hugo and Nebula nominee, lives up to the grandiosity of its title.

Darwinia, Robert Charles Wilson, 1998

One night in 1912 the continent of Europe vanishes and is replaced by a new land, Darwinia, which is similar in topography to Europe but is inhabited by dangerous extraterrestrial plants and beings. An expedition of scientists travels to this wild and unexplored region, taking along photographer Guilford Law to chronicle the journey. Most of the expedition dies, but Guilford survives, which is more than can be said for all the Europeans who went missing when Darwinia appeared. The main plot of this alternate history doesn't include a World War, but a secondary plot does. If you're confused by the complex story line, hang in there—you'll be glad you did.

The Doomsday Book, Connie Willis, 1992

It's the middle of the twenty-first century, and the graduate students at Oxford are able to time-travel to whatever period they're studying. Kivrin Engels, a student who specializes in the Medieval period, plans to travel back to the year 1320 for a couple of weeks. Kivrin's troubles begin when a new, virulent form of flu sweeps across England, afflicting the technician in charge of her time travel. Showing the symptoms of the superbug, the technician accidentally sends Kivrin to 1348, the year of the Black Death. Kivrin is stuck in time, as the disease in current-day England incapacitates anyone who might get her home. This fascinating tale has history repeating itself 700 years later.

> ### An Expert Speaks
>
> "I have recommended this extraordinary book [*The Doomsday Book*] to everyone I know ... It's an outstanding—if grim—work, in whatever genre one places it, and the story will haunt you ..."
> —Jo Manning, author

Dragonflight, Anne McCaffrey, 1968

Dragonflight is the first book in the long-running series "Dragonriders of Pern." Every 250 years the planet Pern is threatened with a threadfall. Thread is an organism that is caustic to carbon-based life. To protect themselves, the humans on Pern have developed a symbiotic relationship with the planet's indigenous flying dragons. Guided by their human riders, the dragons can destroy the thread in midair before it can wreak havoc on the ground. But the last threadfall didn't occur, and 450 years have passed since the last one.

People, believing the threadfalls have ceased for good, have curtailed their support for the Weyrs, where dragons are bred and trained. Lessa, a young girl, is recruited to join the last Weyr and bond with the queen dragon, who is about to hatch. This remarkable classic is also popular with fans of the fantasy genre.

Dune, Frank Herbert, 1965

In a tapestry woven of politics, religion, ecology, and technology, Herbert has created one of the best-selling science fiction novels of all time. In the far future, when mankind has spread across the galaxy, a conflict arises between three imperial houses. House Atreides has been forced to accept the fiefdom of the planet Arrakis, a desert planet also known as Dune. Despite its hostile climate, Arrakis is the sole source of the spice melange, a substance that enables faster-than-light travel. Shortly after settling on Dune, the Atreides are betrayed to their enemies, the Harkonnens. Duke Leto, the leader of the Atreides, dies but his son Paul escapes into the desert with his mother. Paul uses all of his skills to survive and vows revenge by gaining control of the spice production. *Dune* won the 1966 Hugo Award.

Echoes in Time, Andre Norton, 1999

In this installment of Norton's "Time Traders" series (written with Sher-wood Smith), Ross Murdock and his bride Eveleen Riordan are ordered back from their honeymoon to help find a lost Russian time-travel team on the planet Yialayil. They travel back in time to search for the missing time travelers and, during their search, discover what happened to the missing Yialayil races. *Echoes in Time* is a solid time-travel story and a sound choice for any science fiction fan.

Ender's Game, Orson Scott Card, 1985

After two invasions of Earth by the insectoid "buggers" (both barely defeated) the military leaders of Earth are seeking the next generation of military strategists to counter the expected third onslaught. Young Andrew "Ender" Wiggins is selected for the orbiting battle school. The students of the battle school are organized into armies, each with a student commander. In addition to their normal studies, the armies battle each other in a weightless gymnasium. As one of the youngest and smallest students, Ender is harassed by the older youths. Still, Ender prevails and is made commander of his own army. *Ender's Game* was the Hugo winner for 1986.

> **The Rest of the Story**
>
> Card wrote several books about the exploits of Ender Wiggins. Perhaps most interesting, he retells the story in *Ender's Game* from the perspective of one of the students in Ender's army in *Ender's Shadow* (1999). The retelling puts an unexpected twist on the original story.

The Essential Ellison: A 50-Year Retrospective,
Harlan Ellison, 2001

Ellison is best known for his short stories, which have won the Hugo Award an astounding eight times. This massive volume is a thorough representation of Ellison's remarkable career and contains over 80 stories, including all but one of the Hugo winners. Even the titles of his stories are a story within themselves: "I Have No Mouth, and I Must Scream" and "'Repent, Harlequin!' Said the Ticktockman." Perhaps his most famous story is "A Boy and His Dog," which is not the innocent story the title suggests. Vic and his dog, Blood, are trying to survive in a post–World War III America, and a quiet night at the local movie theater takes an unexpected and violent turn.

And the Award Goes to ...

At the 1976 World Science Fiction Convention, the film version of "A Boy and His Dog" (starring Don Johnson) was awarded the Hugo for best dramatic presentation. The award was given to the film's producers, but Ellison argued that as the writer, he should be awarded, too. No extra Hugo was available, but the organizers did locate a wooden base and it was given to mollify him. Ellison now claims he has won the Hugo 8½ times.

The First Book of Lankhmar, Fritz Leiber, 2001

The First Book of Lankhmar is an omnibus containing the first four books in Fritz Leiber's "Sword" series about Fafhrd and the Grey Mouser, two rogues on the planet Nehwon who have a series of adventures in and around the city of Lankhmar. Fafhrd is a giant barbarian warrior, and Grey Mouser is a master thief and swordsman. This collection of stories includes the Hugo-winning "Ill Met in Lankhmar," in which our two heroes run afoul of the Thieves Guild. Leiber is attributed with coining the term "swords and sorcery."

The Rest of the Story

The Lankhmar series was the basis for the interactive game *Dungeons and Dragons*. The royalty checks from sales of the game allowed the Leibers to live very comfortably in their final years.

The Forever War, Joe Haldeman, 1975 (revised 1991, 1997)

William Mandella is drafted into a future army for a war against the alien Taurons. He joins a special task force of elite cadets, survives training with live weapons, and ships out to a base orbiting a collapsed star that has created a wormhole, which allows instantaneous travel across light years. Unfortunately, travel between bases is done at sublight speeds. Due to relativistic effects, for the traveler these trips last only a few months, but back on Earth decades go by. When Mandella finally returns to Earth, he finds a society he no longer understands. Feeling alienated, he reluctantly re-enlists in the military. *The Forever War* won the 1976 Hugo Award.

Gateway, Frederik Pohl, 1977

Robert Broadhead is leading a mundane existence on an overpopulated Earth when he wins a lottery. Taking his winnings, he travels to Gateway, an asteroid near Venus that was once the home of the Heechee. The Heechee's civilization is long gone, and all that remains is a honeycombed asteroid that contains hundreds of faster-than-light ships. The ships are pre-programmed, and no one knows how they work or how long a particular voyage may last. Starvation is a real concern for anyone who boards a Heechee ship, but the financial rewards for a successful mission are huge. Despite his decision to come to Gateway, Broadhead is a very unenthusiastic explorer, yet he has to make a lucrative discovery before his lottery winnings run out. *Gateway* won the 1978 Hugo Award.

The Guns of the South: A Novel of the Civil War,
Harry Turtledove, 1992

How different would life be if the North had lost the Civil War? It's January 1864, and a despondent General Robert E. Lee is writing a letter describing his troop's precarious position. He is startled by rifle fire, with shots in such rapid succession that he assumes a whole battalion is target shooting and wasting precious ammunition. Imagine his surprise when he steps out of his tent and sees only one man, oddly dressed, holding a strange-looking gun—an AK-47. With the southern forces armed with the futuristic weapons, the war shifts in favor of the South. *The Guns of the South* paints a picture of a very different America after the War Between the States. This is only one of Turtledove's highly entertaining alternate histories.

The Hitchhiker's Guide to the Galaxy, Douglas Adams, 1979

The first book of the "five part" trilogy finds Earthman Arthur Dent escaping the demolition of Earth with the aid of Ford Prefect, who, unknown to Arthur, is actually an alien from a small planet near Betelgeuse and a contributor to the Hitchhiker's Guide to the Galaxy. After hitching a ride with the Vogon destructor fleet, the pair end up on the spaceship *Heart of Gold*, which had been stolen by Ford's semicousin, Zaphod Beeblebrox, his girlfriend Trillian, and Marvin, a paranoid and severely depressed android. The spaceship is powered by an "Infinite Improbability Drive" so anything, no matter how improbable, can happen (e.g., a missile might be turned into a whale). The ultimate answer to life, the universe, and everything is also revealed, and even though you may not like the answer, you will find it hilarious. Adams's satirical science fiction has a huge cult following.

Hothouse, Brian W. Aldiss, 1962

In the far future, the sun has expanded. Earth and the moon are now tide-locked, with one face always toward the sun. The sunward side of Earth is a massive jungle inhabited by just a few surviving animal species. The novel describes the adventures of Gren, a young male who undertakes a journey of discovery across the surface of a very different Earth. Aldiss's descriptions of the future ecology are fascinating and sometimes humorous. Many of the events and characters are just a bit off-center, adding to the interest of the story.

The Left Hand of Darkness, Ursula K. Le Guin, 1969

The Left Hand of Darkness features Genly Ai, a representative from a federation of planets called the Ekumen, who travels to the planet Gethen to determine whether it's ready to join the Ekumen. On Gethen, Ai encounters hermaphroditic humans who are gender neutral for all but two days a month. Then they may become either male or female. The book recounts the misadventures of Ai as he tries to understand the Gethen society. *The Left Hand of Darkness* won the 1970 Hugo Award.

Neuromancer, William Gibson, 1984

Gibson is credited with coining the term "cyberspace" at least 10 years before the emergence of the Internet. *Neuromancer* is the story of Henry Case, a talented computer hacker in a high-tech, dystopian future. When his employers catch him stealing from them, they retaliate by damaging his central nervous system. Case is desperate to correct the damage, but he eventually runs out of resources and finds himself living as a street hustler with an active death wish. When an opportunity for a cure comes his way, albeit with numerous strings attached, Case jumps at it. One of the strings is circumventing the artificial intelligence, Neuromancer. *Neuromancer* won both the Hugo and Nebula awards.

Parable of the Talents, Octavia Butler, 1998

In this sequel to *Parable of the Sower,* Butler continues the story of Lauren Oya Olamina, her disapproving daughter Larkin, and Earthseed, the religion Lauren founded. The new religion teaches that God is change and that our destiny is to live among the stars. The story is set in the near future of a war-torn United States whose religious crusader president resorts to fascism and totalitarianism. Christian thugs take over Lauren's town and turn it into a re-education center similar to a concentration camp. *Parable of the Talents* was the 1999 Nebula Award winner.

Ringworld, Larry Niven, 1970

Nessus, a member of an alien species known as "Pierson's Puppeteer," organizes a mission to explore a "ringworld"—an enormous ring nearly a million miles wide with a circumference of 600 million miles that's constructed around a star. All together, the ring's surface area is 3 million times the surface area of Earth. Nessus recruits two humans and another alien to join the expedition. Shortly after arriving near the Ringworld, their spaceship is disabled and crashes. The four explorers must find a way to get their ship back into space and set out across the Ringworld. *Ringworld* won the 1971 Hugo Award.

The Rest of the Story

Niven is careful with his science, but he's not a scientist, and his scientific descriptions don't always stand up to scrutiny. At the 1970 World Science Fiction Convention, MIT students stood in the halls chanting, "The Ringworld is unstable! The Ringworld is unstable!" In the sequel, *Ringworld Engineers*, Niven added massive attitude jets to keep the ring centered around its star. "I did the best I was able" was Niven's answer to his critics.

To Your Scattered Bodies Go, Philip José Farmer, 1971

In this first book in the "Riverworld" series, every human being who ever lived is resurrected and living in a world that has a single million-mile-long river valley. Farmer follows the exploits of English explorer and writer Richard Burton (1821–1890) and others as they try to survive. They suffer attacks by Hermann Göring, although anyone killed is simply resurrected elsewhere along the river. Burton is eventually approached by a stranger working to subvert Riverworld. The interaction between characters from different eras makes this book sparkle. *To Your Scattered Bodies Go* was the Hugo winner in 1972.

The Uplift War, David Brin, 1987

This book is the third novel in the "Uplift Universe" series, in which one species in the galaxy can "uplift" another into sentience. Humans are an anomaly, since they have no "patron" species and have actually uplifted two other species on earth—chimpanzees and dolphins. The three species are collectively known as "Earthclan." In *The Uplift War*, Earthclan has been given the lease to the planet Garth, with the responsibility of restoring its ecosystem. The Gubru invade Garth and claim that Earthclan has mishandled the planet. The Gubru manage to subdue most of the humans, but they underestimate the neo-chimps, whom the Gubru believe will be easily controlled without their human "patrons." The neo-chimps engage in guerilla warfare (yes, this sentence made us giggle, too).

Way Station, Clifford D. Simak, 1963

Enoch Wallace returns from the Civil War and takes up farming again. However, his life takes a dramatic turn when an alien named Ulysses approaches him. Ulysses turns Enoch's home into a way station for galactic travelers, leaving Enoch as the caretaker. While inside his house, Enoch doesn't age. After a hundred years in peaceful isolation, things start to go wrong for Enoch. People begin to notice his long life; the government has stolen the alien body Enoch buried when one of his visitors died; and the peace of the galaxy is being disrupted, threatening to close the way station. *Way Station* was the 1964 Hugo winner.

10

Fantasy Novels: Life After *The Lord of the Rings*

In This Chapter

- ◆ Classics: castles in the sky and other real estate
- ◆ More great reads: flights of the imagination

The fantasy genre is a complete departure from reality and plausibility. Its cousins, science fiction (see Chapter 9) and horror (see Chapter 11), possess an element of possibility, but fantasy is pure imagination, filled with magic, fanciful worlds, and supernatural beings. From ancient myths and legends, such as the *Epic of Gilgamesh* and *The Odyssey*, to fantasies like *The Hobbit* and *Harry Potter*, readers throughout time have enjoyed the escapism, imagery, and subtle metaphor that characterize this genre.

Classics

The Crystal Cave, Mary Stewart, 1971

You know him by his literary stage name, "Merlin the Magician." Prepare to learn the story behind the celebrity. Stewart's biography of the mystic, "Myridden Emrys," reveals the essential Merlin, from his fatherless childhood, to siring Arthur, the most renowned king of all lore.

Dragonsong, Anne McCaffrey, 1976

Far away, in Half Circle Hold on the planet Pern, Menolly, a young, aspiring harpist, runs away after her father forbids her to play her music. She happens upon her planet's fabled fire lizards, who encourage her to become Pern's first female harpist.

Harry Potter and the Sorcerer's Stone, J. K. Rowling, 1997

Harry Potter, orphaned after his parents are killed, must live with his abusive and manipulative aunt and uncle. When one day an owl arrives, delivering an invitation to the young ward, Harry's life is changed forever. He learns he has inherited his parents' unparalleled gift for wizardry, and he travels to Hogwarts, a mind-bending boarding school for magicians in training.

The Rest of the Story

J. K. Rowling's first *Harry Potter* novel—*Harry Potter and the Philosopher's Stone*—was published in England in 1997. The book became an immediate success and won a number of awards including the British Book Award for Best Children's Book of the Year and the Nestle Smarties Gold Award. The book debuted in America the following year with a slight title change to *Harry Potter and the Sorcerer's Apprentice.* Readers were immediately captivated by the magical adventures of Harry and his friends Ron and Hermione. More titles in the Harry Potter series followed, each one selling even more copies than the last, perennially pushing the books onto the *New York Times* bestseller list. The seventh and final book in the series, *Harry Potter and the Deathly Hallows* (scheduled to be published in 2007), will conclude what is certainly one of the most popular and successful fantasy series ever written.

The Hobbit, J.R.R. Tolkein, 1966

Be careful what you wish for. Wealthy hobbit Bilbo Baggins learns this lesson the hard way when wizard Gandalf grants Baggins's wish for wealth that tangles him in a dangerous mission to raid a dragon's treasure trove. This novel is full of good stuff—magic, adventure, and a band of dwarves. *The Hobbit* is a prequel to Tolkein's internationally famous (now a cinematic blockbuster) trilogy, *The Lord of the Rings*.

The Last Unicorn, Peter S. Beagle, 1968

The last unicorn sets out to find more of her kind, but is captured by an evil gypsy who makes her part of "The Midnight Carnival." After the unicorn is freed by the inept magician Schmendrick, they're joined by the intrepid Molly Grue. The story is a wonderful mix of magic, fantasy, and humor.

The Lion, the Witch, and the Wardrobe, C. S. Lewis, 1950

Leave it to kids to find a portal to another world through the back of a piece of furniture! This classic introduces readers to the magical kingdom of Narnia and a golden lion named Aslan. A witch has cast a spell of eternal winter upon the land, and it's Aslan who must confront her.

The Mists of Avalon, Marion Zimmer Bradley, 1982

Fans of Arthurian lore will appreciate Bradley's take on the legendary monarch as told from the perspective of the powerful women behind the royal throne. Morgan le Fay (Morgaine) is forced to sacrifice her virginity during fertility rites, and the man who impregnates her is her younger brother Arthur. Morgaine believes that Arthur has turned against Avalon's ancient religion in favor of Christianity and Gwenhwyfar (Guinevere). *The Mists of Avalon* is a beautifully written variation on the Camelot legend.

The Once and Future King, T. H. White, 1939

White sets the standard for fantasy with this all-time classic of Arthurian lore. *The Sword in the Stone, The Witch in the Wind* (also known as *The Queen of Air and Darkness*), and *The Ill Made Knight* are all included in this one volume, chronicling Arthur's life from his childhood with Merlin to the night before he died. All of the legendary Camelot characters are here, in a magical place where animals talk and anything is possible, even for a boy known as "Wart."

The Princess Bride, William Goldman, 1973

The unusual, larger-than-life characters in this medieval fantasy take you on a rollicking journey. You'll visit such bizarre places as the Cliffs of Insanity, the Fire Swamp, and the Zoo of Death. The peculiar ports-of-call alone in this fanciful love story make it worth the trip.

> **The Rest of the Story** _____
>
> Rob Reiner brought *The Princess Bride* to the big screen with his film of the same name, featuring characters that seem to jump right out of the book, played by Robin Wright, Mandy Patinkin, and Andre the Giant.

Small Gods, Terry Pratchett, 1994

As the peaceful land of Discworld floats through space on the back of a gigantic turtle (top that, Lewis Carroll!), our quiet little hero, Brutha, contentedly tends to his melon patch. But Brutha's simple life gets complicated when he hears a tiny voice of a god calling him to his destiny. This witty, clever satire kicks off the "Discworld" series.

Watership Down, Richard Adams, 1972

Imagine your peaceful homeland threatened by a powerful, destructive intruder, forcing you to flee to foreign lands and an uncertain future. Art imitates life in this tale of a family of rabbits who experience the encroachment of humans into their pastoral habitat of Sandleford Warren.

Wizards' Worlds, Andre Norton, 1989

Norton's collection of 13 short stories, written between 1952 and 1985, introduces readers to a sampling of her prolific fantasy stockpile. Her inventive, mind-bending characters and out-of-this-world settings will set your imagination reeling.

> **An Expert Speaks** _____
>
> "It was unbelievably difficult for me to pick just one favorite in the Fantasy genre, but Andre Norton introduced me to amazing new worlds and has been a lasting influence on many readers, some of whom later become well-known authors in their own right. Norton has written many many stories, and more than 40 years later they are still an unalloyed pleasure for me to reread. As an introduction to the genre and the author, I don't think anyone can do better than *Wizards' Worlds*. Characters and settings from Norton's groundbreaking *Witch World* series are interspersed with those from other places and times she has shared with us, and all are gems of the highest value, together forming a glittering necklace stretching across the universe of the imagination."
>
> —Lynne Welch, librarian

More Great Reads

Biting the Sun, Tanith Lee, 1999

Anything goes in Utopia, especially if you're a teenage girl who's a member of Jang. No pleasure is off limits, and lives can end and restart like characters in a video game. In fact, as hedonism becomes increasingly mundane, the stakes get higher and the behavior even more debauched. When the decadence reaches its pinnacle, there's nowhere to go but down, and suddenly, even the teenagers have to examine their values. This novel features great characters set in a very stylish, well-developed world, and is meant to be read with its companion book, *Sapphire Wine.*

Byzantium, Stephen Lawhead, 1996

After his father's kingdom is lost in conquest, Aidan, the son of Irish royalty, becomes a reclusive monastery scribe. However, his quiet monastic life is forever changed when he is chosen to join a band of monks to deliver a precious manuscript to the Emperor of all Christendom. Leaving the security of the monastery, Aidan embarks on the adventure of a lifetime, and his experiences along the way prepare him to realize his destiny as a gifted leader.

The Charmed Sphere, Catherine Asaro, 2004

In the pastoral hamlet of Jacob's Vale lives a girl named Chime, who discovers she has potential as a "mage," the Vale term for sorceress. Although reluctant, Chime leaves her home to be schooled in the magic arts and to prepare to become the bride of Prince Muller, an unlikely marriage candidate and even more unlikely successor to the throne. Send in the bad guys.

The Compass Rose, Gail Dayton, 2005

Captain Kallista Varyl must invoke a higher being for the strength and ability to defend her countrymen. Once she's "Godstruck," she's endowed with superhuman powers. Kallista learns to harness her mighty gifts, but can she decipher the mysterious Compass Rose and defeat her enemies?

The Curse of Chalion, Lois McMaster Bujold, 2001

Lupe dy Cazaril, once a gallant soldier but now a broken, escaped prisoner of war, returns to the realm of Chalion to quietly serve the monarchy. His courage is tested once again when he's drawn into battle with a dark force that threatens his beloved royal family.

The Dragonbone Chair, Tad Williams, 1988

Some of the greatest heroes come from the most unlikely places. Simon, a lowly kitchen worker, has been taking magic lessons on the side. When King John Presbyter dies and his son Elias assumes power, dark forces are welcomed into the kingdom. It's Simon who intervenes, along with Elias's brother Joshua, to ward off the advancing evil in this battle between good and evil and brother against brother.

Elric of Melnibone, Michael Moorcock, 1976

This is the first story in a long series of dark adventures about the albino warrior, Elric, Emperor of Melnibone. His striking appearance, insightful wisdom, and skills in sorcery make Elric a formidable hero.

The Eye of the World, Robert Jordan, 1990

Primitive monsters called Trollocs attack three friends, who manage to escape to another land with a little help from some rather unusual characters and then embark on a journey of high adventure, wonder, and peril. Inventive characters and complex plotting whisk readers along in this labyrinth of fantasy.

The Eyre Affair, Jasper Fforde, 2002

The barriers between time and reality dissolve in this alternate existence, where literature comes to life. Special Operative Thursday Next is summoned to investigate the disappearance of Jane Eyre, kidnapped from the pages of Charlotte Brontë's novel. Next must enter the classic herself to thwart a murder. The story is highly intellectual and tremendously funny.

A Game of Thrones: Song of Fire and Ice #1, George R.R. Martin, 1996

The seasons are out of whack; the kingdom of Winterfell is experiencing an unusual cold snap; and enemies are amassing all around. Eddard Stark, no stranger to danger, is called to serve the king during this turbulent time and risks both family and homeland in the quest for survival.

His Majesty's Dragon, Naomi Novik, 2006

It's history with a twist as France's squadron of airborne dragons is about to meet its match after the British capture a dragon egg from a French frigate. Captain Will Laurence becomes the dragon's keeper and must master the art of aerial warfare in record time to face Napoleon's impending assault on the kingdom.

Joust, Mercedes Lackey, 2003

A young slave aspires to become a jouster, which in his world is a dragon-riding warrior. When a kindly jouster rescues the abused slave boy to care for his dragon, the boy seizes the opportunity to secretly raise his own dragon in a quest to gain freedom and a better life.

Lord of the Isles, David Drake, 1998

Characters from the past are coming out of the woodwork in this fantasy world, when powerful magic forces reach their cyclical thousand-year peak, enabling survivors from the last peak to traverse time. A large cast of interesting characters inhabit a complex plot filled with danger and romance.

Lord Valentine's Castle, Robert Silverberg, 1980

Prince Valentine launches the Majipoor Chronicles series in this trek to discover his birthright. Accompanied by an odd group of performers, Valentine gets more than he bargained for when his adventurous quest becomes a crusade of courage that tests his integrity and all that he believes.

Neverwhere, Neil Gaiman, 1996

When Richard Mayhew helps a young woman he finds wounded and bleeding on a London sidewalk, it's his ticket into a mysterious, underground city, London Below. Made up of people who "fell through the cracks," as well as mystical creatures (many evil), this netherworld adventure is a dark urban fantasy.

The Rest of the Story

In addition to writing fantasy, horror, science fiction, screenplays, and poetry, Gaiman is the author of a number of graphic novels, including his uniquely original 10-volume *Sandman* series.

Pawn of Prophecy, David Eddings, 1982

Launching Eddings's Belgariad series is young Garion, an ordinary farm boy who gets caught up in a quest to maintain order in the land of the West. A legendary evil god, Torak, is about to be resurrected, and the fate of the people rests in a powerful, protective Orb. The book is full of action-packed fun.

Redwall, Brian Jacques, 1987

All of the essential ingredients for pure fantasy are here, in this story of a young mouse named Mathias, who overcomes his fears to save his friends from a wicked rat, Cluny the Scourge. A badger, a hare, and a wise old mouse share the spotlight in this imaginative tale of courage, self-discovery, and wisdom.

Stolen Magic, Mary Jo Putney, 2005

Discover a land where "Guardians," humans who possess magical powers, are in charge of peacekeeping. Drayton, one of the Guardians, goes bad and abuses his powers by casting an inescapable spell that saps other Guardians' powers.

The Earl of Falconer tracks him down, only to become the next victim. The Earl's rescuer is a woman named Meg, who had also been zapped by Drayton, and together they find the means for revenge.

The Sword of Shannara, Terry Brooks, 2002

Living in the bucolic confines of Shady Vale, half-elfin Shea Ohmsford is blissfully unaware that his world is about to be threatened by the return of an evil warlock bent on destruction. Only the Sword of Shannara can end the warlock's relentless rampage, and only Shea, the last of his bloodline, can wield it.

Talon of the Silver Hawk, Raymond E. Feist, 2003

A boy named Kieli is the sole survivor of a murderous rampage by an army of ruthless marauders under the Duke of Olasko. Rescued and nursed back to health, Kieli receives training in the art of warfare and accepts his destiny as the Talon of the Silver Hawk, intent on avenging his people.

Wicked: The Life and Times of the Wicked Witch of the West, Gregory McGuire, 1995

You've heard Dorothy Gale's side of the story. Now it's wicked witch Elphaba's turn. McGuire flips Baum's classic around, examining the Wonderful Wizard of Oz from a fresh perspective. The curtain is pulled back on the Land of Oz to reveal everything from social status-seeking Munchkins to a misunderstood, green-skinned little girl who grows up to become the Wicked Witch of the West. Fresh and clever, the book is as colorful as the Emerald City itself.

Wintertide, Linnea Sinclair, 2004

Khamsin is a healer with a destiny yet to be discovered. She only knows that a powerful, mysterious force wants her dead. When her village is attacked and her family killed, Khamsin survives. With the help of Rylan the Tinker, she journeys to seek the aid of a wise old healer who can help her develop her skills as a sorceress. Along the way, fantasy becomes romance.

A Wizard of Earthsea, Ursula K. Le Guin, 1968

As a young sorcerer's apprentice, Sparrowhawk irresponsibly oversteps the limits of his abilities and unleashes an evil presence on the land. Now grown and going by the name "Ged," Sparrowhawk must undo the mistake from his past and restore order to the kingdom. This is the first installment of the Earthsea Chronicles.

And the Award Goes to...

While fantasy novels are eligible for, and have won, both the Nebula and Hugo awards, these honors can also be given to books in the science fiction genre. One award given solely to fantasy fiction is the World Fantasy Award, which is bestowed each year at the World Fantasy Convention and was established to recognize outstanding talent in the fantasy genre.

Wolf Who Rules, Wen Spencer, 2006

In Spencer's novels, Pittsburg exists near an inter-dimensional border with the land of the elves. Tinker, a young genius salvage yard owner, does her best to keep local paranormal matters in check with gadgets of her own making, but her plans for her first date are disrupted when she becomes embroiled in a battle with formidable elfin foes intent on making trouble in the burgh. It's as tantalizing as a first kiss.

Chapter 11

Horror Novels: It Was a Dark and Stormy Night

In This Chapter

◆ Classics: 200 years of terror

◆ More great reads: scare me to death

Vampires, ghosts, monsters, demons, werewolves, witches, and hauntings—these are just a few of the horrific images and eerie night-time imaginings that the writers of this genre have seared into our minds. Dating back to 1796 when the first horror novel, *The Monk*, was published (profiled in Classics, and still in print today!), the tantalizing plausibility of this genre's characters has continued to mystify the fans of the macabre. Even though *The Monk's* early Gothic horror was harshly criticized as an affront to decency with its dark, sexual, and shockingly violent content, it was a best-seller for its day. Of course, now these same qualities are considered necessary ingredients of a really good video game.

This list of horrors is a sampling of the award-winning or most widely read works in this genre. You might recognize some of the titles or have seen films based on them, but as any reader will tell you, the book is always better. On a dark and stormy night, do you really want to know what lurks in the shadows where the flickering candlelight doesn't quite reach?

You'd better turn on all the lights before you read these stories. Oh, and by the way, *BOO!*

> **The Rest of the Story**
>
> Do you know where the phrase "It was a dark and stormy night" came from? Edward Bulwer-Lytton (1803–1873), an English dramatist, poet, novelist, critic, and politician, first penned these words in *Paul Clifford* (1830): "It was a dark and stormy night; the rain fell in torrents—except at occasional intervals, when it was checked by a violent gust of wind which swept up the streets (for it is in London that our scene lies), rattling along the housetops, and fiercely agitating the scanty flame of the lamps that struggled against the darkness."

Classics

The Andromeda Strain, Michael Crichton, 1971

Crichton writes horror based on scientific theory, adding a touch of plausibility to his stories that makes them all the more frightening. The reader gets the feeling that if conditions were right, these catastrophes could really happen. In this, Crichton's amazing debut novel, a space probe returns to earth carrying a deadly microbe. In the tiny Arizona town where the probe lands, only two people survive this new cosmic disease. The government quietly activates its anti-pandemic program, Project Wildfire, to retrieve, quarantine, and study the specimen. But is the crisis averted? Hardly. The bug finds a way to escape its containment, and all the scientific minds in Project Wildfire begin a race to find a way to stop the spread of the deadly disease.

Dr. Jekyll and Mr. Hyde, Robert Louis Stevenson, 1885

Does each of us have a monster within us? That's the premise for this classic novella, in which respected Doctor Henry Jekyll samples his own experimental potion, transforming himself into his cruel, sadistic alter ego, Mr. Edward Hyde. The foggy, narrow cobblestone streets of London provide an obliging backdrop for Mr. Hyde's wickedness and Dr. Jekyll's sordid forays into his wilder side.

Dracula, Bram Stoker, 1897

The formidable Count Dracula (modeled after an evil sadist, Vlad the Impaler, a.k.a. Vlad Dracula), is a wily, seductive Transylvanian vampire with an insatiable appetite for the blood of vivacious women. Entrancing his victims with his machismo, he sinks his fangs into their necks, drains them of their essence, and leads them helplessly into the world of the undead. Like many classics, the original ending of this story is quite different from Hollywood's concoction of wooden stakes and garlic.

The Rest of the Story

It's hard to believe the same pen that created the savage Mr. Hyde also composed the beautiful and soothing *A Child's Garden of Verses*. But it's true. Robert Louis Stevenson wrote both books, as well as *Treasure Island* and *Kidnapped*. Born in Scotland, Stevenson spent his last years on his estate in his beloved Samoa. When he died suddenly at age 44, the natives carried the body of their "Teller of Tales" to the top of a cliff for burial and inscribed a nearby tablet with his famous lines, "Home is the sailor, home from the sea, And the hunter home from the hill."

The Exorcist, William Peter Blatty, 1971

Fans of the occult will savor this gripping page-turner about a young girl named Regan who becomes possessed by a demonic spirit that ravages her body and soul. Extremely bizarre physical and behavioral changes occur in Regan that force her mother to turn to the church for help. The violent exorcism that follows is intense, grueling, and not for the squeamish.

Frankenstein or, the Modern Prometheus,
Mary Wollstonecraft Shelley, 1818

To many, Frankenstein's monster is considered the granddaddy of all horror characters, dating back nearly 200 years. Shelley's original story is surprisingly different from later revisions that turn the confused and misunderstood, albeit hideous, outcast into a demented and rampaging monster. This book presents an interesting contrast to the Frankenstein story you thought you knew.

The Fury, John Farris, 1976

The mysterious, untamed power of the human mind is the subject of this story, along with the two next-generation sequels that follow, *The Fury and The Terror* (2001) and *The Fury and the Power* (2003). Two teenagers, Gillian and Robin, each possesses a dangerous and destructive psychic ability that he struggles to control. Powerful forces learn of the unique talents of the two and plan to exploit them as weapons for world domination. In fact, Robin's captivity and brainwashing has already begun. Gillian's father, a highly successful government assassin, steps in to put a stop to the madness and save Robin and Gillian, even though he knows this will make him a moving target for the rest of his life.

The Haunting of Hill House, Shirley Jackson, 1959

Fragile, mousy Eleanor Vance is the leading lady of this gothic horror set in a remote, sprawling, 80-year-old mansion called Hill House. Her prior experiences with the paranormal make Eleanor a prime conduit for this house's extreme hauntedness, ultimately driving her to madness. Hold hands with a trusted friend to read this heart-stopping thriller!

Interview with the Vampire, Anne Rice, 1976

This macabre tale is a "true" confession told from a vampire's perspective. In it, Louis, a vampire, reflects on his existence with fellow undead, Lestat and Claudia, and laments the futility, loneliness, and tedium of immortality. This is the first of Rice's Vampire Chronicles, followed by *Vampire Lestat* (1985), and *Queen of the Damned* (1988). No one can read just one of these shocking, yet disturbingly sensuous, yarns.

Jaws, Peter Benchley, 1975

You'll think twice before getting into the water after reading this chilling account of a great white shark that hunts for humans along the beaches of a resort town. The gigantic, frighteningly clever, and ruthlessly persistent killer shark manages to scare the bejeebers out of us, even without creepy background music.

The Monk, Matthew G. Lewis, 1796

Enough to give Grandma the vapors, this cornucopia of all that is evil is set during the Spanish Inquisition. A highly regarded monk named Ambrosio, a holy man of impeccable character, has lust in his heart and the hots for pure and innocent Antonia. When she spurns him, he rapes and kills her in the crypt of Saint Clare. Facing the death sentence for his crime, he sells his soul to Satan, and things take a really ugly turn from there. The gruesome events and brilliant cast of colorful characters (a gypsy fortune-teller, the infamous Wandering Jew, the Bleeding Nun, the Grand Inquisitor, and special guest star Lucifer) helped Lewis put the horror genre in the mainstream.

> **The Rest of the Story**
>
> Matthew G. Lewis was only 19 years old when he wrote *The Monk,* which he later adopted as his nickname.

"The Rats in the Walls," H.P. Lovecraft, 1923

Lovecraft's classic narratives and short stories are masterful blends of horror, fantasy, and science fiction. Flip open any of this man's books, and you can begin reading some of the best horror fiction ever written. The title of his short story, "The Rats in the Walls," conjures a sickening image all by itself, but the details behind the title are nothing short of revolting. It seems the heir to the well-heeled Massachusetts Delepore family has stumbled upon a big fat skeleton in the family closet. For centuries the Delepores kept a hidden underground city beneath their old English estate, Exham Priory, where generations of humans were cultivated for food and consumed by the inhabitants. And that's not even the icky part!

Rosemary's Baby, Ira Levin, 1967

Levin knows a thing or two about groundbreaking horror. He has won two Edgar Awards from the Mystery Writers of America and the Bram Stoker Award for Lifetime Achievement from the Horror Writers Association. In this daring 1967 shocker, Rosemary and Guy Woodhouse move into an old Manhattan apartment building where they meet an overbearing older couple, the Castavets. When Rosemary discovers she is pregnant, the Castavets show an inordinate amount of interest. Unusual circumstances occur that cause Rosemary to fear her pushy neighbors might be Satanists and that the child she carries is somehow demonic. Raw liver anyone?

The Stand, Stephen King, 1978

The "Complete and Uncut Edition" of this thriller, which came out in 1990, tells about a Defense Department snafu that unleashes a deadly super-virus upon mankind. The few people who survive divide themselves between the forces of good, led by Mother Abigail, and the forces of evil, followers of the sadistic and uber-powerful Randall Flagg. The action is violent, bloody, and in-your-face as the last ones standing inherit the world. Other notable Stephen King horrors include three Bram Stoker Award winners: *Misery,* 1998; *The Green Mile,* 1997; and *Bag of Bones,* 1999. So many horrors, so little time do we have to read King.

You Can Book on It!

The *Stand* is only one example of Stephen King's terrifying works. Creating horror that's every librarian's dream ("The Library Policeman" in *Four Past Midnight*) and every writer's nightmare (Annie Wilkes in *Misery*), King's skewed vision of what could go terribly wrong if things were only a *little* different appeals to a broad spectrum of readers.

The Tell-Tale Heart, Edgar Allen Poe, 1843

Poe's insight into the dark logic of an insane mind makes this disturbing tale, told in first person, a horror reader's favorite. The nameless speaker calmly tells about a kindly old man who shares his house and about the old man's hideous "pale blue eye with a film over it." The speaker is so repulsed by the eye that he devises a plan to extinguish it by killing the old man. He describes the event in chilling detail as he goes skulking about the dark house, night after night, sneaking slowly, silently, painstakingly, carefully into the sleeping old man's room, then allowing only the thinnest shaft of light to escape his lantern to shine on the offending eye, closed in slumber. He is exhilarated by his cleverness, practically giddy, until one night, the eye opens, and he carries out his evil plan. This one will get your heart tin-tin-abulating!

The Werewolf in Paris, Guy Endore, 1933

Bertrand Caillet has werewolf tendencies in his genes, enjoys a sordid sex life, and leaves a trail of mauled corpses in his path. But, as we discover, even werewolves can find love. Bertrand hooks up with an amazingly accommodating canteen girl named Sophie, who goes to unbelievable extremes to stand by her man.

More Great Reads

Anno Dracula, Kim Newman, 1993

By including a cast of Victorian literary and historic figures in the plot, Newman takes the vampire concept to a new level, making this tale entirely entertaining and strangely plausible when he proposes that Count Dracula actually survived death by the stake and relocated to London (being undead and all), where he subdued and ultimately married Queen Victoria. With Dracula behind the throne, London becomes a vampire's paradise. Could Jack the Ripper's real identity be Dr. John Seward, from Bram Stoker's *Dracula*, now in London killing undead prostitutes? And how do Dr. Jekyll and Mr. Hyde factor into this bizarre labyrinth of horror all-stars? Lots of questions, and the answers are all disturbing.

The Between, Tananarive Due, 1995

Hilton James should be dead. He almost drowned when he was a child, but his grandmother rescued him, losing her life to save his. Now Hilton is pushing 40. He's become a successful social worker, a father of two, with a wife who is the first African American judge to sit on the Miami bench. You could say Hilton has led a charmed life. But that's about to change. Lately he's been having horrible nightmares about his grandmother's death, and his family has been receiving increasingly vicious, racist

> **The Rest of the Story**
>
> Tananarive Due is the first major female African American horror writer. Her characters give much-needed diversity to the genre.

hate mail from a vengeful criminal his wife once prosecuted. Hilton wonders if the Grim Reaper is using this dangerous felon to settle an old score with him. Can Hilton cheat death a second time?

Bitten: Book 1, Women of the Otherworld, Kelly Armstrong, 2004

This is a clever departure from the usual werewolf story line. The main character, Elena Michaels, is a she-wolf and member of a nonhuman-eating pack of werewolves. When Elena decides to leave the pack in hopes of finding fulfillment by living as a normal woman, she can't ignore the werewolf inside her. Whenever she feels "the Change" about to overtake her, she quietly slips into the night to conceal her wildness and surrenders to her natural, primal tendencies. Her identities collide, and her loyalties are tested when a renegade gang of "Mutts" begins converting criminals into werewolves who kill for pleasure, unleashing bloody havoc and threatening to implicate Elena's pack.

Blood Lines, Tanya Huff, 1993

There really ought to be a hieroglyphic symbol for "Caution! Do not open!" But that probably wouldn't stop this team of archaeologists who discover a rare, intact sarcophagus and deliver it to the Royal Ontario Museum for further study. In the excitement, they unwittingly undo all the protective measures set in place long ago, that were intended to keep the ancient coffin's evil occupant trapped inside. Now that he's on the loose in modern Toronto, he possesses the locals and manipulates them into building a new empire for his evil god. The only ones aware that this is happening are Huff's recurring characters: private investigator Victory Nelson, her vampire partner Henry Fitzroy, and her former police partner, Detective Mike Celluci.

The Book of Shadows, James Reese, 2002

Where do witches learn their craft? They're home-schooled by other witches, of course. Young Herculine is orphaned and raised in a nineteenth-century French convent. When her classmates discover something bizarre and unnatural about Herculine, she is shunned as a witch and locked away to await trial. But fellow witch Sebastiana d'Azur rescues Herculine and spirits her away to safety. There, Sebastiana teaches the girl the disciplines of witchcraft she will need to carry out her destiny.

Books of Blood, Clive Barker, 1984

Barker's first American hardcover publication is a compilation of 16 short narratives for horror readers who like it fast and gory. Adding to the creepy experience are graphic illustrations by noted cover artists J. K. Potter and Harry O. Morris. Barker's unparalleled brand of gruesome nastiness earned him high praise from fellow horror writers and prompted two more bloody compilations, *Books of Blood #2* (1986) and *Books of Blood #3* (1991). Get the mop.

Dead Until Dark, Charlene Harris, 2001

Can a small-town Louisiana telepathic cocktail waitress find happiness with a vampire? This cleverly humorous "Southern Vampire Series" introduces characters Sookie Stackhouse, the waitress whose spontaneous mind-reading ability is ruining her love life, and vampire Bill Compton, eye-candy with fangs. Sookie notices she is unable to penetrate the thoughts of this handsome new customer and recognizes immediately that he's a vampire. She's willing to dismiss this little flaw, since vampires are now socially accepted and considered legal minorities in the United States. But shortly after Bill's arrival, some of the locals turn up dead, and, of course, Bill becomes the obvious suspect. Is Sookie being duped?

Dead Witch Walking, Kim Harrison, 2004

The first installment in the Rachel Morgan Series, this horror novel features title character Rachel Morgan, a shapely, feisty, leather-clad witch who shatters the broomstick-riding, pointy hat-wearing, hook-nosed stereotype. Rachel is an Inderlander, a class of otherworldly beings who are commonplace in this alternate reality. Rachel knows she's in for a fight when she quits her job as a bounty hunter, something few have lived to talk about, and the repercussions start almost immediately. To survive, she needs the help of her rather unusual friends.

The Descent, Jeff Long, 1988

All hell breaks loose in this page-turner about the physical presence of Satan and his minions right here on earth. A brain trust of scholars and theologians known as the "Beowulf Circle," theorize that the biblical "Satan" is actually one of a species called "Homo hadalis," an evil, primitive branch of the Homo sapiens family that lives inside the earth. Their hypothesis proves true when Ike Crocket, a ski guide leading an expedition in Tibet, discovers a cave that's really the portal to hell.

Guilty Pleasures, Laurell K. Hamilton, 1993

Hamilton's "Anita Blake: Vampire Hunter" series introduces an unusual and sensuous twist to the standard vampire fare. The title character, a licensed vampire executioner and zombie animator, lives in a world parallel to our own, where vampires, werewolves, shape-shifters, and other horror genre regulars are commonplace. In Guilty Pleasures, the first of Hamilton's 14 Vampire Hunter tales, Anita Blake investigates a string of vampire murders and encounters a variety of otherworldly characters who live right in her own city. If you enjoy a little detective fiction mixed in with your horror, Hamilton gives you plenty of both.

The Historian, Elizabeth Kostova, 2005

Oddly, no one has ever seen Vlad the Impaler and Dracula in the same place together. Could they be the same person? Elizabeth Kostova thinks so, in her vampire novel about a teenage girl who stumbles upon some old research documents of her father's that draw the parallel between these two notorious figures. The young heroine takes up the hunt where her father left off, mounting an international search for the truth. Is it possible Vlad the Impaler never died and still walks the earth today? Hidden clues, cryptic references, and subtle hints entwined in ancient traditions take the reader on an intriguing journey of discovery.

An Expert Speaks

"Is it a memoir? A travelogue about Eastern Europe? A coming-of-age story? A vampire yarn? Or a contemplation on the transference of knowledge? Who cares? A story couched in dreamy, sepia-tinted prose, Elizabeth Kostkova's *The Historian* is a seven course meal for the intellect and senses."

—Connie Brockway, author

The Keep, F. Paul Wilson, 1982

Inside a garrison high in the Romanian Alps, something sinister is afoot that's systematically killing off the Nazis stationed there. One by one, the victims' gruesome corpses are left on display for the others to find in the morning. Alarmed and horrified, the commander summons the best minds in the SS to hunt down and exterminate the culprit. But when they discover that the enemy is a powerful, illusive, evil force that they can't subdue, they must call upon an unlikely ally for help, a Jewish folklore expert. At the same time, another stakeholder (pun intended) is prompted through his nightmares to travel to the garrison and fulfill his destiny.

Kitty and the Midnight Hour, Carrie Vaughn, 2005

Nighttime Denver radio personality Kitty Norville has a secret. She's a werewolf. Her listeners don't know this until she confesses on the air one night during her popular talk show, "The Midnight Hour." A local vampire family is seeking to put a stop to Kitty's highly successful show, and they hire an assassin to end Kitty's life as well. Meanwhile, the local police are interested in her unusual canine tracking abilities and seek her help in identifying a serial killer whose crimes have werewolf similarities.

Meg, Steve Alten, 1997

Paleontology professor Jonas Taylor discovers that a ferocious sea creature, Carcharodon Megalodon, which was believed to be extinct since the Ice Age, has only been lying low deep in the thermal warmth of the Marianas Trench off the California coast. This gigantic predecessor of the great white shark is alive and well and manages to make a return trip to the surface where she finds a whole new world of warm-blooded, tasty delights. She's eating for four these days and soon delivers three baby "Megs," which ensure the continuation of the species into Alten's *Meg* sequels.

Minion, L. A. Banks, 2004

Minion, the first of Banks's six tales in the "Vampire Huntress Legend" series, introduces a hip-hop diva named Damali Richards, who moonlights as a vampire huntress. Banks ramps up the vampire action in this one, leaving the victims with more than a couple of tidy puncture wounds—they're shredded beyond recognition. The vampire behind it all is bigger and more powerful than Damali and her Guardian Team have ever encountered, and with Damali next on the hit list, time is running out.

> **The Rest of the Story**
>
> L. A. Banks's "Vampire Huntress Legend" series is the first vampire series developed by a female African American author.

Nazareth Hill, Ramsey Campbell, 1997

Could you live in a skull-like building where insane people were once mercilessly killed? Neither could we, but that's exactly what Oswald and Amy Priestly do in this 1998 International Horror Guild winner. Centuries ago, Nazareth Hill was an insane asylum where mental patients were abused and brutalized to death. Now it's the site of Nazareth House, an apartment building recently reconstructed from a burned-out office complex. The unsuspecting tenants, including Oswald and his daughter Amy, begin experiencing strange things around their building that quickly escalate to terrifying proportions. Leave your security deposit behind and get out while you can!

Nightshade, John Saul, 2000

You can pick your friends, but you can't pick your dead relatives. Fifteen-year-old Matthew Moore is a great kid, with loving parents, a beautiful home, and a budding romance with the prettiest girl at school. But everything changes when Matthew's grandmother, Emily, moves in with the family. The effects of her Alzheimer's disease, her unreasonable demands, and her wickedly sharp tongue become unwelcome burdens. When she insists that the family recreate her dead daughter Cynthia's room in their home, strange things begin to happen. Matthew starts having terrifying nightmares and notices the lingering odor of Cynthia's perfume in the house. Emily's toxic personality drives the family apart, and amiable Matthew becomes a tortured adolescent with a bad attitude. When his stepfather turns up dead, all clues point to Matthew, and the mysterious deaths that follow are laid on his doorstep, too.

Practical Demonkeeping, Christopher Moore, 1993

Think of the worst road trip you've ever been on; then add a large, green, people-eating monster who smokes. Moore explores the funny side of horror using his fine sense of comedic timing and off-beat, absurd humor to tell the story of 20-year-old Travis O'Hearn and his monster, Catch. Travis has been forever young, stuck at age 20 since he acquired Catch, 70 years before. But being perpetually 20 has gotten old. Plus, the constant battle to keep Catch out of trouble has Travis searching for an incantation that will rid him of his traveling partner from hell. So when Travis and Catch arrive in the tourist town of Pine Grove, California, they encounter a boatload of wacky (and tasty) townsfolk. It's a yummy read.

> **An Expert Speaks**
>
> "A scoop of horror, a scoop of science fiction, and a scoop of fantasy, topped with a sprinkling of drama and a dollop of romance, all covered with a generous serving of humor—Christopher Moore satisfies all my literary cravings!"
>
> —Kris Vanderlee, librarian

A Prayer for the Dying, Stewart O'Nan, 2000

What are the limits of human endurance when a good, decent man faces progressively evil, unrelenting tragedy? A mysterious, post–Civil War disease, for which there is no cure, hits the tiny burg of Friendship, Wisconsin. The town's multitasking sheriff-undertaker-minister, Jacob Hansen, has his hands full as the casualty count of dead and dying, which includes his own wife and child, continues to rise. As a wildfire approaches and a group of Spiritualists with a charismatic leader camp at the edge of town, Jacob gets ever closer to his breaking point.

The Relic, Douglas Preston and Lincoln Child, 2005

Something unnatural is happening at the natural history museum. Just before the gala opening of an exciting new exhibit, "Superstition," featuring an Amazonian god named Mbwun, patrons of this New York museum begin turning up dead in gruesome fashion. Considering the trail of death and destruction this stone idol left in its path on its journey to New York, some speculate that Mbwun himself is committing these savage killings. When a team of scientists investigates the Mbwun theory, they discover something even more ancient and sinister is happening—something that will have global implications if it escapes.

The Ruins, Scott Smith, 2006

In what is probably the worst lapse in judgment since the Skipper handed Gilligan the dynamite, four friends vacationing in Cancun, Mexico, abandon logic and agree to venture into the jungle with a German tourist, who asks them to help find his brother, Heinrich. The group sets out in search of a Mayan archaeological site where they expect to find Heinrich, but it isn't long before they become lost in the dense undergrowth. Their lighthearted day trip takes an ominous turn as an eerie presence begins to prey on the group, with deadly consequences. Welcome to the jungle, baby.

Silence of the Lambs, Thomas Harris, 1989

Hannibal Lecter, with his appetite for evil and human flesh, earned this author the Bram Stoker Horror Award in 1989. *Silence of the Lambs* is the dark account of a manhunt to capture a psychopathic serial killer with a fetish for human skin. FBI Agent Clarice Starling enlists the help of the criminally insane "Hannibal the Cannibal" Lecter, probing his twisted mind to better understand the psyche of the serial killer she pursues. But the cunning Dr. Lecter expects something in return. *Quid pro quo.*

The Store, Bentley Little, 1996

The Store, a dark psychological thriller, flirts with the reality of "big box" merchandisers. A retail giant opens a mega-discount store in the fly-speck town of Juniper, Arizona. Low prices and great selection lure customers from all around, as smaller local competitors are driven out of business. The town's politicians become pawns of the retailer, and The Store takes on a life of its own, keeping a stranglehold on the close-knit community while lowering its business practices and ethical standards on a captive clientele. Bill Davis's two teenage daughters take jobs there, ignoring their father's advice, and become caught up in a corporate culture of blind loyalty and ruthless cruelty directed at those who disagree. *Caveat emptor.*

Swan Song, Robert R. McCammon, 1987

It's Armageddon in America, following a nuclear war that lays the country to waste. A sinister force known as the "Man with the Scarlet Eye" is at work, preying on the dark side of humanity in a world where mutants and anarchy rule. The last vestige of purity lies in a child named Swan, who is in danger of being destroyed by Scarlet Eye's minions unless her protectors can prevail against a legion of evil.

The 37th Mandala, Marc Laidlaw, 1996

Frustrated, mediocre freelance writer Derek Crowe finds an opportunity to make a quick buck off of a gullible New Age spiritualist book market by reworking the cosmic occult figures he found in an ancient manuscript into benevolent spirits of joy. The unwitting cult he creates calls upon these spirits for peace and guidance and unleashes instead a vortex of unspeakable evil as the specters emerge in their true forms.

Those Who Hunt the Night, Barbara Hambly, 1988

Someone in Edwardian London is getting away with murder. All over the city, sleeping vampires are being systematically cremated when their coffin lids are torn open, exposing them to the lethal rays of the sun. It's the perfect crime, because instantaneous death prevents any of the "victims" from naming the culprit and no vampire can withstand daylight to retaliate. Can a solution be found? London's most venerable vampire, Simon Ysidro, coerces a former spy, James Asher, to conduct an investigation, threatening to harm Asher's wife if he refuses. But Asher can't help wondering whether, once the exterminator is destroyed, he and his wife will be the next victims because they know too much. This elegant, chilling paradox is a potent mixture of historical fiction and horror.

Threshold, Caitlin R. Kiernan, 2001

Young paleontologist Chance Matthews makes a frightening discovery that sets off a series of terrible tragedies in her life. She finds an unlikely ally in an odd albino girl who claims to be a monster hunter—and ultimately proves it. Eerie things happen in such vivid, spine-tingling detail that the story brings out the nail-biter in all of us.

The Throat, Peter Straub, 1994

Serial killing becomes a family affair in this Bram Stoker Horror Award winner, the third novel in Straub's "Blue Rose Trilogy" (*Koko*, 1988; *Mystery*, 1989). The town of Millhaven is on edge following a brutal murder, *à la* Jeffrey Dahmer, that bears striking similarities to slayings committed in the 1940s by the "Blue Rose" killer. Straub's trilogy regulars, Tim Underhill (*Koko*), and Tom Pasmore (*Mystery*), now unite in Millhaven to investigate this latest murder and discover the apple didn't fall far from the tree.

Watchers, Dean Koontz, 1987

Dog lovers will appreciate this unusual horror story about a dog that escapes from a lab where weird animal experimentation has given it the ability to communicate with humans. A boy who befriends the stray takes on more than he realizes as both the authorities and "The Other," a fierce killer mutant that also escaped from the lab, are closing in on them.

And the Award Goes to...

Named after the creator of Dracula, the Bram Stoker Awards have been given out each year since 1987 by the Horror Writers Association. These are awarded in a number of categories, including novels, short stories, and nonfiction.

Chapter 12

Inspirational Fiction: Have a Little Faith in Your Books

In This Chapter

- ◆ Classics: readings for the righteous
- ◆ More great reads: surely, goodness, and mercy

"Inspirational fiction," a term that is often used interchangeably with "Christian fiction" and "faith fiction," encompasses books written in virtually all the genres, including historical novels, mystery and suspense books, and even romance. The one thing all inspirational fiction has in common is a strong statement of faith. The best authors in this field, like those listed in this chapter, manage to get their messages across while still keeping you entertained with a great story.

Classics

Christy, Catherine Marshall, 1967

In 1912, 19-year-old Christy Huddleston leaves her comfortable home to teach at a mission school in Cutter Gap, a poor hamlet in the Smoky Mountains. Her faith is challenged by the ways of the people and the love of two men. Based on the life of the author's mother, this story, which was also a popular television series and movie, will grab you from page one.

Joshua, Joseph Girzone, 1983

Joshua, a humble carpenter, moves into a small cabin just outside of town. He's a gifted woodworker—the statue of Moses Joshua carved for the local synagogue is an extraordinary work. But there's an air of mystery about him, especially after he heals a sick child. The church leaders are concerned. Who is this man? It's a marvelously written "What if?"

Love Comes Softly, Janet Oke, 1987

Marty, a young pioneer widow, is pregnant and has no train fare to return to her family. Clark Davis needs someone to care for his daughter, so he suggests a marriage in name only until spring, at which time he'll pay Marty's way home. A marriage of convenience evolves into a true love match in this well-written, classic inspirational romance.

An Expert Speaks

"Janette Oke's *Love Comes Softly* series is a joy to read. She brings to life people you would like to know—people living their daily lives with dignity, courage, and faith. She is a talented author who has the ability to write wonderfully interesting stories about people of faith without sacrificing the story line to demonstrate that faith."

—Suella Baird, librarian

This Present Darkness, Frank Peretti, 1988

In this spiritual warfare novel, there's a plot to take over the small town of Ashton and, eventually, the world. It's an all-out battle against the forces of evil, and the unlikely warriors are a newspaper reporter and a minister. This page-turner will capture—and hold—your interest.

More Great Reads

The Affectionate Adversary, Catherine Palmer, 2006

The old question of "Does he love me for my money?" is at the heart of this story about wealthy Sarah Carlyle and Charles Locke, who would give anything to make his tea-trading business a success. Can Sarah, who hates her fortune and believes the love of money is the root of all evil, ever find happiness with a man whose main goal in life is to get rich?

Almost Friends, Philip Gulley, 2006

Probably the most controversial of Gulley's highly popular "Harmony, Indiana" series, this is the story of Krista Riley, a minister who fills in for Pastor Sam Gardner, the regular preacher at the Quaker church, when Gardner's father falls ill. The Friends are quite taken with the spunky Krista ... until rumors begin to fly that she's a lesbian. This tale of acceptance gets the point across with Gulley's trademark gentle humor.

The Amen Sisters, Angela Benson, 2005

Wracked with guilt, minister Francine Amen has a nervous breakdown and has to be hospitalized after her friend Toni commits suicide. Francine had doubted Toni's claims that Bishop Payne had impregnated her. It takes a lot of faith and perseverance for Francine to get her life back on track, especially now that her sister's husband (Francine's old beau) is showing interest in Francine again. The story is a richly textured novel of redemption.

At Home in Medford, Jan Karon, 1994

The first book in the much-loved Medford series introduces the middle-aged Episcopalian rector, Father Tim; Emma Garrett, his feisty secretary; and Barnabas, the huge black dog who adopts Father Tim. There's lots of excitement in Medford—a 60-year-old mystery; a jewel thief; a boy who seems to be as much of a stray as Barnabas; and yes, even love for the bachelor priest. As warm and welcoming as an old friend, Karon's books aren't just for inspirational readers. Anyone who likes a gentle, emotionally nourishing read should add her books to their must-read list!

> **You Can Book on It!**
>
> If you enjoy the television series *Seventh Heaven* or like to read books about ministers, try Jan Karon's uplifting "Medford" series or Philip Gulley's "Harmony, Indiana" series about a Quaker preacher and his quirky congregation.

Autumn Dreams, Gayle Roper, 2003

Cassandra Merton, owner of a bed-and-breakfast in Seaside, New Jersey, cares for her aging parents as well as her teenaged niece and nephew. Single and 40, she's always devoted her life to others, never taking time for herself. Dan Harmon, who's just checked into the inn, is also in his 40s. A successful businessman, Dan has been searching for the reason for his existence since he witnessed the attack on the Twin Towers on 9/11. Will he find his destiny in Seaside? Love is not limited to the young in Roper's thoughtful romance novel, the first in the "Seaside Seasons" series.

Before I Wake, Dee Henderson, 2006

Justice, Illinois, is a quiet little town. At least it was before someone started murdering tourists sleeping in the upscale hotels. Sheriff Nathan Justice is worried about this crime spree—after all, his family founded the town. Former FBI agent Rae Gabriella has set up shop in Justice with her former boyfriend, Bruce Chapel, and Nathan isn't happy when she gets involved with his investigation. It's another one of Henderson's top-notch faith-based thrillers.

Beneath a Southern Sky, Deborah Raney, 2001

After missionary Daria Camfield learns that her husband, Nathan, was killed giving medical aid in Colombia, she takes comfort in the birth of her daughter and her faith in God. After a while, she falls in love again—this time with veterinarian Colson Hunter. But after Daria and Colson tie the knot, she receives word that Nathan is still alive. Which man will she choose?

Blessed Is the Busybody, Emilie Richards, 2005

Award-winning author Emilie Richards begins her "Ministry is Murder" mystery series with this charmingly entertaining novel. Aggie Sloane-Wilcox is the wife of the new pastor of the Consolidate Community Church in Emerald Springs, Ohio. She must contend with the Women's Society Board, whose members think that they should have control over every aspect of the parsonage—even the height of the shrubbery. However, during one of their "inspections" the women are shocked to find a naked female corpse on the parsonage porch. Things go from bad to worse when the evidence points to Aggie's husband as the killer. Richards is one of our favorites!

Boo, Rene Gutteridge, 2003

Reclusive horror novelist Wolfe Boone (known as "Boo") is the most famous citizen of the small town of Skary, Indiana, and fans of the novelist have helped transform the once-struggling town into a major tourist destination. So when Boo decides to retire, the residents of Skary try to figure out a way to get him back into the horror writing business. Don't miss the equally charming and warmly funny sequels, *Boo Hoo* and *Boo Hiss!*

Candle in the Darkness, Lynn Austin, 2002

Caroline Fletcher, the daughter of a rich Virginia slave-holding family, has always been taught that slavery is not only acceptable but also biblically ordained. But when Caroline realizes what an evil institution it is, she's forced to question the beliefs and practices of her parents. This is the story of a woman who's brave enough to seek the truth no matter what the cost.

Deadline, Randy Alcorn, 1994

After journalist Jake Woods is involved in a suspicious car accident that takes the life of his two closest friends, he begins his own investigation. But someone wants Jake dead, too, and the closer he gets to the answers, the closer he comes to his own demise.

Dearest Dorothy, Are We There Yet?,
Charlene Ann Baumbich, 2002

Dorothy Jean Wetstra, an 87-year-old former bandleader, enjoys her role as matriarch of the tiny town of Partonville, Illinois. Humor abounds as Dorothy, who has a direct connection to God, deals with a developer who wants to buy her farm. The characters are so familiar you'll think you know them!

Directed Verdict, Randy Singer, 2002

Charles and Sarah Reed are missionaries in Saudi Arabia when they are captured, tortured, and framed for cocaine possession and use. Charles dies, and when Sarah returns to the United States, their insurance company refuses to pay his death benefit because of his alleged cocaine addiction. Sarah has two children to support and desperately needs the insurance money, so she hires lawyer Brad Carson. Brad sues the government of Saudi Arabia and the leader of their religious police, but the Saudis aren't taking this unprecedented move lying down. This is one legal thriller you won't be able to put down!

The Englisher, Beverly Lewis, 2006

Annie Zook, an Amish preacher's daughter, is asked by her father to give up her art for six months. Annie's father is upset enough about her love of art, but little does he know she's fallen in love with an "Englisher" named Ben Martin. Does Annie love Ben enough to leave her church and forsake her heritage? Lewis is known for her wonderful stories featuring the Amish.

The Friendship Cake, Lynne Hinton, 2002

When the women of the small Hope Springs Community Church in North Carolina decide to put together a cookbook, each recipe has a story. Beatrice, a makeup artist for the local funeral home, comes up with the cookbook idea because she feels it will bring the women closer together. The group is a mixed bag of characters who deal with issues such as interracial relationships, homosexuality, and the death of youth as they share their stories and become friends.

The Great Divide, T. Davis Bunn, 2001

Before his two children were killed in a car accident, Marcus Glenwood was a hotshot corporate attorney. Too depressed to work after their death, he returns home to Rocky Mount, North Carolina, and begins restoring his grandparents' house. Marcus' renovation is interrupted when Gloria Hall's parents beg for his help. Gloria, a grad student looking into the slave labor situation in China, has been put in a Chinese prison. It turns out that the prisoners are used as free labor by an American sports gear company, and the corporation will kill to keep their dirty little secret. Think Grisham, but with a spiritual message.

Grounds to Believe, Shelley Bates, 2004

Police investigator Ross Malcolm's daughter has been taken by a cult, so when a local sect is accused of child endangerment, Ross goes after them. He turns to Julia McNeill, a cult recruit's aunt, for help. There's plenty of danger and suspense in this well-crafted novel as Ross and the cult go head-to-head.

Heavens to Betsy, Beth Pattillo, 2005

Some of Pastor Betsy Blessing's congregants help themselves to money from the collection box, while others set her up on dates … with ex-cons. To make matters worse, she finds herself falling for friend and fellow seminarian David Swenson. Pattillo has made a joyful noise with this hilarious, heartwarming story of a new minister who happens to be female. Don't miss the sequel, *Earth to Betsy!*

And the Award Goes to ...

The RITA award, Romance Writers of America's highest honor, is given in several categories, including Best Inspirational Romance, which Beth Pattillo's *Heavens to Betsy* won in 2006.

If I Had You, Deborah Bedford, 2004

Tess Crabtree is a wild, rebellious teen. But when she gets pregnant, she returns home to her mother, Nora, who sees the baby as a fresh start and thinks that this time she'll get it right. This emotion-filled tale is full of reconciliation and healing.

In His Arms, Robin Lee Hatcher, 2001

Book three of the "Coming to America" series, which gives stories about women who immigrate to the United States, features Mary Emeline Malone who's come from Ireland with her baby. In New York, Mary's boss tries to sexually assault her, so she defends herself. Sure that she's killed him and worried about the law, Mary accompanies a madam with a big heart to Whistle Creek, Idaho. Sheriff Carson Barclay is drawn to Mary, now a bookkeeper at the local saloon, but she seems to be going out of her way to avoid him. In this tale one window closes and another one opens.

Jerusalem Vigil, Bodie and Brock Thoene, 2000

In 1948 when the British withdraw from Jerusalem and the nation of Israel is founded, Moshe and Rachel Sachar are separated—maybe for a lifetime. In this first book of "The Zion Legacy" series, the characters and locations are richly drawn, and as more of the story unfolds, the adventure just gets better.

Just Above a Whisper, Lori Wick, 2005

It's 1839 in Tucker Mills, Massachusetts, and 23-year-old Reese Thackery is working as an indentured servant. When the person who holds her contract dies, the bank gets to decide what will happen to her. Conner Kingsley, the son of the bank's owner, terminates Reese's contract as a bond servant and offers her a job as his housekeeper. Love and a common faith bridge the divide between Reese and Conner in this romantic story of learning to trust again.

The Last Sin Eater, Francine Rivers, 1997

At her beloved grandmother's grave, ten-year-old Cadi Forbes sees the "sin eater," the man who allegedly has the ability to absolve the dead of their sins. Many of the residents of her small Smoky Mountain village believe in him. However, Cadi realizes that the sin eater can't really do what he claims and that too many people are gambling their souls on a fraud. The talented Rivers has penned a gripping tale of the mountain folk of the 1850s and the child who shows them the way to the truth.

Left Behind: A Novel of the Earth's Last Days,
Tim F. LaHaye and Jerry B. Jenkins, 1996

The Book of Revelation is the basis of this thrilling series about the Rapture and its effects on the world. This book begins the series, which has been a huge success in both the secular and religious markets.

The Rest of the Story

Timothy LaHaye, an influential fundamentalist preacher, founded San Diego Christian College in 1971. He came up with the idea for the "Left Behind" series while flying on a plane, wondering what would happen if the Rapture were to take place right then and there. LaHaye co-wrote the series with Jerry B. Jenkins.

The Light of Eidon, Karen Hancock, 2003

Abramm Kalladorne, fifth son of the king of Kiriath, spends eight years study-ing to be a monk but discovers that their religious leader is a charlatan. As he begins to look for the true path to Eidon's light, his brothers sell him (*à la* the biblical Joseph) into slavery in a faraway land. Eidon, a metaphor for Jesus, continues to be Abramm's quest. This is the first book of the "Legends of the Guardian-King" series.

Magdalene, Angela Elwell Hunt, 2006

This certainly isn't *The Da Vinci Code.* In fact, it's a response to it, especially the part of the novel/film that portrays Mary Magdalene as Christ's wife. Hunt's Mary is a former prostitute, yes, but she's also a strong woman who helps and sometimes counsels Jesus. This is a Mary Magdalene you won't forget.

Monday Morning Faith, Lori Copeland, 2006

Johanna Holland, a librarian, falls for Dr. Sam Littleton, a missionary. Unfortunately, Sam's been called to the jungles of New Guinea, and Johanna prefers places that have indoor plumbing. Will she help Sam with his mission or go back home to her books? This hilarious, G-rated chick lit novel takes readers along on Johanna's journey.

The Rest of the Story

In addition to writing for the inspirational market, several of these authors, including Lori Copeland, Emilie Richards, Angela Benson, Felicia Mason, and Robin Lee Hatcher, either were or are popular romance novelists.

Night Light, Terri Blackstock, 2006

In the grip of a global energy crisis, the modern world is plunged into an exis-tence with no electricity, automobiles, or running water. The Brannings face a quandary—should they share their resources and trust God to provide, or keep everything for themselves? The theft of all their food leads to an unexpected discovery and still more difficult decisions. This is Book 2 in the exciting "Restoration" series.

A Promise for Ellie, Lorraine Snelling, 2006

Ellie Wold was separated from her true love, Andrew Bjorklund, when her family moved from Blessing, North Dakota. Upon graduating, Ellie returns to Blessing and her true love. The troubles start even before their wedding, however, when the barn on their new farm burns to the ground. This first installment of the "Daughters of Blessing" series paints a vivid picture of the rural life of Norwegian immigrants at the turn of the century.

Rolling Thunder, Mark Mynheir, 2005

Florida Department of Law Enforcement Agent John Russell is assigned to find a missing boy. In the meantime, John's estranged father, hungry for John's forgiveness, is on his trail. In turns exciting and emotional, this is a story of childhood lost and childhood found.

Santa Fe Woman, Gilbert Morris, 2006

Jori Hayden has had a pretty good life for 22 years. But her fortune changes when her mother dies and her father loses his wealth when an economic depression hits the country. Now Jori's on a wagon train with her father, whose health has deteriorated; her Aunt Kate, an upstanding Christian; and Chad Rocklin, the former prisoner Jori hired to lead them. In this western, there's danger and adventure on the Santa Fe Trail as Jori's faith and courage are tested.

Sisterchicks on the Loose, Robin Jones Gunn, 2003

Penny, a free-spirited former hippie and motorcycle mama, has been best friends for 24 years with Sharon, a conventional mother of four. When Penny decides to go to Finland and find her only living relatives, she buys a ticket for Sharon, too. This amusing, sometimes poignant friendship story started the popular "Sisterchicks" series.

Sweet Devotion, Felicia Mason, 2006

Amber Montgomery leaves the big city and a bad marriage and moves to the small town of Wayside, Oregon, to start over. When Wayside's police chief, Paul Evans, accidentally arrests her, it makes for an awkward first meeting. Between working and trying to raise two orphans, Paul has his hands full. But then he and Amber are asked to be youth chaperones. Before they know it, they're both prisoners of love.

A Tender Touch, Lenora Worth, 2004

Police officer Clay Dempsey moves to Sunset Island after Samson, his much-loved K-9 partner, is seriously injured in the line of duty. Veterinarian Dr. Fredica Hayes seems to be the answer to Samson's problems ... and Clay's. Worth's book is a special treat for dog lovers.

Thorn in My Heart, Liz Curtis Higgs, 2003

The story of Jacob and Esau is given a neat twist when Higgs sets it in 1764 Scotland. Despite the change of venue, the deception is just as devastating in this very clever and entertaining retelling of a favorite Bible story.

Thr3e, Ted Dekker, 2004

Good and evil battle as Kevin Parson, a 28-year-old seminary student, suddenly finds himself fighting a nefarious enemy known as Slater. If Kevin doesn't answer Slater's riddles correctly or acquiesce to his demands (such as making a public confession of a secret sin), death is the punishment in this nail-bitingly suspenseful psychological Christian thriller.

The Whitney Chronicles, Judy Baer, 2004

This Christian version of *Bridget Jones's Diary* features Whitney Blake, who realizes that she isn't getting any younger and vows to lose weight and find Mr. Right. Whitney's perfect man should be handsome, successful, and Christian, but finding all those qualities in one person won't be easy! This wholesome chick lit has a dash of gentle humor.

The Yada Yada Prayer Group, Neta Jackson, 2003

A diverse group that includes Jamaican, Honduran, Anglo, African American, and South African friends pray their way through life's problems. It's a lively beginning to a popular series.

Chapter 13

Inspirational Nonfiction: Food for the Soul

In This Chapter

◆ Classics: wind for your wings

◆ More great reads: faiths of many fathers … and mothers

Most inspirational nonfiction books are written in an effort to enrich the reader's spiritual life. These personal accounts of journeys of faith, religious epiphanies, philosophical enlightenments, and searches for spiritual truths are not always tied to one particular religion or belief, and many of them cross the boundaries of doctrines, dogmas, and denominations. But all these writings have one common goal: a better you.

Classics

The Art of Happiness: A Handbook for Living, Dalai Lama with Howard C. Cutler, M.D. 1998

Tenzin Gyatso, His Holiness the Fourteenth Dalai Lama, winner of the Nobel Peace Prize, the Wallenberg Award, and the Albert Schweitzer Award, believes the true purpose of our lives is to seek happiness. He talks about recognizing the right to happiness and discusses the need for human warmth, compassion, and intimacy, as well as how to see things from another person's perspective. In this uplifting work, the Dalai Lama dissects suffering and tells us how to face and find meaning in it.

The Confessions of St. Augustine, Augustine of Hippo, 2001

A very understandable, contemporary translation by Rex Warner, this edition of St. Augustine's confessions has an introduction and afterword by Martin Emil Marty, an American Lutheran religious scholar and University of Chicago Divinity professor. From stealing fruit to lusting after a woman, Augustine (354–430 A.D.) methodically and honestly lists his sins. The spiritual truths he obtains after this arduous soul-cleansing resonate with such insights as "He loves each of us as if there were only one of us." The book gives an intimate look at a man at prayer.

The Courage to Be, Paul Tillich, 1952

Known as the "Apostle to the Intellectuals" and the "Theologian's Theologian," Paul Tillich taught in German universities until the Nazis stripped him of his academic titles. Fortunately, he left Germany to teach at New York's Union Theological Seminary and, a few years later, at Harvard. This book is based on a series of lectures Tillich gave at Yale that looked at religion "in the light of science and philosophy." And the point where the three connected, Tillich decided, was courage. This is a must-read classic.

Gandhi: An Autobiography: The Stories of My Experiments with Truth, Mohandas Karamchand Gandhi, et. al., 1993

Born to privilege, Mohandas Karamchand "Mahatma" Gandhi gave up his wealth, allied himself with the poor and social outcasts, and changed the world. He talks about his efforts to achieve purity and get closer to the divine truths: simple living, celibacy, "fruitarian" dietary practices, and a nonviolent life. Gandhi's ideas transcend one faith and become universal goals.

The Hiding Place, Corrie Ten Boom, 1971

What makes a woman stand in the middle of a concentration camp and pray that God will forgive the Nazi guards who have stripped off her clothing and are treating her and the other prisoners with brutality unmatched in the human experience? A riveting tale, this shows the strength of faith, courage, and forgiveness.

The Journey: How to Live by Faith in an Uncertain World, Billy Graham, 2006

Probably the most respected and influential evangelist in the last hundred years, 87-year-old Billy Graham outlines his journey of faith in four sections: getting started, gathering strength for the journey, facing challenges on the way, and staying the course. For Christians, this is a blueprint of sorts to help continue one's own journey day by day.

Man's Search for Meaning, Viktor E. Frankl, 1946

Psychiatrist Viktor E. Frankl tells the inside story of a German concentration camp from a prisoner's standpoint. During his years in this man-made hell, Frankl came to believe that what kept him and his fellow survivors alive was their search for meaning. Despite all the insanity and suffering going on around him in the camp, Frankl found inspiration and a reason to carry on in the smallest of victories. This is undoubtedly one of the most profound and power-ful works in this genre, a must-read about the resilience of the human spirit.

Mere Christianity, C. S. Lewis, 1943

During World War II, Lewis spoke on the radio to "explain and defend the belief that has been common to nearly all Christians at all times." This book brings together these talks. Ignoring denominational divisions, Lewis focused on the central tenets of Christianity in such a way that even agnostic intellec-tuals could see its logic and rationality.

The Miracle of Mindfulness, Thich Nhat Hanh, 1987

Thich Nhat Hanh, Zen Master, compassionate Vietnamese monk, and icon of the peace movement (he led the Buddhist delegation to the Paris Peace Talks), tells how to maintain a meditative mind at all times, no matter what you're doing, and live a peaceful life. Thich Nhat Hanh continues to work for world peace and, at age 79, led a peace walk in Los Angeles in 2005. This is one author who definitely practices what he preaches.

> **An Expert Speaks** _____
>
> "Thich Nhat Hanh is probably the most famous Zen Master of our age.... *The Miracle of Mindfulness* makes a perfect introduction to meditation, Buddhism, and the humble monk himself. There are no prerequisites for this book—only an open mind to the possibility of a saner, more peaceful approach to one's life and the world around us. Try it ... you won't be disappointed!"
>
> —Mark Floor, librarian

The Road Less Traveled: A New Psychology of Love, Traditional Values and Spiritual Growth, M. Scott Peck, 1978

With his opening line, "Life is difficult," this noted psychotherapist gets right to the heart of the matter in this best-selling guide to personal development and spiritual growth. He examines how the four key components of discipline, love, religion, and grace contribute to creating balance in relationships and in life. Peck writes that by taking responsibility for the choices we make, loving rightly, discerning truth from religion, and being sensitive to everyday miracles, we continually grow as loving, patient, well-adjusted people. This book is frank, highly readable, and wholly satisfying.

Self-Love: The New Affirmation, Robert Schuller, 1986

As a "positive believer," Schuller has penned what has become a landmark book. This work directly challenges John Calvin's "doctrine of the elect," offering an "I am worthy" theology in its place.

The Way of a Pilgrim: And the Pilgrim Continues His Way, Anonymous (R. M. French, translator), 1972

An anonymous nineteenth-century Russian peasant begins his tale with the following words: "By the grace of God I am a Christian man, by my actions, a great sinner, and by calling a homeless wanderer of the humblest birth who roams from place to place ..." On a quest to discover how to "pray without ceasing" the peasant discovers the "Jesus Prayer" ("Lord Jesus Christ, Son of God, Have Mercy on Me a Sinner"). This masterpiece is a memorable work of Orthodox spirituality.

This Is My God: The Jewish Way of Life, Herman Wouk, 1959

Wouk, the author of such best-selling novels as *The Caine Mutiny, The Winds of War,* and *War and Remembrance,* turns introspective and philosophical as he talks about his Jewish faith and relationship with God. This captivating book from a master storyteller will appeal to readers of all faiths.

An Expert Speaks

"The Way of a Pilgrim is a classic story of a man in search of inner peace and salvation. He finds this inner peace in the ancient Jesus Prayer, and also finds that through the prayer he has a new perspective on life. The pilgrim's spiritual struggle and lessons transcend time and speak to us all. Each time I have read this book, I have found it an inspiration as it pulls you along through the pilgrim's spiritual struggle into a place of genuine peace."

—David Rodriguez, librarian

When Bad Things Happen to Good People,
Rabbi Harold S. Kushner, 1981

When his son was born with progeria, a tragic condition that causes premature and rapid aging, Rabbi Kushner set out to discover why God allows terrible things to happen to people who have led moral, caring lives. Kushner's conclusion, written in a simple but eloquent style, has given comfort to people across the spectrum of religious beliefs.

Words to Love By, Mother Teresa, 2004

Mother Teresa, a humble religious leader who ministered to the "poorest of the poor" on the mean streets of India, impacted the world in a way that few others have. This book, based on a series of interviews she gave in 1981, will give readers who want to understand this truly amazing woman a better idea of her simple yet eloquent philosophy of life.

More Great Reads

The Anatomy of Hope: How People Prevail in the Face of Illness, Jerome Groopman, M.D., 2004

Dr. Groopman, professor at the Harvard Medical School and staff writer for the *New Yorker*, frames the concept of hope and the human spirit with his experiences with patients as well as references to religious scholars and works (Rabbi Yehoshua ben Prachia, Paul Tillich, etc.). He contrasts "false hope" with "true hope" and discusses a person's right to hope. Even his notes at the end of the book are interesting.

An Expert Speaks _____

"Jerome Groopman's *The Anatomy of Hope: How People Prevail in the Face of Illness*, talks about his experiences with his patients. Each patient taught him something different about disease. The ones with hope triumphed against all odds. Without hope, they gave up and died."

—Louise Stephens, librarian

Bad Girls of the Bible and What We Can Learn from Them, Liz Curtis Higgs, 1999

Higgs offers instruction in the righteous life from the Bible's "Bad News Belles." Potiphar's wife, Lot's wife, the woman at the well, Delilah, Sapphira, Rahab, Jezebel, Michal, and the sinful woman—their stories are told in an inspirational, sometimes humorous manner. Higgs has also included a study guide to help readers learn the lessons these strong-willed women teach.

Cure for the Common Life, Max Lucado, 2006

Everyone is unique, and everyone has his or her "sweet spot," as Lucado calls it. But he says that only 13 percent of all workers have found this spot, where they love their work and what they do has meaning for them. He uses S.T.O.R.Y., People Management Inc.'s acronym, to explain each individual's path to the "sweet spot"—strengths, topic, optimal conditions, relationships, and "Yes!" moments. Lucado, Senior Minister of the Oak Hills Church in San Antonio, Texas, says God has a "sweet spot" for all of us.

Driven by Eternity: Making Your Life Count Today and Forever, John Bevere, 2006

Fundamentalist Christian Bevere, founder and host of Messenger International, argues that each day of life needs to be lived with eternity in mind. He includes an allegory featuring Lord Jalyn, ruler of the Kingdom of Affabel, to illustrate his point.

Experiencing Father's Embrace: Finding Acceptance in the Arms of a Loving Father, Jack Frost and John G. Arnott, 2002

This is an ode to God as a father and his unconditional love for humankind. Frost and Arnott talk about this love as the key for healing past hurts and getting rid of pain that runs so deep it has become a part of you.

Experiencing God: Knowing and Doing His Will, Henry Blackaby, 1998

Blackaby's classic reveals "how to live the full adventure of knowing and doing the will of God." He includes the "seven realities of experiencing God." An interesting appendix covers the names, titles, and descriptions of God.

The Faith Club: A Muslim, a Christian, and a Jew—Three Women Search for Understanding, Ranya Idliby, Suzanne Oliver, and Priscilla Warner, 2006

After the terrorist attacks of September 11, 2001, Ranya Idliby, an American Muslim of Palestinian descent, decided to find mothers from the Christian and Jewish faiths to co-author a book for children on the similarities among the three religions. Suzanne Oliver, raised Catholic, is an Episcopalian. The Jewish representative on the project, Priscilla Warner, is a children's author. The three women began writing the book, but ironically, stereotypes and misconceptions from the group itself threatened the viability of the very volume that was supposed to eradicate them. In the end, honesty and good intentions won out, and *The Faith Club* became a reality. It's an absorbing read on interfaith cooperation.

The Father's Blessing, John Arnott, 1995

The pastor of the Toronto Airport Christian Fellowship talks about the renewal of spirituality and the biblical mandate for us to love each other. This story of the "Toronto Blessing," as it's come to be known, is filled with references to Bible verses as well as testimonies of those who have experienced the "Toronto Blessing."

If God Is Love: Rediscovering Grace in an Ungracious World, Philip Gulley and James Mulholland, 2005

These two preachers pose the question: If God is love, why are people so afraid? Examining the three sides of people (personal, social, and spiritual), the authors propose a world based on the concept that God loves everyone. By skipping the dogmas of organized religion and going back to the actual teachings of Christ, this work is considered controversial by some of those in mainstream Christianity.

It Was on Fire When I Lay Down on It, Robert Fulghum, 1988

Robert Fulghum has been a parish minister, folksinger, bartender, and philosopher, just to name a few of his life's experiences. With gentle wit, Fulghum, who wrote *All I Really Need to Know I Learned in Kindergarten*, makes poignant observations on life and the human condition. His homilies, strong messages told in a light vein and conversational style, are occasionally irreverent, almost always thought-provoking, but never disrespectful.

Mother Angelica's Answers, Not Promises: Simple Solutions to Life's Puzzling Problems, Mother Mary Angelica, 1987

Anyone who's watched Mother Angelica's television show knows that this no-nonsense nun isn't afraid to tell it like it is. With its firm basis in traditional Catholicism, this straightforward book offers uncomplicated answers.

Power, Freedom, and Grace: Living from the Source of Lasting Happiness, Deepak Chopra, 2006

Best-selling author Chopra offers his views on becoming one with the universe. Creating a mix of Vedanta, an ancient philosophy, and modern science, he tells how to discover and understand your "true nature," which leads to a state of pure consciousness.

The Purpose-Driven Life: What on Earth Am I Here For?, Rick Warren, 2002

Rick Warren, pastor of Saddleback Church in Lake Forest, California, wrote a popular book for ministers titled *The Purpose-Driven Church*. Using the same five "God-ordained" purposes—worship, community, discipleship, ministry, and evangelism—he extended his message to work with individual lives. This 40-chapter, 40-day program, a publishing phenomena, hit the major bestseller lists and stayed there.

Questions Christians Ask the Rabbi, Ronald H. Isaacs, 2006

Rabbi Ronald H. Isaacs, Ph.D., spiritual leader of Bridgewater, New Jersey's Temple Sholom for more than 30 years, has written more than 60 books on various aspects of Judaism. In this book he attempts to dispel some of the mysteries and misconceptions about his religion. Rabbi Isaacs has divided his book into two dozen subject categories that he addresses in a question-and-answer format. In addition to the obvious (Jewish holidays and customs, Jewish holy days, keeping kosher, the synagogue), there are discussions about Jesus, the Bible, the Dead Sea Scrolls, the lost tribes, and the ten plagues. This fascinating collection of insights and answers will appeal to anyone interested in the Jewish faith.

Reason for Hope: A Spiritual Journey, Jane Goodall and Phillip Berman, 1999

Jane Goodall, known for her work with the chimpanzees of Gombe, Africa, has seen many discouraging things during her life: mistreatment, abuse, and killing of animals; destruction of the environment; even man's inhumanity to man and attempts at genocide. But through all of this evil, she has also seen hope and courage and heroic acts. In this poignant work, Goodall discusses her own 65-year journey (which includes the London Blitz, the death of her husband, the threats to her chimpanzees, and her part of a hostage situation) and calls for a return to hope, even when things look darkest.

That's Funny, You Don't Look Buddhist: On Being a Faithful Jew and a Passionate Buddhist, Sylvia Boorstein, 1998

Practicing psychotherapist, observant Jew, and teacher of Buddhist Insight Meditation, Sylvia Boorstein shows how two different religions can be practiced. Known as "the kindly Jewish grandmother bodhisattva" in meditation circles, Boorstein is proof that Karma, Dharma, and Torah aren't mutually exclusive concepts. A warm and captivating read, it's filled with gentle humor.

Through Gates of Splendor, Elisabeth Elliot, 1995

Elliot tells the story of five missionaries who were murdered by the Auca Indians in the jungles of Ecuador. What makes this story particularly moving is the fact that one of those killed was her husband, Jim. She quotes from his journals and speaks of forgiveness for those who ended his life. The book is a powerful read.

Through the Narrow Gate: A Memoir of Spiritual Discovery, Karen Armstrong, 1981

In the 1960s, Armstrong spent seven years as a Catholic nun in a convent in Great Britain but gradually realized that the strict rules of the convent were not her true calling. Armstrong details her years as a nun in *Through the Narrow Gate*, a poignant and compelling story of her search for faith. She later studied literature at Oxford and recalls those years in *Beginning the World*. As she became an author and expert on world religions, Armstrong continued her personal journey of faith in *The Spiral Staircase: My Climb Out of Darkness*.

The Rest of the Story

Karen Armstrong's 1993 book *A History of God: The 4,000-Year Quest of Judaism, Christianity and Islam* explores the idea of one God from the perspective of the three major world religions.

The Way of the Shaman, Michael Harner, 1980

For readers interested in learning about the religious practices of non-Western cultures, Harner has created this anthology of spiritual writings and the colorful imagery of the deities, myths, rituals, and teachings of a variety of world religions. How do other faiths view death, the afterlife, and human divinity? How do their beliefs differ from yours? Also included are excerpts from religious texts and oral traditions of indigenous cultures around the globe.

> **The Rest of the Story** _____
>
> Shamanism is an ancient practice of using the abilities of mind and spirit to heal. The Foundation for Shamanic Studies, founded by Michael Harner in 1985, conducts over 200 Core Shamanic training courses each year in North America, Europe, and Latin America.

What We Ache for: Creativity and the Unfolding of Your Soul,
Oriah Mountain Dreamer, 2005

This is a heartfelt appeal for people to get in touch with their creative selves, which Dreamer believes is essential to the human condition. She links creativity, spirituality, and sexuality, discussing the interconnectedness of the three. Dreamer (*The Invitation*, *The Dance*, and *The Call*) offers readers contemplations and exercises for their spiritual journeys.

> **An Expert Speaks** _____
>
> "I highly recommend Oriah Mountain Dreamer's *What We Ache for: Creativity and the Unfolding of Your Soul.* This quick read jumps straight to the heart."
>
> —Tara Taylor Quinn, author

When God Is Silent: Choosing to Trust in Life's Trials, Charles Swindoll, 2005

Has life gotten you down? Evangelical minister, radio personality, and president of Dallas Theological Seminary Charles Swindoll says not to give up hope, but look to the example of Job. Using concepts introduced in his biography of Job, Swindoll explores seven things Job teaches us about ourselves as well as seven things Job teaches us about God. Swindoll's upbeat, encouraging book is meant to give support and hope to those who are in a crisis situation or low point in their lives.

Wherever You Go, There You Are: Mindfulness Meditation in Everyday Life, Jon Kabat-Zinn, 1994

In *Full Catastrophe Living: Using the Wisdom of Your Body and Mind to Face Stress, Pain, and Illness,* Jon Kabat-Zinn, Ph.D., the founder and director of the Stress Reduction Clinic at the University of Massachusetts Medical Center, showed how to use basic meditation techniques to reduce stress and facilitate healing. This book, on the other hand, is about meditation for no other reason than going into a state of "mindfulness," and "being" rather than "doing."

Kabat-Zinn offers a way to put your mind in the present, not the past or the future. He sees mindfulness, an ancient Buddhist practice, as a way to get away from the stresses of everyday life and to live a nonjudgmental existence. Kabat-Zinn has written with wit and a sense of humor.

The Wisdom of Islam: A Practical Guide to the Wisdom of Islamic Belief, Robert Frager, 2002

As a convert to the Sufi order of Islam, Frager wrote this book to expand the understanding of his adopted religion by non-Muslims. The importance of pilgrimage, the beauty of prayer, and the spiritual enlightenment coming from the Sufi ceremony of Remembrance of God are only some of the things he covers in this well-illustrated book.

Your Best Life Now: 7 Steps to Living at Your Full Potential, Joel Osteen, 2004

Joel Osteen, upbeat television evangelist and mega-church pastor, brings his message of empowerment in a book that urges readers to "break out of the ordinary and experience the full potential that God intends." Osteen's program is as much motivational as inspirational.

Your God Is Too Safe: Rediscovering the Wonder of a God You Can't Control, Mark Buchanan, 2001

Canadian minister Buchanan investigates the reasons for spiritual burnout and complacency, including his own. One of his theories is that Christians begin to feel God is too safe, cuddly, warm-and-fuzzy, and so on, and they stop trying. Among his tips for "breaking free" is observing fasts.

Chapter 14

Science, Medicine, Nature, and Animals: The Discovery Genre

In This Chapter

- ◆ Science: life on the Euclidian Plane
- ◆ Medicine: writer, heal thyself
- ◆ Nature: down to earth
- ◆ Animals: fine, feathered, finned, and furry

Perhaps more than any other genre, the sciences experience the greatest amount of change. Each new development, discovery, and invention sets off a ripple effect into every direction. Current theories and the newest technologies can be fleeting, while some books speak a truth so basic that they endure for years. Even if you've never considered reading books in these categories, we think you will find something of interest here. We hope to at least whet your appetite for these fascinating subjects.

Science

A Brief History of Time: From the Big Bang to Black Holes, Stephen Hawking, 1988

Hawking, widely regarded as the most profound theorist since Einstein, has a personality as regular as the guy next door. His wit and layman's presentation make this book an entertaining, fascinating read. Because Hawking wrote this book for the masses, it has enjoyed broad appeal; read by scientists and science buffs alike, well over 10 million copies have been sold worldwide.

Cosmos, Carl Sagan, 1980

As Sagan himself would have said, "billions and billions" of years of cosmic evolution are the subject of this immensely popular scientific favorite. Sagan covers a myriad of topics from the dawn of life to the death of the sun; from ancient astronomy to contemporary space exploration; from inside the human mind to the outermost reaches of space. His delivery is easy to follow, and his enthusiasm is positively infectious. Reading *Cosmos* will have you shopping for a telescope!

You Can Book on It!

In 1990 film director Robert Zemeckis made Sagan's 1985 book, *Contact*, about the search for extra-terrestrial intelligence (SETI), into a movie of the same name.

Heisenberg Probably Slept Here: The Lives, Times, and Ideas of the Great Physicists of the 20th Century, Richard P. Brennan, 1997

Was your physics textbook written in Klingon and used as a dorm room door-stop? Here's your chance to see what you missed. In this highly readable history of physics, Brennan depicts seven of the greatest scientific minds of our time, their lives and achievements. Even complex theories such as Heisenberg's Uncertainty Principle and the paradox of "Schrodinger's Cat" are explained in plain, everyday language.

Manhattan Project, Daniel Cohen, 1999

Cohen introduces the people and events that led up to the development and testing of the first atomic bomb. Written from an American perspective, this book examines outside influences as well, including covert attempts by German and Russian agents to acquire the technology and reactions to the Hiroshima and Nagasaki bombings. Selected photos and quotes give you a good feel for the mood and gravity of this volatile, world-altering time in history.

The Right Stuff, Tom Wolfe, 1979

Wolfe recaptures the glory days of America's early space exploration, from the 1940s experimentation with manned flight to Neil Armstrong's walk on the moon in 1969. The book focuses on the pilots of the Mercury Project, blending the drama and humor of the astronauts' training and personal lives with the tragedy and factual intensity of their missions. Read it to experience that era for the first time, or read it to live it all over again.

Rocket Boys: A Memoir, Homer H. Hickam Jr., 1998

You'll want to stand and cheer at this biographical account of NASA engineer Homer Hickam's journey into history. In the small West Virginia coalmining town of Coalwood, where Homer grew up, most boys only aspired to one day take their father's place down in the mines, despite the dangerous, backbreaking work and the probability of eventually developing lung disease. But Homer had other plans. His determination and unwavering pursuit to achieve his goal of launching a missile into outer space is nothing short of inspiring. Homer's quest to reach the stars appeals to the dreamer in all of us.

> **You Can Book on It!**
>
> *Rocket Boys: A Memoir* inspired the 1999 film *October Sky.*

Strange Universe, Bob Berman, 2003

If you're a nonscientist, this is the perfect science book for you. Berman has written his essays specifically for the unscientific among us, as he explores the fascinating and unusual things about the natural world that make it so remarkable. Every section is filled with astonishing facts and little-known tidbits about the universe and its explorers. This book will totally amaze and amuse you, and you may find you're more into science than you thought.

Stiff: The Curious Lives of Human Cadavers, Mary Roach, 2004

Before you sign that organ donor card, you might want to read this book to see what you're getting your former self into. This is a disturbingly hilarious review of the history of cadavers and their bizarre and practical uses over the centuries. From test subjects for the first guillotines to NASA space shuttle cargo, these unwitting volunteers have been on the cutting edge of some of the most significant advances in science and medicine. Roach's humor makes this book a thoroughly fun read.

Surely You're Joking, Mr. Feynman!: Adventures of a Curious Character, Richard Phillips Feynman, 1985

Who says scientists don't have a sense of humor? Nobel Prize–winning physicist and lecturer Richard Feynman is not what you would expect for a serious man of science. This book tells of his life and adventures, his charming yet quirky sense of humor, his fearless audacity, and much more.

The Rest of the Story

The charismatic Richard Phillips Feynman (1918–1988), winner of the Nobel Prize in Physics and one of the key players on the Manhattan project, popularized physics. He conceptualized quantum computing and developed the Feynman diagrams, which explained subatomic particles. He extended the theory of quantum electrodynamics, particle theory, and nanotechnology. The 1996 film *Infinity,* starring Matthew Broderick, chronicles Feynman's life.

Zero: The Biography of a Dangerous Idea, Charles Seife, 2000

It's not easy being zero. Born in Babylonia, growing up in the Middle East, it was slow to gain acceptance in Europe. In fact, the Europeans eventually used the zero to ward off heretics. Banned by the Greeks, worshipped by the Hindus, the grand nothingness of zero and its history is explored by Seife in this clever, entertaining book.

Medicine

And the Band Played On: Politics, People, and the AIDS Epidemic, Randy Shilts, 1987

Anyone who remembers the earliest national publicity about the AIDS virus can recall the media's nonchalant attitude. Who would have thought back then that it would become the greatest medical crisis of our century? Shilts's groundbreaking exposé reveals the political posturing and scientific egomania that prohibited meaningful research, enabling this virus to spread unchecked.

And the Waters Turned to Blood: The Ultimate Biological Threat, Rodney Barker, 1997

You may recall reading articles about a persistent "red tide" forming along the U.S. eastern seaboard. Barker tells what it is and what it means, and both are bad. The organism causing the concern, *Pfiesteria piscicida,* poses a serious environmental threat with potential health repercussions, as toxins produced by this algae invade our food chain. Barker also reveals how scientists studying the phenomenon have encountered political and corporate resistance as they attempt to unravel the cause and effect of this tiny invader.

The Demon in the Freezer, Richard Preston, 2002

This tale sounds like it belongs in science fiction, except it's frighteningly possible. Smallpox, one of the most deadly, feared diseases in all of history, may have been eradicated, but it's not gone. Two tightly guarded (we hope) supplies of the virus still exist, frozen—one in the United States and the other in Russia. Preston speculates what could happen if the virus somehow fell into the wrong hands and became weaponized. Come to think of it, this book belongs in our horror chapter.

Maneater and Other Stories of a Life in Infectious Diseases, Pamela Nagami, M.D., 2001

Ebola virus, flesh-eating bacteria, these diseases only exist in other countries, right? Wrong. This book describes actual cases of people here in America who became infected by the worst kinds of parasites, bacteria, and viruses. Plain old chicken pox contracted by an adult male resulted in a catastrophic skin infection. A simple lunch salad contained an organism that grew into a worm that years later penetrated the victim's brain. Dr. Nagami, a noted authority on infectious disease, shares her stories, educates readers, and describes what it's like to be a medical detective who must make life-and-death decisions with the worst possible circumstances.

My Mother's Keeper, Tara Elgin Holley and Joe Holley, 1997

Had things worked out differently, Dawn Elgin might have become a household name and a jazz diva. But her promising 1940s singing career was cut short when, at the age of 21, after giving birth to her daughter, Dawn began seeing a ghostly figure at her bedside. Diagnosed with acute paranoid schizophrenia, Dawn was institutionalized. Tara, her daughter, was raised by her great-great-aunt, who shielded her from the truth about her mother. Meanwhile, after years of institutions, Dawn was living on the street. This emotionally powerful book describes how Tara, at the age of 17, resolved to rescue her mother, care for her, and restore her dignity, as well as their bond of love.

Nobody, Nowhere: The Extraordinary Autobiography of an Autistic, Donna Williams, 1992

As the title reveals, the author of this amazing autobiography is autistic. She tells her story of a long, self-imposed isolation, of being mistaken as deaf and retarded, and of her constant, frustrating "war against the world." But at the age of 25, Williams finally experienced an "aha" moment when she learned the word "autism" and came to realize its relevance to her. From that point on, Williams began her journey into life. Autism is revealed from the rare perspective of the inside out in this enlightening and thoroughly inspiring read.

The Sociopath Next Door, Martha Stout, Ph.D., 2005

If you think your neighbor is nuts, you may be right. This book examines the type of people who appear to have no conscience, no sense of right or wrong, and no guilt, shame, or remorse. These people are sociopaths and make up 4 percent of the population. Dr. Stout, an instructor at Harvard Medical School, provides compelling insight into the characteristics of sociopaths, and you will likely recognize someone you know in her descriptions. The book contains examples and case studies from everyday life that help to bring the subject into focus.

Splendid Solution: Jonas Salk and the Conquest of Polio, Jeffrey Kluger, 2005

The name Jonas Salk became legendary in the early 1950s, when his namesake polio vaccine was first administered, saving untold thousands of lives since then. This book describes the frustrating uphill battle Salk fought against rival researchers and competing formulas while developing his urgently needed treatment. Inflated egos, medical politics, and warped priorities all collided during the creation of the polio vaccine at a time when every second mattered.

The Rest of the Story

> Franklin Roosevelt, the most widely recognized victim of polio, spon sored the National Foundation for Infantile Paralysis in 1938, known today as the March of Dimes.

Sybil, Flora Rhea Schreiber, 1973

Thanks to this best-seller and the 1976 movie that followed, the story of Sybil is probably the most universally recognized case of multiple personality disorder on record. The book chronicles Sybil's horrifically abusive childhood at the hands of her schizophrenic mother, the mysterious blackouts that signaled the onset of Sybil's disorder, and her groundbreaking therapy that uncovered 16 distinct personalities. The story is riveting, moving, and a tribute to the woman who survived it.

Whose Hands Are These?: A Gifted Healer's Miraculous True Story, Gene Egidio, 1997

Gene Egidio was blessed as a child with a remarkable gift—the ability to see the future and to heal with a simple touch. However, his family was frightened by his unusual abilities, and his pastor considered them evil, describing them as "Powers passed down by Satan." Young Egidio underwent exorcism. When that didn't work, he was subjected to electric shock therapy. It wasn't long before he learned that using his special gifts meant punishment and they were best forgotten. Years later, a chance happening brought his gift back to the surface, and Egidio had to decide for himself. Are his unusual abilities a curse, or are they a God-given gift?

Willow Weep for Me: A Black Woman's Journey Through Depression, Meri Nana-Ama Danquah, 1998

What's it like to suffer from depression? Meri Danquah will tell you it isn't easy, especially for a young, single, African American mother who had to endure cultural biases along with her illness. She reveals her experiences in no-nonsense fashion, from denial, to attempting to hide the unbearable sadness, to even questioning her own sanity. Danquah also tells of her courageous struggle to fight back, regain her life as a young mother, and ultimately, to survive. Inspiring reading it is!

Nature

Blood Diamonds: Tracing the Deadly Path of the World's Most Precious Stones, Greg Campbell, 2002

The price of that diamond sparkling in the jeweler's display case may be much higher than you realize. If it's a "blood diamond," one that was mined in a Sierra Leone war zone, it probably cost someone his life. This book describes the dark path of these coveted gemstones and the ruthless thugs who kill to control, smuggle, and sell them to the highest bidder. And that's just the beginning. These precious stones get even bloodier when the proceeds from their sale get used. It doesn't take a jeweler's loupe to spot the flaws in this deadly trade.

A Country Year: Living the Questions, Sue Hubbell, 1986

Hubbell recounts the quiet joys each different month brings as the seasons change on her 100-acre farm in the Ozarks. Weather, nature, her bees, and her animals are all explored in a wonderfully spare writing style that will enchant and charm you.

Krakatoa: The Day the World Exploded: August 27, 1883, Simon Winchester, 2003

Winchester gives you a front-row seat to witness the incredible, destructive power of the earth as it is unleashed on the Indonesian island of Krakatoa. The violent explosions that rocked the island, and the catastrophic aftermath, are brought into vivid perspective through narrative observations and eyewitness descriptions of ominous events preceding the disaster. From the dramatic accounts of human tragedy to the incredible, far-reaching global impacts, the breadth of this disaster will astound you.

The Origin of Humankind, Richard E. Leakey, 1994

William Jennings Bryant and Clarence Darrow would have a lively debate over this one. Leakey, the foremost paleoanthropologist of our time, examines human origins and our relationship to apes. He proposes that complex social behavior is more likely the primary influence behind human evolution, not tools and weapons as widely believed. In addition to physical and social development, Leakey explores the probable origins of higher thought, such as language, art, and self-awareness, in this provocative presentation of human evolution and prehistoric life.

Silent Spring, Rachel Carson, 1962

Carson launched an environmental movement more than 40 years ago with this then-radical, now-classic, book. She was a marine biologist who began her research on chemical pollution after receiving a letter that told of an alarming number of birds that had died after being exposed to the pesticide DDT. Carson set out to demonstrate that harmful agricultural pesticides and herbicides weren't just killing pests and birds but were poisoning our own food chain! This book changed the way the nation regarded chemicals and spurred legislation to control the use of them. Thanks to Carson, the only place you find "DDT" these days is in crossword puzzles.

Animal Stories

All Creatures Great and Small, James Herriot, 1972

When Yorkshire vet James Alfred Wight first wrote about his experiences as a country vet, he had no idea that it was the start of a writing career that would include 4 books at the top of the bestseller list, 10 children's books, a television series, 2 movies, and an Order of the British Empire decoration. *All Creatures Great and Small*, the best and most successful of his books, opens as Herriot begins his veterinary practice in Yorkshire, working with two other vets. The book is a series of vignettes about the animals he helped and their owners and musings about rural life at the dawn of a new era in veterinary medicine. A keen observer of small-town people and their many quirks, Herriot's love of animals and his profession is evident in each story. Other authors have written animal stories, but Herriot is the gold standard.

Amazing Gracie: A Dog's Tale, Dan Dye, 2000

It was love at first sight when Dye adopted Gracie, a half-blind and deaf albino Great Dane puppy. In addition to her obvious physical problems, Dye soon discovered Gracie had a delicate constitution and couldn't tolerate regular dog food. So he researched recipes and began to make Gracie's food himself, using all natural ingredients. From Gracie's organic, additive-free chow, Dye launched his world-famous Three Dog Bakery. The heartwarming story is wonderful— but keep the tissues handy when it's time to say goodbye to Gracie.

Born Free: A Lioness of Two Worlds, Joy Adamson, 1960

Joy Adamson and her husband George lived in Kenya, where George was a warden in Kenya's Game Department. In 1956, George was sent to track down a man-eating lion, but instead he and his hunting party startled a young lioness, who attacked. Adamson had to shoot the lioness, but he kept the smallest of her cubs, whom they named Elsa. *Born Free* is the story of that cub and how, when she was three years old, she was reintroduced into the wild, something that had never before been attempted. The fascinating story of Elsa and her assimilation into the wild is a loving portrait of an animal adopted by humans but still wild.

The Rest of the Story

Elsa and the Adamsons became even more famous after the release of the movie of *Born Free* in 1964. George Adamson served as an animal trainer for the film. But both Joy and George Adamson met untimely deaths. Joy was murdered in 1980 by a former employee, and George was shot by poachers in 1989.

The Cat Who Came for Christmas, Cleveland Amory, 1987

One cold Christmas Eve in a New York City alley, a beaten and starving cat found an unlikely home when rescued by Amory, an author, critic, animal activist, and self-proclaimed curmudgeon. Amory, who considered himself a "dog person," intended this to be a temporary arrangement, but through patience and understanding, he came to love Polar Bear the cat and learned the joy of sharing his life with the little critter. This book is full of tangents, like cat trivia and history and animal cruelty commentary (which some might find unpleasant to read). Amory and Polar Bear are buried side by side at Black Beauty Ranch in Texas, the animal refuge founded by Amory.

Cod: A Biography of the Fish That Changed the World,
Mark Kurlansky, 1997

Consider the humble cod, the little fish that could. Who would ever guess that the simple codfish could have such a profound impact on the history of humankind? The Vikings chased after it; the Pilgrims survived on it; wars have been fought over it; and entire industries are based on it. But there's trouble on the horizon. This centuries-old dietary mainstay is so loved that it's now approaching extinction. Kurlansky's book will give you a new respect and appreciation for this little staple of history.

The Craggy Hole in My Heart and the Cat Who Fixed It: Over the Edge and Back with My Dad, My Cat, and Me, Geneen Roth, 2004

We animal lovers know it's true—owning a pet can change your life. Roth, author of several books on eating and self-esteem, didn't want a pet because she didn't want to love something that was destined one day to die. But when a friend foists a kitten, Blanche, on Roth, she falls in love with it and opens her heart. In doing so, Roth begins to come to terms with loss, grieving, and saying goodbye. When she loses Blanche and when her father is diagnosed with cancer, Roth allows herself to feel the grief and release the pain. Any animal lover will appreciate this moving and emotionally satisfying book.

Crocodile Hunter: The Incredible Life and Adventures of Steve and Terri Erwin, Steve Erwin and Terri Erwin, 2001

This autobiographical work looks behind the television cameras at crocodile hunters Steve and Terri Irwin. Readers might expect this book to be merely a glossy companion to the Irwins' popular television show, but it's much more. In addition to providing interesting background information on the Irwins, it promotes an awareness of animal conservation and habitat preservation, particularly for animals considered dangerous. The book demonstrates their care and dedication to this cause. In their own words, "Our passion for wildlife is our elixir of life, and we'll die defending animals that others deem dangerous and threatening." The book has now become a poignant legacy to Steve Irwin, who in 2006 lost his life doing exactly that.

Dog Eat Dog: A Very Human Book About Dogs and Dog Shows,
Jane Stern and Michael Stern, 1998

If you ever watched the Westminster Dog Show and are still a bit bewildered when a poodle wins over the cutest little Chihuahua you've ever seen, then you will enjoy this insight into the world of dog shows. The Sterns make sure they get it right—they have expert help in the form of bull mastiff breeder and long-time dog show participant Mimi Einstein. Her knowledge of dog breeding and showing helps make this book an excellent read. The description of a retiring bull mastiff's proud moments parading around the show ring for the last time will put a lump in your throat.

A Dog Year: Twelve Months, Four Dogs, and Me,
Jon Katz, 1991

This book proves that "Katz" and dogs can peacefully coexist. (Sorry.) Jon Katz is accustomed to life with his two gentle Labs, Stanley and Julius, but when he decides to take in Devon, a neurotic, high-strung, emotionally abused Border collie, his life turns upside down. Stanley and Julius are bewildered by Devon, and Katz's patience is tested daily by the animal he affectionately calls "Helldog." The book chronicles how Devon becomes part of the Katz family and is soon joined by another Border collie puppy named Homer. Keep those tissues handy for when it's time to say goodbye to Stanley and Julius.

The Rest of the Story

Katz was a mystery writer and journalist before writing about dogs in 1991, with his book *A Dog Year*. He continues the story of his Border collies with *The Dogs of Bedlam Farm* and *A Good Dog*.

The Good Good Pig: The Extraordinary Life of Christopher Hogwood, Sy Montgomery, 2006

Montgomery, a writer and naturalist, rescues a sickly little piglet she names Christopher Hogwood (like the symphony conductor) and takes him home to live with her in New Hampshire, where he grows as close to her as any 750-pound family member possibly could. Montgomery writes about the sociable, lovable, intelligent porker, his brush with fame, and the lessons about life, and herself, she learns from him.

Gorillas in the Mist, Dian Fossey, 1983

This groundbreaking first-person account covers Dian Fossey's 18-year adventure studying endangered mountain gorillas in the African rain forest. From her remote research outpost in Rwanda, Fossey eased her way into the gorillas' habitat, gained their trust, and was able to move openly among them for years, witnessing their behavior close up. This unprecedented vantage point for scientific observation revealed a surprising structure to the lives, behaviors, and cultures of these remarkable, docile creatures. This unforgettable read brought the plight of the great apes to the world's attention. You'll never think of gorillas the same way again.

> **The Rest of the Story** _____
>
> Fossey was an outspoken activist against the poachers who hunted and killed the great apes for profit. Ironically, like her gorillas, Fossey's greatest threat came from humans. She was found murdered in her outpost in 1985.

I Have Heard You Calling in the Night, Thomas Healy, 2006

Healy was a minor novelist whose life in Glasgow was turning into a series of barroom brawls and drunken stupors. When Healy adopts a Doberman puppy he names Martin, the dog becomes more than a pet—it becomes a true companion and, eventually, a redeemer. This dark, gritty memoir is a revealing account of the power of an animal's love.

Marley and Me: Life and Love with the World's Worst Dog, John Grogan, 2005

When _Philadelphia Inquirer_ columnist John Grogan and his new wife choose Marley from a litter of yellow Labrador puppies, they think he'll grow to be a big, mellow, good-natured goofball like other Labs. But not Marley! He's a hyperactive master of mischief, an obedience school dropout, a destroyer of evil couches, and a faithful companion until his death at age 13. Laughter will turn to tears, and back to laughter, in this touching bestseller.

My Dog Skip, Willie Morris, 1996

In 1943, nine-year-old Morris gets Skip, a smooth-haired fox terrier who becomes Morris's constant companion. With down-home southern charm, Morris tells tales of his best friend, Skip, and their adventures. A diehard dog lover, Morris also penned _My Cat Spit McGee,_ a paean to the cat adopted by Morris and his wife, whom he refers to as "The Cat Woman."

My Fine Feathered Friend, William Grimes, 2002

New York Times restaurant critic Grimes can't believe his eyes the day a chicken suddenly appears in his backyard in Queens. Grimes is fascinated by "Chicken" (obviously a better restaurant critic than pet namer), and watches as it stakes its claim against the owner's cats, making Grimes's backyard its temporary home. Grimes's little book is chock full of tasty factoids on the lore and history of chickens, and you'll learn more about them than you'll ever need, but it's an entertaining read.

The Parrot Who Owns Me: The Story of a Relationship, Joanna Burger, 2002

Did you know parrots are the third most popular pets in the country, after dogs and cats? Parrot owners are a special group, who enjoy a longtime relationship with their pet parrots who can live up to 60 years. Burger, a professor at Rutgers, a renowned ornithologist, and the author of several academic books on bird behavior, adopted Tiko, a 35-year-old Red-Lored Amazon parrot. Burger uses her professional knowledge to do more than anthropomorphize her pet (Tiko's happy, Tiko's bored); she backs up statements with facts. Bird owners will love *The Parrot Who Owns Me*, and the rest of us can appreciate the tidbits of information and Burger's heartwarming relationship with Tiko.

Seabiscuit: An American Legend, Laura Hillenbrand, 2002

Seabiscuit was an unruly, runty little horse that no one could imagine racing against thoroughbred champions, much less winning. But win he did, becoming a symbol of hope for a country mired in the Great Depression. People likened their own struggles and aspirations to the heart and courage of this unlikely hero at a time when the nation needed it most. Hillenbrand brings all the characters in Seabiscuit's legendary tale to life, from owner Charles Howard, to trainer Tom Smith, and especially jockey Red Pollard. *Seabiscuit* will fire your imagination and touch your heart.

A Three Dog Night, Abigail Thomas, 2006

Five years ago, Abigail Thomas's husband was hit by a car, leaving him with a brain injury that destroyed his mind. During those hard times, Thomas received her emotional strength from her three dogs: Rosie, a dachshund-whippet mix; Carolina, a hound; and Harry, a beagle. Emotionally gripping, with moments of humor, this book is an affirmation for animal lovers and an eye-opener for those who aren't.

The Wild Parrots of Telegraph Hill: A Love Story ... with Wings, Mark Bittner, 2004

It's more than evident that animals can give us a sense of purpose and belonging. Mark Bittner found this to be true when he started observing and befriending the wild parrots of San Francisco. Bittner was homeless, a "dharma bum," eking by on odd jobs until he was hired as a caretaker to a mansion on a hill. He started watching the parrots that nested in the trees and befriended them, giving them names and learning each one's personality and quirks. His relationship with the parrots changed his life forever. And it changed even more thanks to a wildly successful documentary about Bittner and his parrots.

Chapter 15

Biographies, Memoirs, and Autobiographies: But Enough About Me ...

In This Chapter

◆ Biographies: real stories about real people

◆ Memoirs and autobiographies: that's my story, and I'm sticking to it

Everyone has a tale to tell. Whether you're a politician, an entertainer, a rebel, a teacher, or an ordinary everyday hero, you have a story. Maybe that's why we enjoy reading biographies, memoirs, and autobiographies so much. Not only are we introduced to new people and different cultures, but we also discover how very much alike all of us really are.

Biographies

A well-written biography breathes life into its often long-dead subject. The reader experiences the culture of the time as well as a glimpse into the very soul of the person the book's about. Although biographies are based on fact, conversations and other details come from the imagination of the writer. The better the storyteller, the more enjoyable the book. We've selected some terrific biographies that have both entertained and educated us.

Ava Gardner: "Love Is Nothing", Lee Server, 2006

Although Gardner was one of the great beauties of our time, she was overshadowed by other starlets (damn you, Marilyn!). Nonetheless, she deserves to be remembered, both for her fabulous life (let us just say, men, men, men) and for her considerable acting ability. With husbands Mickey Rooney, Artie Shaw, and Frank Sinatra, and lovers like Robert Mitchum, Clark Gable, and Burt Lancaster, it's a wonder that she had time to make any films!

Ball of Fire: The Tumultuous Life and Comic Art of Lucille Ball, Stefan Kanfer, 2003

A generation grew up adoring Lucy and her series of sitcoms, including *I Love Lucy* and *The Lucy Show*. As a comedienne, Lucille Ball is still without equal, and many comedic actresses today mention Lucy as their idol. Like most comics, Lucy had a rough life, including a tragic childhood and a failed marriage to Desi Arnaz. *Ball of Fire* is a gossipy treat.

Benjamin Franklin: An American Life, Walter Isaacson, 2003

Yes, Benjamin Franklin was a statesman, an inventor, and one of the Founding Fathers, but Isaacson reveals that he was also a fun guy who loved the ladies—and they loved him, too. Isaacson's lively, chronological approach to Franklin's life provides an excellent introduction to the man with the kite.

Galileo's Daughter: A Historical Memoir of Science, Faith, and Love, Dava Sobel, 1999

To write about science and still keep the reader's interest is not easy. However, Sobel's skillfully crafted story of Galileo, the father of physics, and his much-beloved illegitimate daughter Virginia is not only an introduction to the theories of this scientific genius but also a touching tale of faith and devotion. Using the never-before-published letters of his daughter (Galileo's letters didn't survive), Sobel brings seventeenth-century Italy to life.

The Rest of the Story

A former science reporter for *The New York Times*, Sobel also wrote the nonfiction book *Longitude: The True Story of a Lone Genius Who Solved the Greatest Scientific Problem of His Time*, a surprise best-seller about an eighteenth-century clockmaker determined to devise an accurate way for sailors to measure longitude.

Georgiana: Duchess of Devonshire, Amanda Foreman, 1999

We didn't include a biography of Princess Diana on this list, but this book is the next best thing. Georgiana was the reigning beauty of her era and the great, great, great, great-aunt of the People's Princess. Like Diana, Georgiana was beloved by the common people, and both women used their position to promote good works. Trendsetter, toast of society, and, ultimately, a tragic figure, Georgiana's story is enlightening, entertaining, and engrossing.

Jacqueline Bouvier Kennedy Onassis: A Life, Donald Spoto, 2000

Spoto knows how to tell a good story (he's written entertaining biographies of Elizabeth Taylor, Tennessee Williams, and Ingrid Bergman, among others), and with Jackie (a name she hated), he has lots of material to work with. Yet Spoto's well-researched biography of one of the twentieth century's most famous women is as elegant and refined as the former First Lady herself. Separating myth from fact, Spoto gives readers a complex, contradictory, and wonderfully human Jackie.

The Life of the Party, Christopher Ogden, 1994

There were many men in the life of former U.S. Ambassador to France Pamela Digby Churchill Hayward Harriman (well, just look at all of her names!), and this fun, tell-all biography shows how this naturalized citizen (and ex-wife of Winston Churchill's son, Randolph) used her beauty and wit to advance her own career ... and become a major fundraiser for the Democrats. *The Life of the Party* is filled with juicy details about the wealthy and powerful in the twentieth century. Think *People* magazine meets *Washington Week.*

Lincoln, David Herbert Donald, 1995

Two-time Pulitzer Prize winner and Civil War scholar Donald's biography of one of America's greatest presidents tells of an ambitious man who was not afraid of defeat. If something didn't work, Lincoln would try another approach. This was, perhaps, the key to Lincoln's political genius and his success at keeping the country together during the Civil War. While not the definitive biography of Lincoln (Carl Sandburg's 1951 multivolume classic is often given this designation, but who has time to read all of them?), Donald's book is still one of the best single-volume biographies of Lincoln.

Lindbergh: A Life, A. Scott Berg, 1999

Lindbergh seemed to have it all. He was a hero for his record-breaking plane flights and happily married to Anne Morrow. But then his life came crashing down. First, his infant son was kidnapped and murdered. Then he was vilified for his isolationist stance during World War II. Finally, he ended up hating the very technology that had brought him fame. Utilizing previously unviewed private letters and papers given to him by Anne Morrow, Berg's Pulitzer Prize–winning biography brings new depth to the life of this American legend.

Marilyn Monroe, Barbara Leaming, 1998

Are you tired of all that "Candle in the Wind" junk about Marilyn? Leaming's readable and edifying work offers what may be a more accurate portrait of the legendary beauty. Marilyn was not buffeted by the winds of fate; she was focused, ambitious, and determined to be a star. Leaming also has a plausible theory on Marilyn's suicide (and no, the Kennedys did not have her killed—come on, people!).

Mary, Queen of Scots, Antonia Fraser, 1969

Fraser has written a number of books about history's rich and powerful players, but we love her first book, a captivating look at the tragic Scottish queen, who loved not too wisely and not even too well. With loads of literary license, Fraser dramatically speculates about the life and motivations of the queen who fell for Mr. Wrong (or should that be Lord Wrong?), and was falsely accused of plotting an uprising, which forced her cousin, Elizabeth I, to order Mary's head cut off (which, we agree, is kind of drastic!). Here's another dysfunctional family in action.

My Lady Scandalous: The Amazing Life and Outrageous Times of Grace Dalrymple Elliot, Royal Courtesan,
Jo Manning, 2005

What if Jane Austen wrote *Pride and Prejudice*'s Elizabeth Bennett as a party girl? A notorious courtesan, Grace Dalrymple Elliot used her beauty and wit to survive and thrive in late eighteenth-century England and France. Filled with plenty of interesting details and lots of historic celebrities, this gossipy good read is like *Lifestyles of the Rich and Famous*, but in bonnets!

Nicholas and Alexandra, Robert K. Massie, 1967

In the classic biography of the last tsar and his doomed family, Massie chronicles the Russian Empire's last days before the Revolution. Massie's interest in the Romanov family began as he was researching his son's diagnosis of hemophilia, which Alexei, the tsar's son and heir had. Massie used the disease as the key to understanding the Romanov Dynasty's downfall, bringing a unique perspective to one of history's most tragic tales.

Obsessive Genius: The Inner World of Marie Curie,
Barbara Goldsmith, 2004

Although she won two Nobel prizes and her work in chemistry and physics changed the scientific world forever, Marie Curie still struggled with finding a balance between her home life and her career and constantly fought to earn the respect of the male-dominated scientific community. Goldsmith's remarkably readable biography looks at Curie's amazing achievements and all of the obstacles she had to overcome.

Profiles in Courage: Decisive Moments in the Lives of Celebrated Americans, John F. Kennedy, 1956

Kennedy was a new senator from Massachusetts when he wrote about eight politicians in history and the single act that exemplified each person's courage and integrity. John Quincy Adams and Daniel Webster are just two of the inspiring individuals that Kennedy includes in this book. *Profiles in Courage* won Kennedy the Pulitzer Prize in 1957 and brought him to public attention.

Roots, Alex Haley, 1976

Alex Haley's book, based on his own family history, made a huge splash when it was first published in 1976. Tracing his ancestry as far back as Africa in 1750, Haley uses one family to bring a time in history alive. Exhilarating and poignant, this is a masterpiece of storytelling, and even the excellent television miniseries didn't do the book justice.

Shakespeare: The Biography, Peter Ackroyd, 2005

A noted novelist and biographer, Ackroyd uses his own literary talents to give readers an insightful look at one of the world's most famous writers. An abundance of details about sixteenth-century politics, society, commerce, and theater all give depth and color to Shakespeare's story.

Son of the Morning Star: Custer and the Little Bighorn, Evan S. Connell, 1984

The Battle of Little Bighorn is one of the defining moments in the history of the American West. While many conflicting accounts of the battle exist, critics have judged Connell's version as the most accurate. With an elegant writing style, Connell distills a wealth of historical minutiae into an engrossing tale of not only the famous battle and its participants but also of the conflict between the two cultures.

Titan: the Life of John D. Rockefeller, Sr., Ron Chernow, 1998

Rockefeller was the world's first billionaire and a business mogul who ruthlessly crushed any rivals to his monopolistic Standard Oil Company. Yet in his later years of life, he gave away millions of his personal wealth. Chernow skillfully captures the complex nature of John D. Rockefeller Sr. in this lengthy yet entertaining narrative of the founder of the Rockefeller dynasty.

To the Scaffold: The Life of Marie Antoinette,
Carolly Erickson, 1991

Erickson has written an immensely readable biography of the tragic French queen. While some historians fault Erickson for occasionally veering into the realm of speculation (she even wrote a novel about Marie's secret diary in 2006), readers will appreciate her lively writing style. And, by the way, she never said that stupid thing about eating cake.

Truman, David McCullough, 1992

This spellbinding and surprisingly fast-paced biography covers the life of America's thirty-third president. From his early failed business ventures as a farmer and haberdasher, to his years as a soldier during World War I and later a Missouri state senator, through his term as FDR's vice president and, ultimately, to his service as president of the United States, McCullough vividly captures Truman's plain-speaking, no-nonsense character, which was just what the country needed (and could still use today!).

> **An Expert Speaks**
>
> "There is properly no history, only biography."
>
> —Ralph Waldo Emerson

Memoirs and Autobiographies

An autobiography is a book about a person's life, written by that person. A memoir is a person's recollections of his or her life or particular experiences. Memoirs often focus on one specific period of that person's life and his or her relationship with other people (usually famous) and/or historical events. Whether an autobiography or a memoir, these books are only as accurate as the writer's memories. (Who remembers what someone said 20 days ago, let alone 20 years ago?) We've selected a few of our favorite memoirs and autobiographies, featuring both the famous and the not-so-famous.

The Andy Warhol Diaries, Andy Warhol, 1989

Why do we like this book? Studio 54. Jerry Hall and Bianca Jagger. Liza Minnelli when she was cool. These gossipy tidbits and more fill this diary of an artist whose work defined a generation and chronicled an era of parties and excess. Warhol was an established artist when he had his assistant condense 20,000 pages of his diary into 900 pages of rambling yet revealing entries that give a tiny glimpse into the life of a legendary artist.

Angela's Ashes: A Memoir, Frank McCourt, 1996

McCourt, the oldest of Angela and Malachy's eight children, was born in Brooklyn in the 1920s, but his family emigrated back to Ireland four years later. There, the family grew up in extreme poverty during the 1930s and 1940s. Although realistically and relentlessly depressing, McCourt's compelling story forces you to read on.

Anne Frank: The Diary of a Young Girl, Anne Frank, 1967

On her thirteenth birthday, Anne Frank received a blank diary. In it, she wrote about her life during an extraordinary and harrowing time. For 25 months, Anne and her family hid from the Nazis in German-occupied Amsterdam. Through her diary, you learn that Anne is both a chronicler of her life under Nazi rule and a normal teenager with hopes and dreams. It's impossible to read this book and not be moved.

The Color of Water: A Black Man's Tribute to His White Mother, James McBride, 1996

Journalist McBride first published a piece about his mother, Ruth Jordan McBride, in the *Boston Globe* on Mother's Day in 1981. Readers loved the article so much that he was encouraged to write a book about her. A Jewish woman who married two different African American men, Jordan helped her first husband establish an all-Black Baptist church in their home, raised 12 children in low-income neighborhoods in Brooklyn and Queens, and saw to it that each of her children had a chance at a college education. The book is a touching tribute to an exceptional woman.

Don't Let's Go to the Dogs Tonight: An African Childhood, Alexandra Fuller, 2001

Fuller describes growing up in Africa during the Rhodesian civil wars of the 1970s. Her father and mother were white farmers in Zimbabwe (it was called Rhodesia then), and were quite confident in their superiority to black Africans. Constantly on the move (from Zimbabwe, to Zambia, to Malawi) as white supremacy was fading, Fuller experienced an amazing childhood. Her youthful memories of her racist parents and the triumphs and tragedies of her life are nonjudgmental and matter-of-fact.

Dreams from My Father: A Story of Race and Inheritance, Barack Obama, 1995

Obama was not famous when he published his memoir in 1995, but after he galvanized the country with his speech at the 2004 Democratic Convention, everyone wanted to read about his life. His parents, African father and white midwestern mom, divorced when he was quite young, and Obama was raised in a white household. Despite little contact with his father, who had returned to Africa, Obama wanted to know more about his African heritage. This articulate memoir depicts a charismatic individual.

The Glass Castle, Jeanette Wall, 2005

You think your parents are bad? Wall's parents thought that being homeless was an adventure, and having four children didn't change their opinion. Wall and her three siblings had to survive constant uprooting and an existence you wouldn't wish on a dog. Despite these challenges, Wall managed to succeed in life, but the real question is how she could still care about her parents when they obviously only cared about themselves.

I Know Why the Caged Bird Sings, Maya Angelou, 1969

Poet, playwright, actress, activist, professor, author, Pulitzer Prize nominee, dancer, composer, screenwriter, director, Grammy Award winner Maya Angelou is a multitalented wonder. In this, the first of a six-volume autobiography, Angelou tells the story of her childhood, being raised by her grandmother in Arkansas, visiting her mother in St. Louis, and moving to California. When she was seven years old, she was raped by her mother's boyfriend and stopped speaking for five years. Angelou endured tragedy and heartache throughout her life, and the story of her struggle still resonates with readers nearly 40 years later.

Julie and Julia 365 Days, 524 Recipes, 1 Tiny Apartment Kitchen: How One Girl Risked Her Marriage, Her Job, and Her Sanity to Master the Art of Living, Julie Powell, 2005

One day Julie Powell came home exhausted from her "soul-sucking" job as a secretary and the general monotony of her life. After cooking a wonderfully restorative bowl of potato soup, Powell decided that the perfect solution to her dull life would be to cook every dish in Julia Child's classic *Mastering the Art of French Cooking*, the source of the fabulous soup recipe. Thus, in 2004, Powell began her Julie/Julia project, and the end result is this delightfully acerbic culinary memoir in which Powell blends tales of her experiences trying to complete her project with equally amusing stories about her own life, marriage, family, and friends.

A Leap of Faith: Memoirs of an Unexpected Life, Queen Noor, 2003

Born in America in 1951, Lisa Najeeb Halaby eventually attended Princeton (she was one of the first women to graduate from that Ivy League school), but a chance meeting with King Hussein of Jordan in 1976 changed her future. After a two-year courtship, Halaby became the King's fourth wife, converted to Islam, changed her name to Noor Al Hussein (Light of Hussein), and moved to Jordan. In this gracefully written memoir, Noor details the story of her marriage, her husband's struggles to bring peace to the Middle East, and her own efforts to bring change in her new adopted country. The book is an affecting look at a uniquely courageous woman.

Madame Secretary: A Memoir, Madeleine Albright, 2003

For eight years in the 1990s as the Secretary of State, Madeleine Albright was the most powerful woman in Washington, D.C. The precocious daughter of a Czech diplomat, Albright could speak four languages by age 11. Her family had to flee from Czechoslovakia twice—first from the Nazis and then from the Communists. Albright experienced firsthand the American dream of immigrants coming to a new land to be free, and she never forgot that lesson. Always a diplomat, Albright's shrewd perspective as she describes her career and influence in major world affairs is even-handed and insightful.

Me: Stories of My Life, Katharine Hepburn, 1991

For 60 years, Hepburn kept her private life just that—private. Like Garbo, she shunned the press and publicity, but in 1991 she decided to tell, if not quite all, much more than we had ever known previously. In a charming, rambling style, Hepburn recounts her childhood, her legendary career, and that famous 27-year affair with Spencer Tracy. It's a winning portrait of a classy lady.

My American Journey, Colin L. Powell, 1995

Powell, whose parents were immigrants from Jamaica, grew up in a poor neighborhood in Harlem. He didn't excel at sports or in his studies, and only after he joined the Army did he find his true calling. As the National Security Advisor to Reagan, chairman of the Joint Chiefs of Staff, and Secretary of State under Bush, Powell's autobiography is straightforward and honest, much like the man himself.

My Life in France, Julia Child, 2006

Before she came to France with her brand-new husband in 1948, Julia Child knew nothing about French cooking. But after one superb meal, she was inspired to enroll in the celebrated Cordon Bleu Cooking Academy. There she met Simone Beck and Louisette Bertholle, and together they would write the legendary cookbook *Mastering the Art of French Cooking*. With warmth and wit, the always-practical Child relates the fascinating story of writing her first cookbook, her journey as a chef and culinary teacher, her love of French cuisine, and most of all, her enduring love for her husband.

> **The Rest of the Story** _____
>
> Julia Child a spy? Yes! Child met her future husband Paul Child during World War II when they were both stationed in Thailand working in the OSS (the precursor to the CIA).

Never Have Your Dog Stuffed: And Other Things I've Learned, Alan Alda, 2005

Any book that starts out, "My mother didn't try to stab my father until I was six," hooks us from the get-go! Add to that the fact that it's the wonderfully witty autobiography of beloved actor Alan Alda, and you get a book you won't want to miss. Born Alphonso D'Abruzza, Alda writes of his mentally ill mother, his dead, stuffed cocker spaniel, and his childhood spent in a burlesque theater. Fans will be interested in his social activism (particularly the E.R.A. and rights of women), and will be delighted to read the inside scoop on M*A*S*H, *The West Wing*, his movies, and Broadway shows. Alda tells his story with his trademark self-deprecating humor and warmth, which makes a most excellent read.

Personal History, Katherine Graham, 1997

Katharine Meyer Graham was born into a life of wealth and privilege. Though she had a background in journalism, when she inherited *The Washington Post*, her husband Philip Graham took over the family's newspaper. When he committed suicide at their country estate, Graham was left to pick up the pieces of their lives, and she became chairman and CEO of the Washington Post Media Empire. Replete with stories of the rich and powerful of the 1960s through the 1990s, Graham tells her story with keen insight and sharp wit.

A Pirate Looks at Fifty, Jimmy Buffett, 1998

Feel the island breeze and grab a cold one while Jimmy sings us a ballad about his life. Buffett, known for his good-natured songs about beaches, boats, and margaritas, looks back on his life and his remarkable career. Born in Mississippi, Buffett eventually landed in Key West. After putting out several moderately successful albums, he hit the big time in 1977 with "Margaritaville." Fruitcakes, Banana Wind, and Volcano—if you don't know what they are, you're no parrothead!

Reading Lolita in Tehran: A Memoir, Azar Nafisi, 2003

Sent from her home in Iran to England to complete her studies, Nafisi returned to Iran to discover that the country had changed. No longer given the freedom to teach the way she wished at the University of Tehran, Nafisi decided to hold illicit classes in her own home. Seven women joined her for discussions on some of the world's great literature, and in the process, they discovered more about each other and themselves. This combined memoir and reading guide gives insights into the oppression of the women of Tehran but is also a testament to the power of books.

The Road from Coorain, Jill Ker Conway, 1989

Conway, who would become the first female president of Smith College, tells the story of her early years growing up in the harsh Australian outback in the 1930s and her school years in Sydney. In evocative prose, Conway takes a literary approach to describing her life, from childhood to her eventual departure for Harvard, a story continued in *True North* (2005).

Saving Graces: Finding Solace and Strength from Friends and Strangers, Elizabeth Edwards, 2006

Elizabeth Edwards, wife of John Edwards, a former United States senator and John Kerry's 2004 running mate, has been through some devastating experiences—each one alone capable of breaking a person's heart and shredding her soul. The first was the death of her teenage son in a car accident. Then, while on the campaign trail, she found a cancerous lump in her breast. Told in a straightforward, candid style, Edwards's memoir shows how she was able to deal with life's tragedies through the support of the community. Full of hope and absent of self-pity, this brave woman's story will inspire you.

Seldom Disappointed: A Memoir, Tony Hillerman, 2001

Best-selling mystery author Hillerman recounts his own life story from growing up on an Oklahoma farm during the Great Depression to his stint in the Army during World War II to his years as a journalist and academician. And he did all of this before he wrote his first novel! Filled with interesting details about his writing process and penned with a quiet sense of humor, this biography is a treat for everyone, especially mystery readers.

Tender at the Bone: Growing Up at the Table, Ruth Reichl, 1998

Former *New York Times* restaurant critic and current editor of *Gourmet Magazine*, Reichl writes deliciously about her growing-up years, her marriage, and her first job as a food critic. Reichl's droll stories about her own attempts at learning how to cook and some of the comical disasters that resulted will endear her to struggling cooks everywhere.

The Tender Bar: A Memoir, J. R. Moehringer, 2005

You know that drunk who sits on the stool in the corner of your favorite bar and has a story for every occasion? Yale graduate, Harvard fellow, and Pulitzer Prize–winning journalist Moehringer learned about life from just such an assortment of those guys in the Publican, a local Long Island watering hole. His coming-of-age story is written with warmth and humor. Norm!

West with the Night, Beryl Markham, 1942

Beryl Markham had such an incredible life that she felt compelled to write her autobiography. Born in England in 1902, Markham grew up in East Africa. She became a racehorse trainer and a bush pilot who was the first woman to fly the Atlantic from east to west. Her autobiography is beautifully written, filled with so much more than "I was born" and "then I met ..." As Ernest Hemingway said, "a bloody good read."

Wild Swans: Three Daughters of China, Jung Chang, 1991

Chang's grandmother was a warlord's concubine; her mother married a Communist guerilla soldier; and she herself was sent to the country to be "re-educated" during the Cultural Revolution. In 1978, Chang left China for a new life in England, but she never forgot the stories and the struggles of the women in her family. This dramatic tale of three generations of Chinese women, whose lives mirrored the changes occurring in twentieth- century China, is like an Amy Tan novel come to life.

And the Award Goes to ...

Several books in this chapter won the Pulitzer Prize for Biography or Autobiography:

◆ *Profiles in Courage* by John F. Kennedy (1957)

◆ *Truman* by David McCullough (1993)

◆ *Angela's Ashes: A Memoir* by Frank McCourt (1997)

◆ *Personal History* by Katherine Graham (1998)

◆ *Lindbergh* by A. Scott Berg (1999)

16

History: Four Score and Lots of Years Ago

In This Chapter

- ◆ U.S.A.: let freedom ring
- ◆ World: events that rocked the globe

A good author can bring history alive, turning a dull bunch of dates and people long dead into an enthralling adventure that you don't want to end. These books will make you love history!

American History

From the original people to those who followed, the history of the United States is a fascinating one. These books will tell you more about the familiar events in this country's past and maybe even introduce you to some new ones.

1491: New Revelations of the Americas Before Columbus, Charles C. Mann, 2005

According to Mann's myth-shattering history, pre-Columbian America probably had more people and a more sophisticated system of agriculture than Europe at the same time. Drawing on decades' worth of archaeological research, Mann explores the famous Native American cultures—such as the Mayans, Aztecs, and Incans, showing just how advanced these nations were.

An Expert Speaks

"I highly recommend *1491: New Revelations of the Americas Before Columbus.* Starting from the interesting premise that 'everything we know is wrong,' this eminently readable book discusses new archaeological and historical findings that challenge the conventional wisdom about the pre-Columbian Americas."

—Wesley Munsil, Ph.D., writer

1776, David McCullough, 2005

Focusing on the major players of the American Revolution—like General George Washington and King George III—McCullough, a two-time Pulitzer Prize winner, offers a compelling look at the year in which the tide shifted in favor of the determined Americans. No matter what subject McCullough tackles—the Panama Canal, the Brooklyn Bridge, or John Adams—he has a way of turning a potentially dull topic into an exciting story.

Bound for Canaan: The Underground Railroad and the War for the Soul of America, Fergus Bordewich, 2005

No trains ran on this railroad, but almost 100,000 people used it to escape from the tyranny of slavery. In the 1840s, a diverse group of individuals began to help slaves escape to the North and, eventually, Canada and freedom. In this thoroughly researched and engaging book, Bordewich introduces readers to an interesting variety of characters, from the famous to the unknown, each of whom played an essential role in keeping this train running.

The Civil War, Shelby Foote, 1958–1974

Foote's epic three-volume account offers a detailed description of the complicated conflict that ripped the country apart. Not bogged down by an overabundance of dates and figures (a feature that some historians have criticized), Foote emphasizes the military side of the conflict, but with a Southern bias (for which he has also been criticized). Foote's appearance in Ken Burns's PBS series on the Civil War has revived an interest in his work.

Manhunt: The 12-Day Chase for Lincoln's Killer,
James L. Swanson, 2006

John Wilkes Booth, a famous actor with matinee idol looks (think Johnny Depp in Civil War–era attire) and Confederate sympathies, assassinated

President Lincoln on April 14, 1865, and changed the country and the world forever. After shooting Lincoln at Ford's Theater, Booth took flight, which led to a 12-day manhunt that ended with his death in Virginia. In a cinematic style, Swanson describes the event in detail, setting it against the backdrop of a country left without a leader.

Mayflower: A Story of Courage, Community, and War, Nathaniel Philbrick, 2006

Forget everything you know about the Pilgrims. Philbrick shakes up the traditional American myth of a pious, meek people, to reveal the real individuals (the good, the bad, and the ugly) involved in the founding of Plymouth Colony. In this National Book Award–winning history, Philbrick narrates the Pilgrims' dramatic journey from England to America, detailing all the blood, sweat, and tears that went into creating a permanent home in the wilderness.

Midnight in the Garden of Good and Evil, John Berendt, 1994

What is it about the South? Is it the steamy weather or the jazz that produces these eccentric characters who do the most outrageous things? In 1981, wealthy antiques dealer Jim Williams shot his lover in Savannah, Georgia. In stylish and witty prose, Berendt describes how he insinuates himself into Savannah society and becomes part of the social scene as he chronicles the murder, and along the way introduces you to the unforgettable denizens of this southern town. Mint Julep, anyone?

No Ordinary Time: Franklin and Eleanor Roosevelt: The Home Front in World War II, Doris Kearns Goodwin, 1994

Goodwin has given us a superb, truly fascinating look at the public and private lives of FDR and his wife, First Lady Eleanor, during the 1930s and 1940s. Filled with rich details (yet never boring!), this Pulitzer Prize–winning book captures both the unique partnership that was the Roosevelts' marriage and the big stakes for which they and the free world were fighting. Goodwin is the author of a number of other excellent popular histories, including her recent *Team of Rivals,* the story of Abraham Lincoln and his cabinet.

The Perfect Storm: A True Story of Men Against the Sea, Sebastian Junger, 1997

The *Andrea Gale* was a fishing boat working out of Gloucester, Massachusetts. In October 1991, on its way home from Canada with a crew of six and a full load of swordfish, the boat ran into the "perfect storm." This storm was actually a combination of three different things: a hurricane blowing up from Bermuda, a cold front coming down from Canada, and a dangerous storm brewing over the Great Lakes, and it sank the *Andrea Gale* and everyone on board. This thrilling blend of science, weather, fishing, courage, and danger will keep you spellbound.

The River of Doubt: Theodore Roosevelt's Darkest Journey, Candice Millard, 2005

Most presidential hopefuls, after losing an election, simply return to their private-sector lives and begin writing their memoirs. Teddy Roosevelt had loftier goals and, after his defeat in the presidential election of 1912, Roosevelt, his son Kermit, and Candido Mariano da Silva Rondon, Brazil's most famous explorer, set out to chart the "River of Doubt," an unexplored tributary of the Amazon River. From whitewater rapids, to angry natives, to deadly diseases, to hungry piranhas, the journey would prove to be one of the most dangerous Roosevelt ever took. The account of it is an enthralling adventure tale!

Shadow Divers: The True Adventures of Two Americans Who Risked Everything to Solve One of the Last Mysteries of World War II, Robert Kurson, 2004

In the fall of 1991, two amateur scuba divers, Richie Kohler and John Chatterton, discover a ruined German U-boat at the bottom of the Atlantic 60 miles off the coast of New Jersey. For seven years, they searched history books, archives, and the wreck itself for the identity of the U-boat, enduring physical hardships and losing three divers to the sea. This rousing tale reads more like fiction but is actually fact.

Ship of Gold in the Deep Blue Sea, Gary Kinder, 1998

When the steamship *Central America* sank off the South Carolina coast in 1857, more than $2 million (more than $1 billion in today's figures) in gold was lost. Kinder takes the story of the *Central America* from its departure from San Francisco and the California gold fields to its watery grave. He then picks up the story of rogue inventor Tommy Thompson, who spent more than a decade searching for the shipwreck before eventually finding it and salvaging the treasure in 1989. This story is pure gold.

Six Frigates: The Epic History of the Founding of the U.S. Navy, Ian W. Toll, 2006

Fans of Patrick O'Brien and C. S. Forester will love this real-life account of the founding of the U.S. Navy. In 1794, the U.S. Congress approved the funds to build six frigates, including the USS *Constitution*, to fight the pesky pirates of the Barbary Coast who had been raiding U.S. merchant ships. The fledgling fleet proved their mettle through the War of 1812 and the permanent establishment of America's naval power. Pirates, sailors, and ships with big guns—could you ask for more?

A Stillness at Appomattox, Bruce Catton, 1953

In this book, the third of Catton's trilogy about the Army of the Potomac, the journalist turned historian recounts the final year of the American Civil War. *A Stillness at Appomattox* won both the Pulitzer Prize and the National Book Award, making Catton the premier historian of his time, but he never forgot how to tell a good story. If you only read one book about the Civil War, choose Catton for his crisp prose and gifted storytelling.

A Thousand Days: John F. Kennedy in the White House, Arthur M. Schlesinger, 1965

Originally, John F. Kennedy wanted no one to keep a written record of what went on during his presidency but, after the Bay of Pigs affair, Kennedy worried that other people (like the CIA) would tell his story and tell it wrong. So he instructed Schlesinger to keep a journal of events, which eventually became this Pulitzer Prize and National Book Award–winning chronicle of America's Camelot. If you are young enough to only know about Kennedy from that grainy Zapruder film or Oliver Stone's *JFK,* Schlesinger's book will illustrate why JFK was idolized by Americans who hoped his presidency would be the start of a new age for the country.

Undaunted Courage: Meriwether Lewis, Thomas Jefferson, and the Opening of the American West, Stephen Ambrose, 1996

While essentially a biography of one half of the famous American exploring duo, Ambrose's book is not only about Lewis but also about all the key participants—Clark, Sacagawea, and Jefferson—in the historic 1803–1806 expedition to the West and back. Ambrose is another author who brings history to life. (His other best-sellers include biographies of Nixon and Eisenhower and perhaps the definitive history of D-Day.)

Washington's Crossing, David Hackett Fischer, 2004

Six months after declaring independence from Great Britain, the newly formed United States of America was in danger of losing the revolution. But General George Washington and his loyal band of soldiers refused to give up. With an impeccable sense of historical detail, Fischer covers the New York and New Jersey campaigns of 1776–1777 that included Washington's famous crossing of the Delaware River.

World History

This planet's a pretty big place, and a lot of interesting things have happened on it. These fantastic books will not only take you back in time but will also transport you to the four corners of the earth.

1421: How China Discovered America, Gavin Menzies, 2003

Seventy years before Columbus claimed America and a century before Magellan circumnavigated the globe, a fleet of Chinese ships set sail on a journey around the world. When they returned to China in 1423 after their two-year expedition, the political climate had shifted and their achievements were forgotten. Historians are divided on Menzies's theory—that a Chinese Muslim explorer discovered the New World—but the story is still an action-packed tale certain to make you think twice about Columbus Day.

Black Hawk Down: A Story of Modern War, Mark Bowden, 1999

In a real-life counterpoint to the novels of Tom Clancy, *Black Hawk Down* is the story of what was supposed to be a quick mission by U.S. Rangers to capture two lieutenants of a Somalian warlord in Mogadishu, but instead turned into a rescue mission when the American troops became trapped in the city. In this intense, gritty, and testosterone-driven story, Bowden gives you a glimpse into the dangers American troops abroad face every day.

Bounty: The True Story of the Mutiny on the Bounty, Caroline Alexander, 2003

If your only knowledge of the infamous mutiny led by Fletcher Christian against the temperamental tyrant Captain William Bligh comes from Charles Nordhoff's classic novel or the Clark Gable film (or, even worse, the hideous remake with Marlon Brando), then this book will be a real treat. Alexander's fast-moving, riveting account (which draws from a plethora of historical sources), covers every detail from the moment the *Bounty* sets sail from England to the court-martial trial of the century (and, for the record, Alexander thinks Bligh got a bum rap).

A Bright Shining Lie: John Paul Vann and America in Vietnam, Neil Sheehan, 1988

This Pulitzer Prize and National Book Award–winning best-seller explores America's gradual involvement in the Vietnam War. Sheehan, a journalist who obtained the secret archive of government documents known as the Pentagon Papers, brilliantly captures the complexity of this tragic war. *A Bright Shining Lie* is *the* definitive story of the Vietnam Conflict, from its moments of courage and hope to its senseless deaths and needless destruction.

A Distant Mirror: The Calamitous Fourteenth Century, Barbara Tuchman, 1978

If you think living in today's world is difficult, try living in the fourteenth century! Europe was consumed in almost constant warfare; everyone's confidence in the government and the Church (the two foundations of their world) had crumbled; and that annoying Black Death threatened to kill one in three people. Tuchman, a two-time winner of the Pulitzer Prize, focuses on one man—French knight and nobleman Enguerrand de Coucy VII—who used the upheavals of the time to become wealthy and powerful. If you've never considered the fourteenth century a landmark time in history (or if you've never even given the century a second thought), *A Distant Mirror* will open your eyes to the parallels between that distant time and today.

Elizabeth and Mary: Cousins, Rivals, Queens, Jane Dunn, 2003

They could not be more different. Cool, calculating Elizabeth I put her position as queen above all else in her life, while her proud and beautiful cousin Mary's unwise personal choices would ultimately cost her the Scottish crown and her life. This compelling tale relates the real-life battle of two of history's most fascinating women—Mary, who loved too well, and Elizabeth, who loved only England—to secure their thrones.

From Beirut to Jerusalem, Thomas L. Friedman, 1989

Pulitzer Prize–winning *New York Times* journalist Friedman, who has spent six years in Beirut and Jerusalem, has written one of the most even-handed accounts of the Middle East crisis. Written from firsthand experience, his articulate history will help readers make sense of the tangled conflict that continues to this day.

Ghost Soldiers: The Forgotten Epic Story of World War II's Most Dramatic Mission, Hampton Sides, 2001

In January 1945, a small group of American Rangers marched 30 miles behind enemy lines in the Philippines to rescue 500 American and Allied POWs from the Japanese Cabanatuan prison camp. This daring and dramatic story was almost forgotten until Sides brought it to life in this well-researched book. With its thrilling tale of danger and heroism, Sides's cinematic prose will make you feel as though you're watching one of the classic WWII movies, like *The Great Escape* or *The Bridge on the River Kwai.*

The Great Influenza: The Epic Story of the Deadliest Plague in History, John M. Barry, 2004

It killed more people than all the plagues in the Middle Ages. It killed more people than AIDS. And yet not many people know about the Great Influenza Plague of 1918, which killed as many as 100 million people. Barry introduces a huge cast of characters involved in the pandemic, from President Wilson, who focused only on fighting World War I while the disease ran rampant, to William Welch and the other doctors at Johns Hopkins, who worked to understand the virus and find a cure before it wiped out the world. It's an epic chronicle of a virus whose mutations kill even today. Did we just hear you sneeze?

The Greatest Generation, Tom Brokaw, 1998

Television news anchor Brokaw went to Normandy to research an NBC documentary on the fortieth anniversary of D-Day, and he was so moved by a generation who gave everything so we could win the war that, 10 years later, when he returned for the fiftieth anniversary, he felt he had to tell their stories. This tribute to a time in America's history will make you thank all the old people you know.

Guns, Germs, and Steel: The Fates of Human Societies,
Jared Diamond, 1997

In this mesmerizing book, evolutionary biologist Diamond gives his theory as to why some nations (specifically those in Europe and the Americas) have succeeded and why others fail in history. He believes that agriculture is the key, noting that civilizations that developed with a strong agricultural foundation (as opposed to hunter-gathers) were able to create classes of society that led to the development of weapons. These weapons later helped them conquer the world. Those native populations not killed by weapons were decimated by the germs brought by these conquering countries. It sounds deadly dull (remember World History 101?), but we know you will find this Pulitzer Prize winner utterly compelling.

An Expert Speaks

"Jared Diamond's *Guns, Germs and Steel: The Fates of Human Societies,* explains why and how Western culture has come to be the dominant culture of our world. It's fascinating reading, and I highly recommend it."

—Denise Domning, author

How the Irish Saved Civilization: The Untold Story of Ireland's Heroic Role from the Fall of Rome to the Rise of Medieval Europe, Thomas Cahill, 1995

Cahill entertainingly details the important role Ireland played during the Dark Ages in preserving the great literary works and knowledge of the Greeks and Romans. If you like Cahill's engaging writing style and historical insights, you'll be pleased to know that he's working on a series of books that focus on different cultures and turning points in history, including the ancient Greeks and the Middle Ages.

How the Scots Invented the Modern World: The True Story of How Western Europe's Poorest Nation Created Our World and Everything In It, Arthur Herman, 2001

The Scots gave the world more than bagpipes and whiskey, as is proved in this compelling look at the achievements of this industrious and notoriously thrifty band of people. From politics and economics to science and technology, Smithsonian historian Herman fills us in on the Scots' many contributions to world history. Now, about those bagpipes …

The Ice Masters: The Doomed 1913 Voyage of the Karluk, Jennifer Niven, 2000

This ill-fated voyage makes the Shackleton Expedition look like a weekend at Vail. Vilhjalmur Stefansson, the noted explorer leading the Karluk expedition, sets out on an ambitious quest to deliver the first scientific team to the Arctic polar ice cap. In his rush to make history, Stefansson fails to provide his crew with polar survival training and forgoes the protective winter clothing he promised them. A few weeks into the journey, disaster strikes and, incredibly, Stefansson abandons his crew, leaving them to drift into the heart of the Arctic Ocean. Niven uses crewmembers' journals and commentary from the last living survivor and the descendents of others to create a riveting story.

King Leopold's Ghost: A Story of Greed, Terror, and Heroism in Colonial Africa, Adam Hochchilds, 1998

The twentieth century doesn't have a monopoly on greed and genocide, as readers will discover in this compelling but grim account of King Leopold II of Belgium's willful destruction of an African country. The Republic of the Congo was plundered for its rubber, and an estimated 10 million people died in the reign of terror beginning in the 1880s and lasting three decades. British shipping agent turned investigative reporter Edmund Morel launched a reform movement (whose members included Mark Twain) that eventually stopped Leopold's vicious rule. A brutal but gripping account, it will haunt you.

Kon-Tiki, Thor Heyerdahl, 1950

There was really only one way to validate the legends and artifacts that suggest ancient Incans sailed primitive rafts across thousands of miles of open ocean from South America to Polynesia. Heyerdahl and his crew of five attempted the voyage themselves, aboard a balsawood craft christened *Kon-Tiki.* This is a captivating account of Heyerdahl's historic expedition and the lessons he learned about the early seagoers who first made the trip.

The Last Empire: De Beers, Diamonds, and the World,
Stefan Kanfer, 1993

Beautiful but deadly, you wouldn't think of using those terms to describe diamonds, would you? Kanfer records the bloody history of these gemstones and the ruthless company that exploited the people who mined them. From 1867, when the first rough diamond was discovered, through the twentieth century as the company's monopoly starts to slip, Kanfer's book gives the reader all the juicy details. A diamond might be forever, but after reading *The Last Empire*, they won't look quite so shiny.

The Longest Day: A Classic Epic of D-Day, Cornelius Ryan, 1959

Journalist Ryan drew on firsthand accounts of the invasion from the soldiers who survived it to write this vivid account of the Allied invasion of Normandy on June 6, 1944. *The Longest Day* was made into a Hollywood epic in 1962, starring dozens of film greats, including John Wayne and Sean Connery.

An Expert Speaks

"This classic ranks among the best, if not the best, books on D-Day, June 6, 1944. Ryan's superb narrative concentrates on the experiences of many participants while giving enough information about the strategy to provide context. I value this book because of its personal focus on individuals caught up in a momentous event in history."

—Russell Sears, librarian

A Night to Remember, Walter Lord, 1955

A renewed interest in the *Titanic* and the fiftieth anniversary of the tragedy brought Lord's classic best-seller—which has nothing to do with Leonardo Di Caprio—back into print. This minute-by-minute account of an unsinkable boat that sinks on its first voyage puts you right there on the *Titanic* (like us, probably in steerage), as the tragedy unfolds. If anyone is King of the World, it's Lord with his poignant and eloquent account of the ship of dreams.

Paris 1919: Six Months That Changed the World, Margaret
MacMillan, 2002

In vivid detail, Canadian historian and professor MacMillan explores the crucial first six months of the Paris Peace Conference of 1919. Focusing on American President Woodrow Wilson, French Premier Georges Clemenceau, and British Prime Minister David Lloyd George, MacMillan disputes the commonly held historical theory that this peace treaty was the cause of World War II. It's not a light read, but MacMillan has obviously done her homework.

The Rape of Nanking: The Forgotten Holocaust of World War II, Iris Chang, 1997

When the Japanese captured the Chinese capital of Nanking in 1937, they began a systematic slaughter of almost 300,000 Chinese. As with the Holocaust, many of the survivors owe their lives to heroic individuals, many of whose stories are included in this shocking account of the horrors of war. The Japanese, who had long denied this massacre, only recently recognized this little-known historical travesty.

The Rise and Fall of the Third Reich, William Shirer, 1960

How could a civilized country like Germany have allowed Hitler and the Holocaust to have happened? Journalist, novelist, and historian Shirer, who was stationed in Europe in the 1920s and 1930s, explains why in his highly readable history. Despite the daunting length—1,200 pages—you'll never feel overwhelmed. Instead, you'll be simultaneously fascinated and horrified in this page-turner.

The Six Wives of Henry VIII, Alison Weir, 1992

This richly researched yet wonderfully readable account presents the six women—intellectual Katherine of Aragon (divorced), ambitious Anne Boleyn (beheaded), fragile Jane Seymour (died), practical Anne of Cleves (divorced), sexy Catherine Howard (beheaded), and adaptable Catherine Parr (survived)—who married Tudor King Henry VIII. Filled with love and betrayal, scandal and politics, and ambition and greed, Weir's classic tale has all the ingredients of a good Jackie Collins novel, but with much better clothes.

The White Headhunter, Nigel Randell, 2003

As a young Scottish sailor in 1876, Jack Renton found more adventure and rotten luck than he ever could have imagined. After being shanghaied in San Francisco, he managed to escape on a whaleboat, traveling over 2,000 miles of open sea until he reached the Solomon Islands. Unfortunately, Jack landed on Malaita, an island inhabited by headhunters. His memoirs and the oral history accounts gathered by the author from Malaita descendents provide startling details of Renton's survival and the events of his eight-year captivity.

And the Award Goes to...

Two of the books on this list were given the Pulitzer Prize for History:

- *A Stillness at Appomattox* by Bruce Catton (1954)
- *No Ordinary Time: Franklin and Eleanor Roosevelt: The Home Front in World War II* by Doris Kearns Goodwin (1995)

In addition, this book won the Pulitzer Prize for General Non-Fiction:

- *Guns, Germs and Steel: The Fates of Human Societies* by Jared Diamond (1998)

Chapter

Travel: Your Literary Passport to the World

In This Chapter

◆ Classics: adventures in traveling

◆ More great reads: way to go!

Are you a seasoned traveler, or do you prefer to experience the world from the comfort of your favorite chair with the help of a good book? Whatever your preference, this section has an assortment sure to appeal to your inner wanderer. You'll find stories of foreign expeditions, road trips, historic places, and famous faces. For readers inspired by human drama, we've got incredibly harrowing tales of survival, reaching from the high seas to the peaks of the Andes. We've included first-person accounts of journeys to every continent written by travelers who will enrich, elucidate, and entertain you.

What makes a good travel memoir? It's the richness of details, the strong sense of place, and the author's ability to re-create his or her experiences so you can imagine yourself right there. So jump aboard with these travel books!

Classics

Coming into the Country, John McPhee, 1976

Alaska didn't become a state until 1959. Seventeen years later, McPhee wrote this eloquent work about his travels there, and how the modern world was encroaching on this relatively untouched paradise. This volume is actually three "books": "At the Northern Tree Line: The Encircled River" (the controversial establishment of the Gates of the Arctic National Park); "In Urban Alaska: What They Were Hunting For" (political bargaining and the attempts to move the state capital); and "In the Bush: Coming into the Country" (the lives of the citizens in Eagle, Alaska). McPhee's lush details and thoughtful insights will give readers a taste of the true Alaska.

The Great Railway Bazaar: By Train Through Asia, Paul Theroux, 1975

In the mad rush to get where we're going in today's world, we seem to have lost the appreciation of traveling by train. Fortunately for us, Theroux hasn't forgotten this appealing form of travel, where one can watch the countryside slip by yet still feel a part of the landscape. Theroux, a successful novelist and biographer before writing about his travels, dropped off the manuscript of his latest novel, went to London's Victoria Station, and began a trip that would last four months and take him across continents. From the legendary Orient Express to the fabled Trans-Siberian Express, Theroux brilliantly details both the lost pleasures of train travel and the wonder of the exotic countries he visited.

Out of Africa, Isak Dinesen, 1937

Baroness Karen Blixen, a Danish aristocrat, lived on a 4,000-acre coffee plantation in the Kenyan hills near Nairobi from 1914 to 1931. Lush, poetic descriptions of Africa, from the deserts to the hill country, fill the pages of this book. The people, land, vegetation, and animals of what was then British East Africa take on almost an otherworldly aura thanks to Blixen's gorgeous prose. Blixen lost her farm and returned to Denmark, where she wrote these remarkable reminisces using the pen name Isak Dinesen. This is truly a captivating read.

The Snow Leopard, Peter Matthiessen, 1978

In 1973, Peter Matthiessen, field biologist George Schaller, four sherpas, and fourteen porters left Pokhara, a city in central Nepal, and headed to the Himalayas to study the Himalayan blue sheep and possibly catch sight of the extremely rare but magnificent white snow leopard. This is also a spiritual pilgrimage for Matthiessen, a Zen Buddhist, who goes to the ancient Buddhist shrine at Crystal Mountain to meet the venerated Lama of Shey. Matthiessen kept this diary of his experiences, and his eloquent, emotion-filled descriptions make readers feel as though they, too, are part of this incredible expedition.

And the Award Goes to ...

The Snow Leopard won the 1980 National Book Award for General Nonfiction.

Zen and the Art of Motorcycle Maintenance: An Inquiry into Values, Robert M. Pirsig, 1974

Robert Pirsig and his 11-year-old son embark on a cross-country motorcycle trip. The pair travel from Minneapolis across the Great Plains to the Dakotas, the Rockies, and ultimately, the Pacific Ocean, and there are marvelous descriptions of these areas, but this is more than a geography lesson. It is a quest for truth and inner peace. If Thoreau had had a chopper, he might very well have written a book much like this one.

More Great Reads

Braving Home: Dispatches from the Underwater Town, The Lava-Slide Inn, and Other Extreme Locales, Jake Halpern, 2003

The places Halpern writes about aren't even nice places to visit, so why would anyone want to live there? Halpern travels to some of the oddest, most inhospitable locations in America to meet the locals and find out why they choose to call these places home. Through his viewpoint and vivid, dead-on descriptions, you'll get a clear sense for the people, their surroundings, and the unsavory features that make each place a realtor's worst nightmare.

Driving Over Lemons: An Optimist in Andalucia, Chris Stewart, 1999

When you decide to pick up everything and move to a remote area in the foothills of the Alpujarras region in southern Spain, you would hope that your new home would at least have the basics, like electricity and running water. When Chris Stewart, former drummer for Genesis, discovers that this isn't always the case when he buys a dilapidated estate called El Valero and must spend months and months (and months) renovating it. Along the way, Stewart spins some wonderful, often hysterically funny, tales of his growing love for Andalucia and its people.

Eat, Pray, Love: One Woman's Search for Everything Across Italy, India and Indonesia, Elizabeth Gilbert, 2006

Gilbert was an award-winning author when she decided that the life she was leading was not the one she wanted. So she divorced her husband and now undertakes a quest to reclaim herself. Her first stop is Italy, a land overflowing with emotions, food, and passion, which she embraces. Her next stop, an ashram in India, is almost a complete opposite to her Italian journey. In India, she meditates, focuses on the internal, and gets closer to the peace she is seeking. Her last stop is Indonesia, the island of Bali, where she studies with a medicine man. With each of these sojourns, Gilbert articulates her apprehension and her joy and eventually brings all the pieces of this newly found self-knowledge together.

The Endurance: Shackleton's Legendary Antarctic Expedition,
Caroline Alexander and Frank Hurley, 1998

The year was 1914 when celebrated explorer Ernest Shackleton and his crew of 27 set sail on the most extreme voyage of their lives. They wanted to be the first to walk across the Antarctic continent, but instead they were forced into a fight for their very survival when their ship, *The Endurance*, became ice-bound, crushed, and scuttled in the frigid Weddell Sea. Now stranded on the floes in freezing conditions with no means of communication, no shelter, and limited provisions, the crew of *The Endurance* face the grim reality of an uncertain future. This is an absolutely incredible, heart-wrenching story.

The Rest of the Story

Cameraman Frank Hurley took actual motion picture footage of the expedition and planned to chronicle the crew's triumphant Antarctic crossing on film. Instead, his camera captured the dramatic events of one of the most astonishing exhibits of human courage and survival ever recorded. Hurley first showed his footage in his 1919 silent film *South: Ernest Shackleton and The Endurance Expedition*. More recent movie adaptations have also made use of Hurley's original camera work.

Fried Eggs with Chopsticks: One Woman's Hilarious Adventure into a Country and a Culture Not Her Own,
Polly Evans, 2006

The next time you think your trip is ruined because the airport Starbucks is out of chocolate croissants, just picture Polly Evans in China and count your blessings. Here's a woman who experienced the dark underbelly of foreign travel accommodations and lived to write about them. From her white-knuckle mountain excursion on muleback, to her no-frills, extreme ferry ride down the Yangtze, Evans recounts her daunting trip in delightfully hilarious detail.

The Ice Cave: A Woman's Adventures from the Mojave to the Antarctic, Lucy Jane Bledsoe, 2006

For many people, like this author, the beauty, peace, and solitude experienced in nature are a welcome respite. But it's the exhilarating dangers, unexpected surprises, and spiritual growth she finds that keep Bledsoe coming back for more. In this book you'll read about her experiences in a survival camp on the Ross Ice Shelf in Antarctica, her confrontation with wolves in Alaska, her encounter with a woman cycling across the Mojave Desert to escape an abusive husband, and many more fascinating stories of Bledsoe's remarkable travels.

In a Sunburned Country, Bill Bryson, 2001

Outdoor adventurist Bryson takes a trip Down Under to explore Australia. Join Bryson as he hikes the best of the continent, from beaches, to deserts, to ancient rain forests, with a spiritual pause at "Uluru" (a.k.a. Ayer's Rock) and a swim at the Great Barrier Reef. Bryson reviews the island's fascinating history, its flora and fauna, its quirky charms, and its wonderful people. His humorous style only makes the adventure all the more fun. Let Barbie grill her own shrimp. You've got a book to read!

The Rest of the Story

Bryson and his out-of-shape friend Stephen Katz (a frequent companion in Bryson's travels) decided to hike the 2,000+ mile Appalachian Trail. Not far into their hike, the two discover that this was probably not the best idea. Their 1998 account, *A Walk in the Woods: Rediscovering America on the Appalachian Trail,* will have you laughing all the way.

Into Thin Air: A Personal Account of the Mount Everest Disaster, Jon Krakauer, 1997

Reaching the summit of Mount Everest was Krakauer's lifelong dream. But even as he celebrated his victory at the top of the world on May 10, 1996, storm clouds were brewing in the Himalayas that would turn deadly for the unsuspecting expedition. Krakauer takes you on the arduous ascent, introducing you to his fellow climbers, many of whom did not survive the treacherous descent. This moving account of the sudden, unrelenting blizzard that struck the group and the horrible fate of its victims is a sobering reminder of nature's awesome fury.

Journeys, Jan Morris, 1984

Jan Morris, a prolific author of fiction as well as history, has profiled Venice, Spain, and Oxford, and authored numerous books of travel essays. Her keen observations and attention to the little details that define a location have made her a literary star in this genre. *Journeys* highlights a wide variety of locations, showcasing Morris's colorful and meticulous prose.

Miracle in the Andes: 72 Days on the Mountain and My Long Trek Home, Nando Parrado and Vince Rause, 2006

This is a first-person account of the challenges the Uruguayan rugby team faced when their plane crashed on a glacial slope in the Andes Mountains in October 1972. After two heartbreaking, grueling months without rescue, the few passengers left alive were forced to take extremely desperate measures to survive, including eating the flesh of the dead. Passenger Nando Parrado tells of this harrowing ordeal, an incredible story of sheer determination.

You Can Book on It!

The story of the Uruguayan rugby team's plane crash is the subject of the 1993 film *Alive*, featuring Ethan Hawke, Vincent Spano, Josh Hamilton, and Bruce Ramsey.

Mirrors of the Unseen: Journeys in Iran, Jason Elliot, 2006

When you picture Iran, what do you see? Elliot shows us both sides of the Iranian identity as he recounts his travels in this country rich in ancient history. Teetering between Western culture and Eastern tradition, progressive society and religious extremism, the Iran you see depends on which side of the door you're on. Elliot's experiences with the Iranian people, those you don't see on the nightly news, will surprise you.

The Olive Farm: A Memoir of Life, Love, and Olive Oil in the South of France, Carol Drinkwater, 2004

After a successful career as an actress and novelist, Drinkwater and her husband buy a 10-acre hillside olive farm in a village near Cannes. The farm, called "Appassionata," is an abandoned and moldy relic with a leaking roof and myriad other problems, but Drinkwater and her husband fall in love with the place. Eventually, they bring it back to life, achieving their dream of making it a working olive farm again. For anyone looking for an escape, *The Olive Farm* is the way to go.

On Mexican Time: A New Life in San Miguel, Tony Cohan, 2000

Cohan and his wife lived the good life in Los Angeles but felt something was missing. When they visited San Miguel de Allende, they felt a kinship and love so deep they packed up everything and moved to this colorful town in central Mexico. Here, they bought a charming, rustic fixer-upper and learned the truth about Mexican time, where the pace slows, the lunches are long … and perhaps the workers will come back. The renovation turned into a comedy of negotiations, but they found it worth all the wrangling. Word to the wise: it's important to find these quiet little towns before anyone else does because once you write a book about yours, well, that's the end of the quaintness.

1,000 Places to See Before You Die, Patricia Schultz, 2003

Need some fresh vacation ideas? Wherever your interests lie, from ancient castles to sacred ruins or lively festivals to stately opera houses, this book has something for every taste. Schultz tells you the best places to visit anywhere on the globe, the ways to get there, and the best times to go. But wait, there's more! Schultz gives the addresses, telephone numbers, and websites for her list of 1,000 destinations. Good for interesting armchair perusal, you may even use it to plan the real thing.

You Can Book on It!

Did you like *1,000 Places to See Before You Die?* Try *Unforgettable Places to See Before You Die,* by Steve Davey and Marc Schlossman (2004), and *Unforgettable Journeys to Take Before You Die,* by Steve Watkins and Clare Jones (2006).

Paris to the Moon, Adam Gopnik, 2000

In 1995, Gopnik was offered a job to write the "Paris Journals" columns for *The New Yorker* magazine. So with his wife Martha and his son Luke he moved to Paris, where he lived from 1995 to 2000, becoming a keen observer of the Parisian lifestyle. Gopnik loves the little cafés and shops and the unexpected adventures that just buying a Thanksgiving turkey can create. He contrasts the arrogance of the French with their concerns that their cultural dominance in many areas—high fashion, food, and romance—is waning. Gopnik brings his keen eye and clever wit to this narrative.

Roads: Driving America's Great Highways, Larry McMurtry, 2003

This McMurtry title is a departure from his normal writing style, without the focus on characters and details. *Roads* is a windshield assessment of America, a cross-country cruise with brief stops in interesting ports-of-call along America's historic highways. McMurtry muses behind the wheel, recollecting places he's read about and people he's met, offering frank commentary about each destination he passes.

Route 66: The Mother Road, Michael Wallis, 1990

Buckle up, adjust your seatback, and let Wallis do the driving in this state-by-state road trip along America's most historic highway. Learn about the origin, decline, and rebirth of this celebrated route, and experience the romance of the open road once traveled by legends like Jack Kerouak, Woody Guthrie, and John Steinbeck. The pioneering spirit of that era still jumps off the pages of this nostalgic classic of Americana.

You Can Book on It!

Route 66 linked Chicago and Los Angeles, meandering across eight states. It opened in 1926 and has been traversed by everyone from dust bowl migrants to troop convoys to songwriters seeking inspiration and maybe getting some "kicks."

Songlines, Bruce Chatwin, 1987

Songlines, the strings of invisible pathways that crisscross all of Australia, define the area of significant events for the Aborigines, like a wedding or a hunt, and delineate a man's territory. For the Aborigines, songlines are the footprints of their ancestors. Chatwin's theory is that their language started out as song, and reading his book is like entering into a time when the world and everything in it was "sung" into existence.

The Rest of the Story

Bruce Chatwin was considered the golden boy of travel writers. Educated in England, he worked at Sotheby's and studied archaeology at Edinburgh. When he landed a job with the *Sunday Times Magazine* as an advisor for art and architecture, it gave him an excuse to travel. Some have criticized Chatwin for mixing fiction with his non-fiction, but you won't care because his writing is so vivid. In 1989, Chatwin died of AIDS at 48.

Storyville, USA, Dale Peterson, 1999

We've all seen them, the small towns with unusual and often quirky names that pepper the map. What's the story behind their peculiar names? This book can give you the answers and a lot more about the places that Dale Peterson has visited in his 20,000 mile trek across the United States. Each destination's unique history and quaint local lifestyle is described in colorful detail, along with interesting information about the industries, economies, and politics of the area, courtesy of the good folks who live there. See what life is like in these Small Towns, USA.

Tracks, Robyn Davidson, 1981

Walking across 700 miles of arid desert in Western Australia with only a dog and four camels doesn't sound like much of a vacation to us, but Davidson's gritty story of her odyssey has become a cult classic. This is a fascinating account of one woman's determination.

Traveling with Che Guevara: The Making of a Revolutionary, Alberto Granado, 1978

Two wild and crazy guys, Alberto Granado and his friend, Ernesto "Che" Guevara, set out on an eight-month journey of discovery in 1952, traveling across South America on a 500cc Norton motorcycle. Their various odd jobs and experiences along the way range from humorous to tragic, and Granada captures them all in his journal. During this odyssey Guevara learned firsthand of the widespread poverty and injustice inflicted on the local people, which ignited his passion for revolution.

> ### You Can Book on It!
> Alberto Granado's journals inspired the 2003 Walter Salles movie *The Motorcycle Diaries.*

Travels with Charlie, John Steinbeck, 1962

After years of writing about Americans, Pulitzer Prize–winning author Steinbeck and his poodle Charlie set out on a coast-to-coast adventure to meet some of them. Traveling from Maine to the Monterrey Peninsula, Steinbeck stopped to experience the local lifestyles along the way and reflected on the collective mood and character of the people who shape the nation. Written over 40 years ago, this journey poses an interesting contrast to the American society of the twenty-first century.

A Trip to the Beach: Living on Island Time in the Caribbean, Melinda and Bob Blanchard, 2000

Ah, we all want to run away to a tropical island, lie in the sun, and drink Mai Tais. Restaurant owners Melinda and Bob run away to Anguilla—and open a restaurant! Sure, they have some problems, just as they had with their Vermont restaurant, but these are way more exotic, like cooking for a packed house with no electricity and surviving a hurricane. This chatty book includes some of their recipes, so you can experience a taste of the islands (without the hurricane!).

Under the Tuscan Sun: At Home in Italy, Frances Mayes, 1996

While Peter Mayle might have begun the trend of travel memoirs, Mayes perfected it. A writer and a professor, Mayes decided after years of renting summer homes that she wanted to buy a place in Tuscany. As she re-creates her love of Italy, she also describes the horrors involved in renovating a dilapidated villa called "Bramasole" ("yearning for the sun"). It's a *bella* book.

The Rest of the Story

Taking a break from home improvements on her Tuscan villa, Mayes leads us on a sweeping tour of the Mediterranean region in *A Year in the World: Journeys of a Passionate Traveler*, 2006. From Portugal to Turkey, with plenty of stops in between, she shows you what it's like to live there—the art, the food, the history, and the scenery. Mayes's imagery of the people, cultures, and local flavors will leave you hungry for more.

Video Night in Kathmandu: And Other Reports from the Not-So-Far East, Pico Iyer, 1988, revised in 2001

Cultures collide in this fascinating account of the effects of Western society on the Far East. In the 2001 revised edition, Iyer, a reporter for *Time* magazine, writes about India, Japan, Burma, China, and other Asian countries and how they have changed even more since the publication of his classic work in the late 1980s. Iyer's writing style is perceptive and entertaining, and his provocative essays show how the influence of the West has been absorbed and adopted by the centuries-old countries of Asia.

A Walk Across America, Peter Jenkins, 1979

There's nothing like taking a long walk, alone with your thoughts, to restore your peace of mind. This author was so cynical about life in America in the 1970s that he walked clear across the country! This book describes Jenkins's experiences in his journey to renew his faith in Americans through the things he learned from the people he met in the places he stopped along the way. Read it. Live it. Love it.

Winterdance: The Fine Madness of Running the Iditerod, Gary Paulson, 1995

Few athletic events are as demanding as the Alaskan Iditerod, a 1,150-mile dogsled race across the frozen wilderness. Paulson takes you through his experiences training for and participating in this annual event and his memorable 17-day odyssey of peril and wonder. You'll get an insider's view of what motivates mushers to participate in this daunting test of wills, what it's like to race alone across a thousand miles of ice and snow, and what powerful bonds form between the mushers and their dogs.

The Rest of the Story

The Alaskan Iditarod has come to be called "The Last Great Race on Earth." Each sled team consists of the "musher" and 12 to 16 dogs, who must cover a distance of over 1,150 miles in 10 to 17 days. The route, now a National Historic Trail, was originally used for bringing mail and supplies into Alaska and hauling gold out!

Without Reservations: The Travels of an Independent Woman, Alice Steinbach, 2000

When it comes to traveling, there's comfort in knowing exactly where you're going, where you're staying, and how long you will be traveling. However, traveling can also be delightful when your itinerary is open and your plans are changeable, as readers will discover in this elegantly written travelogue. Steinbach, an award-winning journalist with *The Baltimore Sun*, decided to take a solo sabbatical because, according to her, when you travel alone, you find out who you are. *Without Reservations* is not a guidebook, it's the introspective meanderings of someone who is on an adventure and open to all the possibilities that linger around each corner. And as a charming part of the book, each chapter opens with a postcard that the author mailed home to herself to remind her of the small but important things that are so easy to forget. But Steinbach doesn't. And you won't either.

A Year in Provençe, Peter Mayle, 1989

It's the perfect fairy tale, saying goodbye to your everyday, boring job and moving to the south of France into a 200-year-old farmhouse. Columnist Mayle lives the dream when he and his wife leave England to take up residence and renovate a farmhouse in a small town at the base of the Luberon Mountains.

With love drenched in wit (or is it wit drenched with love?), Mayle recounts his many misadventures in home renovations *à la francaise*. While some things have changed in Provence since his book was first published (just try finding a parking place, much less a home there!), Mayle's literary debut still exudes a timeless charm.

Chapter 18

Humor: Take My Joke. Please!

In This Chapter

- ◆ Classics: stop me if you've heard this one ...
- ◆ General humor: laugh, and the world laughs at you
- ◆ Political humor: a donkey and an elephant go into a bar
- ◆ Laughing at language: shooting an elephant in your pajamas

Humor is a very personal thing. What's funny to one person might not even make the next person crack a smile. But no matter what tickles your fancy, humor is a vital part of the human condition. With so many top-notch humorists around, we can only offer you a sampling of what's available from the writings of some of the best. Without the humorists' delivery or their comedic onstage timing, the words alone have to convey the humor. If at least one book on this list doesn't make you grin, giggle, or guffaw, call your doctor—you need a funny bone transplant!

Classics

Some of the books listed in this section might be recent, but these writers are considered pioneers and groundbreakers, thus earning them a place with the classics.

The Best of Will Rogers: A Collection of Rogers' Wisdom, Astonishingly Relevant for Today, Bryan B. Sterling, 2000

Clever as a fox, Will Rogers (1879–1935), a Native American cowboy-philosopher, a guy who "never met a man he didn't like," had a razor-sharp wit hidden in a folksy, friendly style. Even after Rogers became famous, his humble, affable attitude seemed unaffected. His amazing observations about people and politics are right-on, even 70-plus years after his untimely death.

Bob Hope: My Life in Jokes, Bob Hope, 2003

Hope was a veritable encyclopedia of jokes. In 2003, when Hope turned 100 years old (the same year he died), his daughter, Linda Hope, organized and published his jokes and other humorous tidbits to tell her father's life story. From his birth ("When the doctor slapped me, I thought it was applause.") to getting old ("Age is only a number. However, in my case, it is a rather large number.) A century was never so much fun.

But Seriously ... Steve Allen Speaks His Mind, Steve Allen, 1996

A comic with a love of humanity, Allen approached everything in a logical, thoughtful manner. With essays ranging from "A Nuclear War Would Just Ruin My Day" to "The Confessions of the Tortilla Priest," this collection reveals the social conscience behind Allen's analytical mind and legendary wit.

Cannibalism in the Cars: The Best of Mark Twain's Humorous Sketches, Mark Twain, 2000

Twain lampooned everything and everyone—nothing was sacred or safe from his barbs. His early works of humor (1863–1872) are collected in this delightful volume. Some are well known, such as "The Celebrated Jumping Frog of Calaveras County." Some are less familiar, like "A Touching Story of George Washington's Boyhood," which has absolutely nothing to do with the first president. You'll love these treasures from one of our most famous humorists when he was young and already very irreverent!

You Can Book on It!

Still funny after all these years, Twain's pointed, sometimes acerbic observations include the following:

> "I became a newspaperman. I hated to do it, but I couldn't find honest employment."

> "Last week I stated this woman was the ugliest woman I had ever seen. I have since been visited by her sister and now wish to withdraw that statement."

> "I looked as out of place as a Presbyterian in hell."

Common Nonsense, Andy Rooney, 2002

Andy Rooney has long epitomized the term "curmudgeon." He's always ready to share what ticks him off (that's just about everything) and why. Rooney, the comic jewel of the long-running television news program *60 Minutes*, has opinions about politics, sports, entertainment, the arts, learning, work, success, the writing life, home life, animals, travel, and progress. It's an impressive bunch of crankiness, but you still find yourself wanting more.

Fatherhood, Bill Cosby, 1986

As the parent of five children, amiable comic Bill Cosby knows more about fatherhood than most of us, and he doesn't hesitate to share what he's learned. For example, "Everything's okay, Dad," really means: "I haven't killed anyone." And the First Law of Intergenerational Perversity means that "No matter what you tell your child to do, he will always do the opposite." Full of humor, Cosby's down-to-earth advice always rings true. This best-selling book topped *The New York Times* Bestseller List for more than a year.

You Can Book on It!

Bill Cosby doesn't use race as a subject in his comedy. He once offered the following explanation for this decision: "I don't think you can bring the races together by joking about the differences between them. I'd rather talk about the similarities, about what's universal in their experiences."

The Funny Thing Is ..., Ellen DeGeneres, 2003

DeGeneres offers humorous counsel about many things, including "smartishness" or how to seem smarter and a list of assurances why prison wouldn't be so bad. From the useful chapter, "Gift Exchange or the Art of Believable Acting" to "Making Your Life Count (And Other Fun Things to Do with Your Time!")," you can be sure that somewhere in her hilarious, effusive prose there are real words of wisdom.

The Grass Is Always Greener over the Septic Tank, Erma Bombeck, 1976

With her wry observations on everyday life in the suburbs, this beloved writer became synonymous with humor for the average American, especially women. In this book, Bombeck laughs at everything from her own imperfections to her husband's addiction to televised sports. Thirty years later, her suburban observations still ring true.

I Shouldn't Even Be Doing This!: And Other Things That Strike Me as Funny, Bob Newhart, 2006

Bob Newhart wrote this, his first book, at the ripe old age of 77. Newhart's signature deadpan delivery carries over into the tone of his work. Fans of the guy who made telephone conversations works of comic art and created two hit television comedies won't want to miss this!

Napalm and Silly Putty, George Carlin, 2001

George Carlin, long known for his satiric, edgy observations about the absurdities of life, calls *Napalm and Silly Putty* a "metaphor for man's dual nature." This book is classic Carlin. Quips ("An art thief is a man who takes pictures") and one-liners ("Just when I discovered the meaning of life, they changed it") fill the pages. Carlin moves seamlessly between lighthearted spoofs (his irreverent "The Miscellaneous Ailments Foundation" supports cures for conditions that are often overlooked, including small pox, medium pox, and large pox) to more serious harangues against society ("Golf is an arrogant, elitist game that takes up entirely too much space in this country"). Whether adopting an amusing or scolding tone, there's no doubt that Carlin is one of the best.

100 Years: 100 Stories, George Burns, 1996

In this, his tenth book, George Burns actually tells 102 stories. Included are anecdotes about his own life and family, especially his wife, Gracie Allen. Burns spins yarns about the many friends he made over his incredibly long stint in show business—Ann Margaret, Jack Benny, Carol Channing, Sammy Davis Jr., W.C. Fields, Goldie Hawn, Bob Hope, Al Jolson, Groucho Marx … well, you get the idea. As you read these stories, you can almost see Burns taking time to puff his cigar and make that devilish grin that the world has come to love.

Lake Wobegone Days, Garrison Keillor, 1986

The genius behind *A Prairie Home Companion* radio show, Garrison offers a selection of down-home tales from the fictional town of Lake Wobegone, Minnesota ("1418 alt., 942 pop."), a failed nineteenth-century Utopian experiment now populated by Germans and Swedes. These stories are full of delightful descriptions and exaggerations ("Most men wear their belts low here, there being so many outstanding bellies, some big enough to have names of their own and be formally introduced"). Keillor's droll humor and expert prose will captivate you from page one.

Life Is Like a Dogsled Team ...: If You're Not the Lead Dog, the Scenery Never Changes—The Wit and Wisdom of Lewis Grizzard, Lewis Grizzard, 2001

Here is the quintessential Grizzard, who wrote such gems as *Elvis Is Dead, and I Don't Feel So Good Myself*; *It Wasn't Always Easy, but I Sure Had Fun*; *Southern by the Grace of God*; and *They Tore Out My Heart and Stomped That Sucker Flat*. This collection showcases Lewis's one-liners, anecdotes, and observations. It's the perfect introduction to a man who understood down-home humor.

Memoirs of a Mangy Lover, Groucho Marx, 1963

Julius "Groucho" Marx (1890–1977) was the master of the insulting quip ("I never forget a face, but in your case I'll be glad to make an exception.") long before Don Rickles took to the stage. Groucho made 26 hilarious movies, 15 with his brothers, Chico and Harpo, and later hosted the popular television show *You Bet Your Life*. The book begins with a section on animal-inspired tales of love ("Horsing Around with My Hormones"). His "Social Notes from a Social Outcast" is pure Groucho, especially "How I Beat the Social Game." Tantalizing tidbits of Groucho's personal memoirs mingle with his outrageous theories of life. He wraps up the book with "Marxist Philosophy, According to Groucho," a very brave title to use in a book that came out at the height of the Cold War fervor. From extreme physical slapstick to cunning, erudite observations, Groucho could do it all.

Pure Drivel, Steve Martin, 1999

Pure Drivel is a collection of zany essays filled with quirky characters described in madly creative terms. Consider Lola, a woman Martin meets at a Mensa party, who has a body "the shape of a Doric column, the earlier ones, preinvasion." As you sample the selections in this book ("Mars Probe Finds Kittens," "Times Roman Font Announces Shortage of Periods," and "The Paparazzi of Plato"), you'll soon see that underneath Martin's façade of silliness lies the soul of a sophisticated wit.

The 2000 Year Old Man in the Year 2000,
Mel Brooks and Carl Reiner, 1997

The 2000 Year Old Man, a classic character created by the incomparable Brooks and Reiner in 1950, always has an opinion about something. After all, he knew most of the important figures in history. In this book of wisdom for the new millennium, the old guy puts in his two cents about diets, infomercials, rap music, and automated telephone attendants, just to name a few. It's a welcome book from a cult favorite.

Without Feathers, Woody Allen, 1975

Musings from Allen's incredible mind include such treasures as "The Whore of Mensa," "God (A Play)," "No Kaddish for Weinstein," "Selections from the Allen Notebooks," "The Early Essays," and "Scrolls." Selections cover a heady mix of absurdist stream-of-consciousness observations as well as his brilliant one-liners.

> **You Can Book on It!**
>
> Woody Allen's humor ranges from the ridiculous to the absurd:
>
> > "He had been a precocious child. An intellectual. At twelve, he had translated the poems of T.S. Eliot into English, after some vandals had broken into the library and translated them into French."
> >
> > "The lion and the calf shall lie down together, but the calf won't get much sleep."

General Humor

The Areas of My Expertise, John Hodgman, 2006

Daily Show regular John Hodgman shares his vast knowledge of the world— "matters historical, matters literary, matters cryptozoological, hobo matters, food, drink, cheese (a kind of food), squirrels and lobsters and eels, haircuts, utopia, what will happen in the future, and most other subjects." Must-have "information," all of it fabricated by Hodgman, includes a list of 700 hobo names and the basics of snow and ice warfare. If you like offbeat humor, you'll adore this book.

Babyhood, Paul Reiser, 1997

Comic/actor/writer Reiser chronicles every step of having a baby, from the decision to have children to "I have never been this tired ever." For anyone who's ever had a baby in the house (or is thinking about having one), these honest, laugh-out-loud, new father insights about parenting will hit home.

The Darwin Awards: Evolution in Action,
Wendy Northcutt, 2002

This first book in the popular "Darwin Awards" series commemorates "those individuals who ensure the long-term survival of our species by removing themselves from the gene pool in a sublimely idiotic fashion." Tales of fatal or near-fatal goofs include: wife tossing in Buenos Aires; six Egyptian men drowning by going into a well to retrieve a chicken (the chicken lived); and a fisherman throwing a stick of dynamite … that his dog retrieves. These unbelievable but true stories of people with no common sense will make you shake your head with amazement and wonder if we're evolving backward.

Dave Berry Is Not Taking This Sitting Down, Dave Berry, 2002

Pulitzer Prize winner Dave Berry has had it, and he shows it with such in-your-face pieces as "My Final Answer Is … Go Back to Your Spaceship, Regis;" "From Now on, Let Women Kill Their Own Spiders;" and "The Gulf Between Father and Son is Called 'Quantum Physics.'" The book includes 70-plus short, comical, highly enjoyable essays.

The Dilbert Future, Scott Adams, 1997

With the help of his famous friend, Dilbert, Adams explains how to predict the future. He offers specific rules: "Adams's Rule of the Unexpected," "Adams's Rule of Self-Defeating Prophecies," and "Adams's Rule of Logical Limits." Adams predicts many things: aging, technology ("In the future, technology will be the leading cause of death"), gender relation work, and "social stuff." He tells us that some things won't improve, such as airlines and bicycle seats. Lots of "true story" anecdotes and Dilbert comic strips help make Adams's points.

Don't Make a Black Woman Take Off Her Earrings, Tyler Perry, 2006

Tyler, a talented writer and actor, is famous for his portrayal of Madea (a.k.a. Mabel Simmons), a sassy, straight-talking, gun-toting granny. Madea, who has something to say about everything, offers "uninhibited commentaries on love and life." Her opinions are specific, as seen in "Madea on Love and Marriage (Often Two Completely Separate Topics)." Want to know about the Bible, kids, or beauty tips? Madea is the expert, and she's hilarious.

Everything and a Kite, Ray Romano, 1998

The star of *Everyone Loves Raymond*, Romano begins the book sharing his trademark insecurities, telling the story of his frantic search for the perfect font for this book (he decides to save the funniest one for when he writes his will). Single life, married life, parent life—Romano discusses all in his congenial, self-deprecating style.

Grown-Ass Man, Cedric the Entertainer, 2002

Cedric the Entertainer, one of Spike Lee's "Kings of Comedy," uses his euphemism for "grown-up" to skewer the quirks of so-called adults. Told in two parts, "The Making of a Grown-Ass Man" and "The Wisdom of a Grown-Ass Man," this book has riffs on everything from race to riches. He draws on experiences and people from his own life, such as his religious grandmother who does everything the Lord tells her—including running red lights—to make his points. It's sharp humor with an inviting, personal touch.

The History of White People, Martin Mull and Allen Rucker, 1985

Mull and Rucker lampoon every aspect of white culture: a typical white family, white people food (Cheese Whiz and gumdrops), and white people's contribution to this country. This good-natured spoof brings together all the stereotypes about "whiteness" and wraps them up in one hilarious package.

I Feel Bad About My Neck: And Other Thoughts on Being a Woman, Nora Ephron, 2006

Nora Ephron is known for her entertaining screenplays, including *You've Got Mail, Sleepless in Seattle,* and *When Harry Met Sally.* Now, Ephron finds the humor hidden amidst all the angst of aging—menopause, empty nests, and yes, wrinkled necks. Although Ephron's observations are written for middle-aged women, men who lived with women going through these things will appreciate the humor, too!

An Expert Speaks

"My newest favorite book (the honor changes quickly!) is Nora Ephron's *I Feel Bad About My Neck: And Other Thoughts on Being a Woman,* because it makes getting old and being a woman something to laugh about instead of cry over. She had me from the moment she said that she hated the writers of books that say 'it's great to be old ... I can't stand people who say things like this ... What can they be thinking? Don't they have necks?' She hits the highlights of getting older—reminiscing, remembering things as better than they were, remembering that some things really *were* better—with just the right combination of wistfulness and humor. I think I'll go read it again."

—Stevi Mittman, author

I Have Chosen to Stay and Fight, Margaret Cho, 2005

There are cranky comedians. There are ticked-off comedians. And then there's Cho. Her blistering one-liners and raw observations are nothing if not angry. Everything's a target—her parents, her body, rich white people, even Andy Rooney. In a world full of safe humor, this is oddly refreshing.

I Like You: Hospitality Under the Influence, Amy Sedaris, 2006

Want to throw a party? Here's some outrageous advice from Amy Sedaris, writer, comic, and actress (*Strangers with Candy*). Sedaris's recipes and some of the tips in this book are real—she has a background as a caterer. However, everything else is pure entertainment.

I Love Everybody (and Other Atrocious Lies): True Tales of a Loudmouth Girl, Laurie Notaro, 2004

Notaro's keen eye finds humor in the most mundane aspects of life. Anyone who's visited the Magic Kingdom will appreciate "Disneyland: A Tragedy in Four Acts." And who can't identify with "Putting the Die in Diet"? Notaro makes a mundane trip to Costco a spiritual mecca when she uses it as an opportunity to clear her kharma by loving everyone ... and telling them so. This down-to-earth humor has universal appeal.

If You Can't Say Something Nice, Calvin Trillin, 1987

An accomplished writer, Trillin penned the long-running humor column, "Uncivil Liberties" for *The Nation*. Here, Trillin discusses such things as getting rid of raccoons, uncovering the fate of chicken à la king, and managing the scandal of George Washington and the cherry tree. Each piece is a small treasure.

Me Talk Pretty One Day, David Sedaris, 2000

This is a hilarious, occasionally poignant memoir of Sedaris's time in France, among other things. Who else would begin to learn a language with such vocabulary words as "exorcism, facial swelling, and death penalty"? Sedaris might talk about his "Giant Dreams, Midget Abilities," but his talent is huge.

> **An Expert Speaks**
>
> "I'm a David Sedaris fan. Although Sedaris's audio books are abridged, he does his own reading, which makes the audio versions a real treat because he has such a unique voice ... I've read all of his books and listened to three of them. I especially liked *Me Talk Pretty One Day* in the audio version. I was laughing so hard while listening to it that I literally had to lie down on the floor."
>
> —Tom Stevens, editor

Naked Beneath My Clothes: Tales of a Revealing Nature, Rita Rudner, 1992

Rudner shares her sometimes oddball observations about men and women in 40 or so succinct essays. She talks candidly about women and the things they encounter in their everyday life. A perpetually quizzical comic, Rudner's musings will keep you entertained from cover to cover.

The Sinner's Guide to the Evangelical Right, Robert Lanham, 2006

Nothing is sacred for Lanham, who delights in skewering the culture of the extreme far-right evangelicals. Lanham's targets include Jerry Falwell, Colorado Springs ("The Evangelical Vatican"), wealthy megachurches, and fancified Bibles. This side-splittingly funny satire is sure to generate controversy, sure to offend … and sure to entertain.

The Sweet Potato Queens' Book of Love: A Fallen Southern Belle's Look at Love, Life, Men, Marriage, and Being Prepared, Jill Conner Browne, 1999

This manual includes humble tidbits intended to help women get and keep the upper hand in all aspects of life. For instance, Conner Browne imparts the "true magic words guaranteed to get any man to do your bidding" and offers insights on how to recognize and deal with "men who may need killing, quite frankly." You don't need to be Southern to laugh out loud.

Texas Hold 'Em: How I Was Born in a Manger, Died in the Saddle, and Came Back as a Horny Toad, Kinky Friedman, 2006

This is Friedman's sort-of political autobiography. A Texan from an upper-class Jewish family, Friedman sees the humor in politics: "The question is whether my candidacy is a joke or whether the current crop of politicians is a joke." His meandering comments cover everything from "You know you're from West Texas if …" to Texas prison slang. Friedman becomes everyman with his most universal statement, "I believe the Internet is the work of Satan." It's a rowdy good time. Yee haw!

Yeah, I Said It, Wanda Sykes, 2004

Feisty and in-your-face, Emmy-winning comedian Wanda Sykes's sarcastic sense of humor makes short work of Martha Stewart, Bill Clinton, George Bush, vanity license plates, homeland security, and breaking up. Nothing is safe from her barbs. Sykes's riffs on sports and the behavior of the fans are especially good, thanks to her career as a sports commentator.

Political Humor

Humor can be used to make a political or social statement. Whatever administration is in power is always fair game, no matter what party they represent. Clever political humorists, such as those that follow, poke fun at the current affairs of state and make you laugh … when what you really might want to do is cry.

Beating Around the Bush: Political Humor 2000–2006, Art Buchwald, 2005

Buchwald, a Pulitzer Prize–winning *Washington Post* columnist, comments on politics and the realities of the modern world: Saudis suing the American tobacco industry for all the smoking-related medical treatments they've covered in the past 25 years; Asian sweatshops making the presents we give for Christmas; and Michael Jackson doing, well, just about anything. Buchwald's comment: "…if weapons are the tip of the iceberg, then Mr. Bush is the captain of the *Titanic*," leads into a satiric piece with just that scenario. He gives humorous thoughts about truly disturbing things.

The Daily Show with Jon Stewart Presents America the Book: A Citizen's Guide to Democracy Inaction, Jon Stewart, Ben Karlin, David Javerbaum, with the Staff of *The Daily Show*, 2004

Fashioned to look like a high school history textbook, this irreverent, in-your-face satire includes such gems as extreme revisionist accounts of historical events and cut-out robes for naked paper-doll Supreme Court justices. Iconoclasm at its rowdiest, this is sure to offend you or make you laugh your socks off—or both. This innovative masterpiece is a worthy winner of the Thurber Humor Award. A "Teacher's Edition" is now available.

Lies and the Lying Liars Who Tell Them: A Fair and Balanced Look at the Right, Al Franken, 2003

Franken's humor shines in these "gotcha" accounts of the political right. Not beneath name-calling ("Ann Coulter: Nutcase"), Franken uses every weapon at hand, including people's own words, to expose what he considers "big ones" told by such notables as Bernie Goldberg, Bill O'Reilly, and George W. Bush.

New Rules: Polite Musings from a Timid Observer, Bill Maher, 2005

The many photos in this book don't leave much room for text, but the few words are cleverly irreverent. Take Maher's New Rule, "Abigail Van Buried:" "… Dear Abby has been dead for years, yet she continues her daily syndicated column. If I want to hear what a corpse thinks, I'll read Robert Novak." It's a fast, fun read.

Nothing's Sacred, Lewis Black, 2005

Using his saber-sharp wit, this perpetually outraged humorist takes aim at the misrepresentations, absurdities, and peculiarities of our so-called "sacred" institutions—and hits the target every time. Beginning with amusing anecdotes from his Cold War childhood, Black's book never fails to entertain. Once you pick it up, you can't put it down. Even Black can't be cranky about that.

What the L?, Kate Clinton, 2005

This is a book with two themes. A columnist for *The Progressive* and *The Advocate*, Clinton uses the first part of the book to lambast everything Bush. The second part of the book deals with lesbianism and Clinton's own choice of an alternative lifestyle, among other things. Intelligent, impudent, and insightful, this will prompt lots of laughter ... and serious discussions.

Who Let the Dogs In? Incredible Political Animals I Have Known, Molly Ivins, 2004

This "lifelong Texas liberal," who has been a columnist for *Mother Jones, Ms, The Nation,* and *The Progressive,* skewers two decades worth of political figures, both "Heroes and Heels." No president escapes her scrutiny—Carter, Reagan, both Bushes, and Clinton. When Ivins says, "I realize that the only people in America having a good time right now are political reporters," you know we're in trouble, but you can't help laughing.

The Rant Zone: An All-Out Blitz Against Soul-Sucking Jobs, Twisted Child Stars, Holistic Loons, and People Who Eat Their Dogs, Dennis Miller, 2001

Miller, a staunchly conservative pundit who has written several "Rant" books, once again makes use of his unbelievably extensive vocabulary to blast society. Hollywood ("Show Business: Hollywood and Vain") and the Clintons ("The Clintons: Is He Gone Yet?" are just a few of his targets. Some of Miller's metaphors might whiz right past the reader's head ("... they make William Randolph Hearst look like Jeff Spicolli"). Miller's ticked-off puns, plays on words, and multisyllabic aphorisms, cogitations, and articulations are very funny—but sometimes, you need a dictionary to get the punch line.

Laughing at Language

Some words are just plain funny (think googoleplex and onomatopoeia). Some are funny in context. In both its use and misuse, language is always good for a laugh!

Anguished English: An Anthology of Accidental Assaults Upon Our Language, Richard Lederer, 1987

Hilarious student bloopers, court "disorders," and advertising gaffes are only a few of the gems that fill the pages of this collection of what Lederer calls "assaults upon our language." With examples like "I am forwarding my marriage certificate and three children, one of which is a mistake as you can see," Lederer's examples will make you grin and giggle.

The Devil's Dictionary, Ambrose Bierce, 1911

This book began as pieces in the newspaper that were collected and published as *Cynic's Word Book* in 1906 and re-published with its current name in 1911. The droll, satirical definitions in *The Devil's Dictionary*, penned a hundred years ago, could have been written today ("bore, *n*. a person who talks when you wish him to listen"). Bierce was the ultimate cynic, so this is perfect for pessimists!

The Rest of the Story

Ambrose Bierce was so jaded and cynical that his contemporaries dubbed him "Bitter Bierce."

The Joys of Yiddish, Leo Rosten, 1968

American English is enriched with words from the Yiddish language. Rosten's classic volume offers humorous definitions as well as many insights into the Jewish culture. Arranged in dictionary format, anecdotes and/or jokes accompany each Yiddish word or phrase and its definition. *Chutzpah*, for example, is when a man murders his parents and throws himself on the mercy of the court because he's an orphan. If this book leaves you wanting more, and it will, try *The Joys of Yenglish*, too.

Chapter 19

True Crime: Blood, Guts, and a Darned Good Story

In This Chapter

- ◆ Classics: no use crying over spilled blood
- ◆ Historical true crime: blood under the bridge
- ◆ Organized crime: as opposed to disorganized crime
- ◆ Serial killers and other murderers: killing by the numbers
- ◆ Theft and white-collar crime: when good boys go bad

People have always had a morbid fascination with true crimes: the more violent, the better. There's a shady side of human nature that has that slow-down-by-the-car-accident-and-take-a-look element. Often gruesome, gory, grisly, graphic, and grotesque, the true crime genre is neither for the faint of heart nor the weak of stomach. From the sordid to the sensational, these titles should please even the most bloodthirsty reader.

Classics

Fatal Vision, Joe McGinnis, 1984

Dr. Jeffrey MacDonald, a former Green Beret, told police a group of hippies broke into his house and killed his two little girls and his pregnant wife. MacDonald even had wounds—all superficial—that he claimed to have suffered at the hands of the long-haired intruders. This nightmare-inducing story tells of a man who killed his family and thought he could get away with it.

Helter Skelter: The True Story of the Manson Murders by the District Attorney Who Put the Puzzle Together, Vincent Bugliosi, 1975

No detail escapes Bugliosi's eye as he recounts the August night in 1969 when Steven Earl Parent, Jay Sebring, Abigail Folger, Voyteck Frykowski, and pregnant actress Sharon Tate were savagely murdered by Charles Manson's infamous "family." An edition published in 1994, the twenty-fifth anniversary of the massacre, gives updated information on the criminals.

In Cold Blood, Truman Capote, 1965

The same author who gave us *Breakfast at Tiffany's* brings us the grisly tale of a shocking murder that took place on November 15, 1959, in the peaceful, remote village of Holcomb, Kansas. The Clutter family—the parents and two of their children—were viciously slain by two men who broke into their home. In this brilliant but disturbing book, Capote regales readers with the entire story, from the brutal murders to the execution of the killers.

The Nutcracker: Money, Madness, and Murder—A Family Album, Shana Alexander, 1985

Frances Schreuder was a wealthy woman who lived off the largesse of her father, Franklin Bradshaw. When Frances became worried about being disinherited, she hired a hit man (who turned out to be a fake) to take out her dad. For Frances's next attempt, she gave her teenage sons poison to add to her father's food. On July 23, 1978, Frances got her wish when her son, Marc, shot and killed his grandfather. Alexander's tone for this gruesome murder is light and sometimes humorous. *The Nutcracker* was made into a six-part television miniseries in 1987, starring Lee Remick and Inga Swenson.

The Onion Field, Joseph Wambaugh, 1973

Former LAPD detective Joseph Wambaugh tells the story of the 1963 kidnapping of two LAPD officers by two criminals. Officers Karl Hettinger and Ian James Campbell pulled over robbers Gregory Ulas Powell and Jimmy Lee Smith (a.k.a. "Jimmy Youngblood") for a broken taillight. Powell pulled a gun on the officers, forced them into his car, and drove to an onion field near Bakersfield, where he killed Campbell. Hettinger escaped, but suffered much derision from his fellow cops, later becoming the subject of a training film on what not to do. The crime, the capture, the trial, the conviction, and the appeal are all chronicled in vivid detail and excellent narration.

Savage Grace, Natalie Robins and Steven M.L. Aronsen, 1985

Brooks Baekeland, grandson of the man who invented the synthetic plastic Bakelite, and his wife Barbara were filthy rich. When their only son Tony announced that he was gay, Barbara went on a mission to "cure" him, even going so far as sleeping with him. In response, Tony turned to drugs and stabbed his mother with a kitchen knife. For eight years, he was in a British institution for the criminally insane, but when released, he returned to New York and committed another crime. It's a modern-day Greek tragedy.

The Stranger Beside Me, Ann Rule, 1980

Brilliant in law school, a rising star in the Republican Party, good-looking and polite, Ted Bundy was the last person anyone would suspect of being a serial killer responsible for at least 38 murders. Even his friend, Ann Rule, had no idea, at first. Exceptionally written, this will chill you to the bone.

The Rest of the Story

Former Seattle police officer Ann Rule was exposed to criminals from an early age when she helped her grandmother prepare meals for prisoners. In college, Rule majored in creative writing, with minors in psychology, criminology, and penology. Considered an expert on crime and criminals, Rule was on the U.S. Justice Department Task Force that set up VI-CAP, the Violent Criminal Apprehension Program.

Historical True Crime

Anton Woode: The Boy Murderer, Dick Kreck, 2006

Small for his age, 11-year-old Anton Woode had the face of an angel but the heart of a killer. Kreck examines this 1893 case of a child who purposely shot Joe Smith in the back because he wouldn't give him his gold watch. (In the nineteenth century, unlike today, juvenile murderers were an oddity.) Incarcerated for 12 years, Anton was the youngest murderer convicted in Colorado as an adult. Kreck uses Anton's story as a vehicle to discuss the lack of progress the juvenile justice system has made in the last 100 years.

The Rest of the Story _____

After his release, Anton Woode went to New York and earned his living as a painter.

The Devil in the White City: Murder, Magic, and Madness at the Fair That Changed America, Erik Larson, 2003

The 1893 Columbian Exhibition in Chicago featured the latest and greatest from the rapidly industrializing, constantly modernizing United States. Unfortunately, scam artist and serial killer Herman Webster Mudgett, a.k.a. Dr. H.H. Holmes, used the World's Fair as a chance to lure unsuspecting women to their deaths. Mudgett imprisoned, tortured, and killed guests at his Chicago hotel, which he opened specifically for the 1893 World's Fair. He confessed to 27 murders, although there may have been more. The author sets Mudgett's gruesome story against an exquisitely detailed description of the creation of the Fair. If you only have time to read one historical true crime book, choose this one.

Sunk Without a Sound: The Tragic Colorado River Honeymoon of Glen and Bessie Hyde, Brad Dimock, 2001

Their October 1928 river trip was to double as a honeymoon for Glen and Bessie Hyde as they set out in the flat-bottomed boat they'd made. A month later, the couple hadn't returned home. Forty-three years later, a woman claiming to be Bessie said she'd killed her abusive husband. This book covers the couple's childhood years as well as the more recent searches for the pair, none of which has solved the mystery of their disappearance.

Organized Crime

Black Mass: The True Story of an Unholy Alliance Between the FBI and the Irish Mob, Dick Lehr and Gerard O'Neill, 2000

What happens when the line between good and evil becomes blurry for the forces of justice? Childhood friends John Connolly from the FBI's Boston field office and James "Whitey" Bulger, godfather of the Irish mob, joined forces to take down the Italian mob, and the whole project lost its moral compass. The two authors, *Boston Globe* reporters, covered this case from beginning to end. They put together a huge cast of principals by affiliation and name—the Bulger Gang, the Original Winter Hill Gang, the Boston Mafia, the Boston Field Office of the FBI, and federal, state, and local authorities.

Gotti: Rise and Fall, Jerry Capeci and Gene Mustain, 1996

John Gotti, "The Teflon Don," was the picture of arrogance as he laughed at the law's failed attempts to convict him. The head of the nation's most powerful crime family, the Gambinos, Gotti was a womanizer, killer, and family man. Then Sammy "The Bull" Gravano defected, and his testimony nailed the once untouchable mafioso. The authors, both reporters for the *New York Daily News*, worked nine years on this well-researched cautionary tale that proves the old saying, "He who laughs last, laughs best."

Underboss: Sammy the Bull Gravano's Story of Life in the Mafia, Peter Maas, 1997

Of all the mafioso to defect, Sammy "The Bull" Gravano, John Gotti's second in command, held the highest rank. Responsible for the conviction of dozens of Costa Nostra members, among them Tommy Gambino, John Gotti, and members of the Locasio, Colombo, and DeCalvacante families, Sammy himself was sentenced on September 26, 1994. (For his cooperation, Sammy was put into Witness Protection but has since left.) This book provides an intimate look at the inner workings of organized crime.

Serial Killers and Other Murderers

Bitter Blood: A True Story of Southern Family Pride, Madness, and Multiple Murder, Jerry Bledsoe, 1989

Cute, wealthy Susie Sharp Newson Lynch was a fraternity sweetheart at Wake Forest University … and a cold-hearted killer. With accomplice Fritz Klenner, her first cousin—and lover—Susie proved she'd do anything for money, even if it meant killing relatives.

Blood Lust: Portrait of a Serial Sex Killer, Gary C. King, 1992

In this true-life horror story, Dayton Leroy Rogers, like Dr. Jekyll, was a model citizen by day. But at night, he turned into a monster as evil as Mr. Hyde. No woman in Portland, Oregon, felt safe from his heinous deeds as he raped, mutilated, tortured, and killed at least eight females. He slashed the last victim to death in a parking lot in plain view of the diners at the nearby Denny's. The book is illustrated with eight pages of "shocking photos."

A Death in Belmont, Sebastian Junger, 2006

In 1963, Junger, author of *The Perfect Storm*, was a year old and his family was having their home renovated. At the same time, Bessie Goldberg, a neighbor, was raped and murdered. Although Roy Smith, an African American cleaning man, was convicted of the crime, Junger theorizes that one of the men doing the work on their home, Al DeSalvo, was the actual murderer. In one particularly chilling scene, DeSalvo tries to corner Junger's mother in the cellar. Two years later DeSalvo confessed to strangling 13 women in the Boston area. It's hard to find good help, but when one of your workers is the Boston Strangler, you should think about doing it yourself.

The Innocent Man: Murder and Injustice in a Small Town, John Grisham, 2006

In his first nonfiction work, best-selling author Grisham tells the story of quiet little Ada, Oklahoma, and how a murder set the town reeling. Local boy Ron Williamson became a hero the day the Oakland A's recruited him. However, only a few years later he returned home, his arm no longer any good and his body battered from drugs and alcohol. In 1987, Ron and his friend Dennis Fritz were arrested for the 1982 rape and murder of 21-year-old cocktail waitress Debra Sue Carter. What happens when there's no physical evidence, you're wrongly convicted, and you are sent to death row? It reads like fiction, but it really happened.

Last Rampage: The Shocking, True Story of an Escaped Convict's Killing Spree, James W. Clarke, 1988

On July 30, 1978, aided by his three sons, Donny, Ricky, and Ray, Gary Tison, who was doing time for killing a prison guard, escaped from the state prison in Florence, Arizona. Randy Greenawalt, another inmate who also escaped, joined the four Tisons for a murderous spree that lasted 12 days and ended with six innocent people, including a honeymooning couple, dead.

You Can Book on It! _____

True crime can be written from any number of points of view. This includes the omniscient narrator, the criminal, the victim, friends and relatives of the victim, friends and relatives of the criminal, the attorneys, the judge, the jurors, and even the coroner.

The Misbegotten Son, a Serial Killer and His Victims: The True Story of Arthur J. Shawcross, Jack Olsen, 1993

In 1972, Arthur J. Shawcross killed two boys with his bare hands. Caught and convicted the same year, he was sent to prison for the murders. When he was released in 1987, he began a murder spree that left at least 11 prostitutes dead. Very well written, the character details, rich descriptions, and comprehensive background information (including psychiatric interviews and court testimonies) make this work a cut above.

Sleep My Child, Forever, John Coston, 1995

Two-year-old David Brian Boehm and four-year-old Steven Michael Boehm didn't stand a chance when their mother, Ellen, used the cushions of her rose-colored sofa to smother them. The murders were 11 months apart. Greedy for even more insurance money, the nefarious mom put a hair dryer in her eight-year-old daughter's bath water. However, this did not kill the little girl, and the child's testimony helped nail the evil mother.

St. Joseph's Children: A True Story of Terror and Justice, Terry Ganey, 1989

In 1978, four-year-old Eric Christgen was kidnapped and killed in St. Joseph, Missouri. When Melvin Reynolds, a bisexual, was convicted of the crime and given a life sentence, the community gave a collective sigh of relief. Their relief was short-lived, however, when four years later, an 11-year-old girl was killed. Drifter Charles Hatcher was eventually arrested for the crime and confessed to 16 murders, including little Eric Christgen's. This disturbing portrait of a genuine sociopath also came out in paperback as *Innocent Blood: A True Story of Terror and Justice*.

Such Good Boys: The True Story of a Mother, Two Sons, and a Horrifying Murder, Tina Dirmann, 2005

Jason Bautista's mom was far from the ideal parent. In fact, she beat him so severely that he was sent to the emergency room. After 23 years of abuse, something snapped. Inspired by the popular television series *The Sopranos*, Jason strangled his mother and then cut off her head and hands so no one could identify the corpse. His 15-year-old half-brother, Matthew, helped him by driving around to find the perfect place to dump the torso. Life imitates art ... and the results are tragic.

Teach Me to Kill, Stephen Sawicki, 1991

There are no apples for Pamela Wojas Smart, a popular "with it" high school teacher. Her curriculum included lurid sex and premeditated murder. This riveting story tells of a beautiful young woman who convinced her students to murder the man she'd been married to for less than a year.

Whatever Mother Says: A True Story of a Mother, Madness, and Murder, Wensley Clarkson, 1995

Theresa Cross Knorr, a single mother of five, was a monster. Jealous of her two beautiful older daughters, Knorr enlisted her sons' help in burning one of the girls alive after Knorr had shot her and allowed the wounds to get infected. Knorr locked the next daughter in the broom closet, keeping her there until she starved to death. The crimes were so heinous that it was five years before the police began to believe the youngest daughter's tale of this unbelievable horror.

Who Killed My Daughter?, Lois Duncan, 1992

Award-winning young adult author Lois Duncan writes about her own anguished, relentless search for her daughter's murderer. Eighteen-year-old honor student Kaitlyn Clare Arquette was gunned down on her way home from a friend's house. The police wrote it off as a random act of violence, but Duncan wasn't convinced. Using every avenue, including psychic readings, she finally convinced the police her daughter had had a hit put on her and members of a Vietnamese gang were the likely suspects.

> **The Rest of the Story**
>
> Lois Duncan is the author of *I Know What You Did Last Summer*, *Killing Mr. Griffin*, and *Summer of Fear*.

Zodiac Unmasked, Robert Graysmith, 2002

After 30 years of research, Robert Graysmith reveals the identity of one of America's "most elusive" serial killers. From 1968 to 1969, San Francisco was under a cloud of terror. Stories of 37 murders, as well as bizarre warnings, eerie dares, and weird cryptograms, filled the city's newspapers. Then the killings stopped as suddenly as they had started. The FBI was stumped, but schoolteacher Donald Gene Harden decoded the cryptograms. This book is the ultimate coverage of a crime. There are images of the killer's notes and cryptograms as well as photos of most of the principals. There's also an extensive list of resources, so you can research to your heart's delight.

Theft and White-Collar Crime

Ballad of the Whiskey Robber: A True Story of Bank Heists, Ice Hockey, Transylvanian Pelt Smuggling, Moonlighting Detectives, and Broken Hearts, Julian Rubinstein, 2005

Hockey-player-gone-bad Attila Ambrus became a Hungarian folk hero during the 1990s when he sneaked over the border from Romania into Hungary, joined a Hungarian hockey team, and committed heist after heist. He continued this double life for several years. This lively and witty tale tells of a truly innovative crook.

Bringing Down the House: The Inside Story of Six M.I.T. Students Who Took Vegas for Millions, Ben Mezrich, 2003

A former math instructor founded the M.I.T. Blackjack Team, telling them, "Blackjack is beatable." After perfecting a system, they checked into hotels in Vegas under fake names. The M.I.T. "gamblers" used secret gestures and code words based on card counts. The students made millions before the casinos realized what they were doing. Who said geniuses were boring?

Confessions of a Master Jewel Thief, Bill Mason with Lee Gruenfeld, 2003

During a criminal career spanning 35 years, Bill Mason, the "most successful jewel thief this country has ever known," stole over $35 million worth of jewels from the likes of Bob Hope, Phyllis Diller, Robert Goulet, Margaux Hemingway, and Truman Capote. Mason even conned Sotheby's and Christies into fencing his goods. By day, Mason was a family man who made a living as a real estate manager and investor. But by night … . Here is a fascinating look at what it takes to be a thief.

The Rescue Artist: A True Story of Art, Thieves, and the Hunt for a Missing Masterpiece, Edward Dolnick, 2005

Edvard Munch's *The Scream* is perhaps one of the most famous paintings of all time. You'd think that with that sort of popularity, it would be under heavy security. But it wasn't, and in 1994, Munch's masterpiece was stolen with incredible ease from Norway's National Gallery in Oslo. To add insult to injury, the theft occurred the same morning the Winter Olympics began … in that city. Don't miss this exciting tale of the theft and recovery of *The Scream*.

Appendix A

Glossary

anthology   A collection of works written by one person or several people and compiled into one book.

autobiography   A book about a person's life, written by that person.

bibliography   A list of books and/or articles on a subject. May also be a list of works by a particular author.

bibliomaniac   A person driven to collect books.

bibliophile   A person who loves books.

biography   The story of a person's life written by some other person.

chick lit   Fun, flirty, contemporary stories, usually written with a humorous tone, of women in their twenties or thirties who are looking for "Mr. Right Now" as opposed to "Mr. Right."

cliff-hanger   A writing technique that leaves the reader in suspense. Authors frequently use this at the end of a chapter so readers will want to continue on to the next chapter.

cloak-and-dagger   Also known as cloak-and-sword, these novels are full of espionage or intrigue.

cozy   A term most often used to describe mysteries in the amateur sleuth subgenre. In a cozy mystery, graphic violence and language are kept to a minimum and the mood of the story is one of gentle, civilized refinement. Most of the characters know one another and the murder takes place in a closed environment, such as a country estate or a small town.

fantasy   Fantasy novels are pure imagination, filled with magic, fanciful worlds, and supernatural beings.

genre   A major category of books, such as romance, westerns, science fiction, mysteries, horror, and fantasy.

gothic   A novel in which an innocent young woman, often a governess, finds herself in an eerie, forbidding castle or mansion with her life in danger.

hard-boiled   A term that is most frequently used to describe private investigator mysteries that take a realistically gritty approach to murder. Violence and graphic language can be a part of the story.

historical fiction   Novels set in the past in which actual historical people and real historical events are part of the story.

inspirational fiction   Also known as "faith fiction" or "Christian fiction," these novels carry a strong religious message.

inspirational nonfiction   Unlike inspirational fiction, this genre crosses denominational boundaries and can represent many faiths and beliefs.

literary fiction   In this fiction the writing style is as important as the story.

memoir   A book about a person's recollections of his or her life or particular experiences. Memoirs often focus on one period of a person's life and his or her relationship with other people (usually famous) and/or historical events.

mystery   In these stories, a crime has already taken place or happens early in the book. The focus of the story is on solving the mystery. Mystery subgenres include amateur sleuths, private detectives, police procedurals, and historical sleuths.

noir mystery   The tone or mood of these mysteries is dark and gritty.

nom de plume   *See* pseudonym.

popular fiction   In these novels the story line is more important than the writing style.

pseudonym   Also known as pen name, allonym, or nom de plume, this term identifies the assumed name under which one writes. Famous pseudonyms include Dr. Seuss and Mark Twain.

Regency   A romance set during the Napoleonic Era when King George's son served as Regent. Jane Austen's books are the inspiration for this genre.

roman à clef   A novel in which one or more characters is based on a real person.

romance   A book in which the central focus of the story is on the developing romantic relationship between the two main characters. Romance subgrenres include historical romances, Regencies, contemporary romances, romantic suspense, paranormal, futuristic and time travel.

saga   A long story that often spans several generations.

science fiction   A story that takes a scientific or pseudo-scientific theory and shows what happens if it were to become a reality.

soft-boiled   A mystery in which the violence is softened so that the story isn't as dark or intense as a hard-boiled mystery.

subgenre   A category within a major genre, such as paranormal romances or historical mysteries.

suspense   A novel in which a crime has not yet taken place and the protagonist must either prevent the crime from happening or escape from it. Suspense novels appeal to the reader's emotions since the reader feels the anxiety of the main character(s).

thriller   Although similar to suspense novels, thrillers are different in scope. In thrillers, the stakes are bigger because not just one or two people are in jeopardy, but a city, government, or even the whole world.

tour de force   Some deed done with brilliance or extraordinary skill.

tragedy   A story in which events are carried to a disastrous, sometimes fatal, conclusion.

true crime   Stories of actual misdeeds, which can include everything from serial murder to white-collar crime.

westerns   Stories set in the American West from the beginning of western expansion in 1830 to the beginning of the twentieth century. The good guy wins, but he's battered in the end. Settings are as simple as the main street of a small western town.

women's fiction   Written for women, about women, and usually by women, these books explore the many roles women play—wife, friend, lover, mother, daughter, and so on.

Websites for Book Lovers

The web is a treasure trove of resources on books and reading. These few websites will get you started!

Read Free Books Online

Page By Page Books
www.pagebypagebooks.com

Page By Page Books provides free access to hundreds of classic books online.

Project Gutenberg
www.gutenberg.org

Project Gutenberg, the first producer of free ebooks, provides access to more than 20,000 online titles.

Digital Book Index
www.digitalbookindex.com

The Digital Book Index has links to more than 130,000 online titles, about 90,000 of which are available free.

Genre-Specific Authors and Awards

Horror Writers Association
www.horror.org

Mystery Writers of America
www.mysterywriters.org

Romance Writers of America
www.rwanational.org

Science Fiction and Fantasy Writers of America
www.sfwa.org

Western Writers of America
www.westernwriters.org

Oprah's Picks

Oprah's Book Club
www.oprah.com/books/books_landing.jhtml

Title Index

C

J

K

N

T

X-Y-Z

Author Index

G

S

T

U–V

My Books to Read

My Books to Read

_____

_____

_____

_____

_____

_____

_____

_____

_____

_____

_____

_____

_____

_____

_____

_____

_____

_____

_____

_____

_____

_____

My Books to Read

_____

_____

_____

_____

_____

_____

_____

_____

_____

_____

_____

_____

_____

_____

_____

_____

_____

_____

_____

_____

_____

My Books to Read

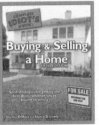